ETHICS AND PUBLIC HISTORY:
An Anthology

The National Council on Public History seeks to promote the utility of history through professional practice. Public history brings the skills and expertise of professional historians to bear on contemporary problems and issues. As part of that work, the NCPH is pleased to work with the Robert E. Krieger Publishing Co., Inc., to arrange for the printing of this volume.

ETHICS AND PUBLIC HISTORY:
An Anthology

edited by

Theodore J. Karamanski

ROBERT E. KRIEGER PUBLISHING COMPANY
MALABAR, FLORIDA
1990

Original Edition 1990

Printed and Published by
ROBERT E. KRIEGER PUBLISHING COMPANY, INC.
KRIEGER DRIVE
MALABAR, FLORIDA 32950

Library of Congress Cataloging in Publication Data

Ethics and Public History / [edited] by Theodore J. Karamanski.
    p. cm.
  "Sponsored by the National Council on Public History."
  ISBN 0-89464-362-2 (alk. paper)
  1. History—Moral and ethical aspects 2. Historians-
-Professional ethics. I. Karamanski, Theodore J., 1953–
II. National Council on Public History (U.S.)
D16.9.E87 1990
174′.997—dc20   89–34145
                          MAR 2 1999   CIP

10 9 8 7 6 5 4 3 2

CONTENTS

v

PART I:
ETHICS AND THE PUBLIC
HISTORIAN

1
INTRODUCTION:
ETHICS AND THE USE OF HISTORY

Theodore J. Karamanski

What are the ethical responsibilities of a historian? What constitutes proper professional conduct for historians toward their sources, colleagues, or the public? These are not novel questions. Every generation of historians has reflected on the practice of its craft. Cicero summarized historical ethics succinctly when he proclaimed that the first law of a historian was "never to dare utter an untruth, and the second, never to suppress anything true." Yet the great Roman rhetorician himself was not above twisting the facts in the interest of his political fortunes. During the first century, B.C., history and tradition were tools Cicero openly used to preserve his vision of the Roman state and its social structure. Breaches in historical ethics are always more apparent when history is being utilized than in purely scholarly situations. The greatest fear of historians who work on a monograph in monastic isolation is that they might be accused of getting the story wrong. Yet being wrong has never been grounds for historical malpractice. Everyone is open to some error. As Polybius noted in his *Histories,* the challenge was to avoid "deliberate misstatements in the interest of country or of friends or for favor." Such behavior even then was equated with those who made "their living by their pens," who inevitably judged the past "by the standard of profit."[1]

The rise of the public history movement, particularly in the United States but in Europe and Australia as well, inevitably brought a renewed interest on the part of historians in the question of ethics. Would "the standard of profit" which ruled the marketplace erode the cool detachment of the scientific investigator? The question was raised by a letter-to-the-editor in the premiere issue of *The Public Historian,* the journal intended to be the mouthpiece of the movement. Bob McKenzie chided public historians' emphasis on "the explication of skills, methodologies, and areas of application" while the central question was rather ". . . how the historian maintains objectivity without the traditional protection of distance from the subject under study."[2] In short order, this question blossomed into a critique of public history which stirred debate among both academic and practicing historians.

PUBLIC HISTORY AND THE ETHICS DEBATE

Nonacademic historians who had anticipated the 1976 phrase "public history" by pursuing career tracks in museums, archives, or government service were familiar with ethical objections from university-based scholars. Their responsibilities involved them with problems unlike those of scholarly investigation. By necessity these groups pioneered the systematic consideration of the ethics of public history. As early as 1968, the Oral History Association issued a pioneering set of goals and guidelines. This led to a decade of debate among practitioners of oral history and paved the way for the famous Wingspread Conference. Out of that conference came clear, well-thought-out guidelines on how oral historians should conduct their work.[3] Throughout the 1970s, museum curators discussed the ethical problems of historic-resource collection, display, and disposal. An earlier code of ethics, issued by the American Association of Museums (AAM) in 1925, seemed out-of-date. Funds available under the National Museum Act and from private sources allowed the AAM to draft the most comprehensive ethical statement for any field of history. Yet even the publication of *Museum Ethics* in 1978 did not end the debate over ethics among curators. Rather, the committee's report seems to have stimulated even more reflection on the subject.[4] In the summer of 1980, the Society of American Archivists issued a formal statement of ethics. Archival students had long been exposed to Wayne C. Grover's informal code. But Grover, who was a former head of the National Archives, made an unfortunate distinction between the archivist and the manuscript curator. The SAA's code of ethics was an official statement addressed not only to all archivists but also to the researchers who utilized their collections. Like the oral historians and the museum curators, the archivists sought to lay down guidelines. No group set up procedures for the enforcement of ethical conduct.[5]

In 1981 the Society of Professional Archaeologists (SOPA) took a decidedly more aggressive stance on ethics. The society was founded in 1976 to ensure that only qualified researchers conduct archaeological excavations. SOPA issued a directory of archaeologists who met its requirements of experience and education and who agreed to abide by its "Code of Ethics and Standards of Performance." Under that code was the proviso that all SOPA members would report knowledge of violations of the code to the "proper authorities." To deal with such reports, the society set up a formal grievance and censure apparatus. While SOPA's experience as a watchdog has not been a happy one, the society remains committed to strict enforcement of its code and standards.[6]

The Society of Professional Archaeologists linked its code of ethics with the certification of researchers. A similar approach has been taken by the California Committee for the Promotion of History (CCPH). Founded in 1981, the California Committee for the Promotion of History is a group of public historians who seek to foster the preservation, interpretation, and management of that state's historical resources.

Those resources, the CCPH felt, were threatened by a lack of standards for public historians which consequently led to a "case of poor historical practice." The CCPH consciously sought to limit the access of those without historical training to history jobs. Many CCPH members also felt that public historians faced different ethical challenges from their university colleagues. Contract historians, the CCPH contended, were inevitably influenced "by nonscholarly interests." Those interests needed to be addressed in order to assure the integrity of historical research reports. In 1984 the CCPH adopted its "Standards of Professional Conduct." While the committee did not at that time set up a formal grievance procedure, its standards did require that members "report violations of these standards to proper authorities."[7] The committee also established the CCPH Register of Professional Historians, prescribing specific eligibility and training requirements. The register, which included only those historians who agreed to follow the professional standards, was distributed to contract-letting agencies.[8]

Among the most rigorous proponents of the CCPH standards were independent history contractors. These free-lance researchers had been pioneers of the public history movement and had succeeded in placing themselves in a wide range of corporate and community settings. In the process, they became lightning rods for much of the criticism of public history, most particularly concerning ethics. In December of 1982, several historical consultants approached the National Council on Public History with the request that it investigate the desirability of a Code of Ethics. The suggestion was warmly received, particularly by the graduate programs in public history. The task of orienting students to history and its public applications necessarily involved many teachers with thorny issues such as contract negotiations, client relations, confidentiality, and the nature of historical truth. Discussion of these matters brought up the question of ethics. Some individual professors addressed such questions as they arose, in light of the case under discussion and their own experience. A statement of general principles could serve to guide teachers through the tricky crosscurrents of the ethics issue.

The National Council on Public History (NCPH) established an ethics committee. For two years, the committee worked to encourage discussion of the ethics issue among historians. Panels were organized at public history conferences and at the 1984 Organization of American Historians Conference in Los Angeles. There was considerable dissent over the ethics issue. Some public historians argued that as archivists, oral historians, or planners, they were already covered by codes of ethics. Others were uneasy with the notion of creating absolute standards and argued for the primacy of the individual investigator's personal ethics. In April of 1985, the board of directors of the NCPH approved a document titled "Ethical Guidelines for the Historian." The guidelines did not seek to touch upon issues covered by existing codes for curators, archivists, and oral historians. Rather, they established general principles to govern the conduct of researchers and professionals.[9]

While the NCPH document recognized the similarity between the ethical problems of academic and public historians, a sister organization, the Society for History in the Federal Government, has recently detailed the special responsibilities of historians employed by, or contracting with, the federal government. Their "Principles and Standards for Federal Historical Programs" represents a conscientious attempt to balance the legitimate security needs of many agencies with the historian's need for access to source material and peer review. Perhaps no other historical-ethics document deals with so many delicate issues.[10]

The blossoming debate over ethics in the various fields of public history has taken place in the context of a revival of concern with moral practice in all aspects of American life. New publications such as *Applied Philosophy, Business and Professional Ethics, Environmental Ethics,* and *The Journal of Value Inquiry* have ridden a wave of discourse over the clash of values. Organizations like the Westminster Institute, the Hastings Center, and state humanities councils have championed discussion of ethical questions. There is even a new organization known as the Center for Business Ethics (something only the bitterest of satirists would have envisioned twenty years ago). According to philosopher Edmund Pincoffs, there is nothing short of "an ethics industry" loose in the marketplace.[11]

ACADEMIC HISTORY AND PROFESSIONAL ETHICS

Yet in spite of this rich debate, some major historical organizations, such as the Organization of American Historians, have moved at a glacial pace on the question of professional ethics. Perhaps this is because the majority of the members of those organizations are academic historians who fancy themselves insulated from the compromises of relationships beyond the cloister of the college. But concern over the propriety of professional conduct has increasingly been directed toward academic life. The academician's chorus demanding accountability from government and business has come echoing back. Trustees, courts, and legislators — to say nothing of students — have become restless with the often vague definition of a professor's duties and responsibilities. In 1982 the *Journal of Higher Education* devoted an entire issue to ethics and the academic profession. George M. Schurr concluded his contribution to the discussion with the assertion that "it is high time for academics to get their ethics in order."[12]

In the recent past, the American Historical Association itself has been faced with several vexing ethical problems. These issues reveal a striking similarity to the types of problems which led public historians to initiate discussion of professional ethics.

Perhaps the most celebrated incident of alleged historical malpractice was the Loewenheim affair. In December of 1968, Francis L. Loewenheim of Rice University charged that the Franklin D. Roosevelt Library staff withheld from him six documents which they knew to be vital to his research. The documents, which were declassified and open to research, were kept from him, Loewenheim contended, so that a member of the library staff could first publish them as part of a documentary series with Harvard University Press. Later Loewenheim charged that he had been personally maligned by the Archivist of the United States and the Assistant Executive Secretary of the American Historical Association. He also questioned the involvement of a private university press with the copyrighting of government documents. The seriousness of these charges and the vigor with which Loewenheim pressed them in print and political circles impelled the American Historical Association and the Organization of American Historians to form a joint investigation committee.

The political atmosphere of the late 1960s influenced the profession's response to Loewenheim's charges. Emotions were easily stirred by the image of a government conspiracy against an independent researcher. Faced with a vocal minority of historians anxious to storm the barricades, the joint committee found its work difficult. Neither the AHA nor the OAH had guidelines for pursuing such an inquiry. In the end, the committee—composed of Dewey W. Grantham, Alfred D. Chandler, and Richard W. Leopold—went about its work of sorting out the truth in a typically historical manner—through a careful analysis of the record. In spite of being overwhelmed by an avalanche of correspondence, the committee eventually completed its report. Most of Loewenheim's charges, particularly those directed against the Roosevelt Library, were determined to be unfounded. However, the legacy of the affair was increased suspicion between historians and archivists, a modest improvement in the AHA's ability to handle such issues, and a pile of legal bills for the two largest historical associations.[13]

More recently, the academy has been shaken by the charges and counterclaims of the Abraham case. David Abraham's *The Collapse of the Weimar Republic,* a structural analysis of the role of capital and labor in the fall of republican Germany, has been assailed by critics on both sides of the Atlantic as "a tendentious misconstrual of evidence." While Abraham admits to mistakes in his footnotes and text, he maintains that there was no conscious effort to deceive his readers. Nor does he feel his arguments have been undermined by the "shortcomings born of inexperience and rush." Yet Professors Henry Turner and Gerald Feldman felt that the issue compromised the very nature of historical research. To stress the seriousness of the matter, they circulated their strongly negative view of Abraham's work. This informal criticism proved more damaging to Abraham than published reviews. Feldman later said, "I am pleased to say I was directly or indirectly involved in stopping four places from hiring Abraham."[14] As one reviewer recently noted, "It has turned into a kind of historical Dreyfus Affair . . . in which the original issues have often been obscured by the personal virulence and moral indignation with which Abraham has been attacked and the bitter and polemical tone of his replies."[15] In December of 1984, the American Historical Association was pressed by several leading scholars to investigate the matter. Although the association's Professional Division began to review the general question of ethics, the AHA decided to steer clear of a case where emotions had spilled over the normal boundaries for scholarly debate.

No less divisive was the controversy surrounding the role of two prominent academic historians in the 1986 case of the *Equal Employment Opportunity Commission (EEOC) v. Sears, Roebuck and Company.* Alice Kessler-Harris of Hofstra University offered testimony in support of the EEOC's charge of hiring discrimination against the giant retailer. Rosalind Rosenberg of Barnard College offered expert testimony in defense of Sears. For more than a year following the trial, the field of women's history was rent by charges of unethical conduct, the betrayal of "women struggling for equity," as well as debate over the role of the historian in the courtroom. The incident served to remind all historians of the broader ramifications of professional practice outside the classroom.

The controversy over access to classified materials is less spectacular than the Loewenheim or the Sears affairs, but in the end it presents more significant ethical challenges. What is particularly vexing is that the issue often pits academic historian versus public historian as the university-based researcher seeks access to restricted documents under the management of a government historian. The potential conflict of interest between the government historians' duty to preserve the historical record, serve the public, and serve their agency has only been partially resolved by the Society for History in the Federal Government's "Principles and Standards." Research historians also are caught in a dilemma. As Joan Hoff-Wilson of the Organization of American Historians has recently pointed out: "One . . . pitfall professional historical organizations in particular must confront is a classic kind of conflict of interest. . . . It is symbolically represented in the FOIA (Freedom of Information Act) and the Privacy Act . . . the former symbolizes the 'public's right to know about government conduct,' and the latter guarantees 'the equally important right to . . . control the flow of personal information.'"[16] As of yet, there are no clear-cut guidelines to help the researcher reconcile these competing social goods.

The controversy over access to restricted information—like concern for the manner in which scholars conduct their disagreements, represent their sources, and punish wrongdoers—cannot be dismissed as unimportant. Ethics is an issue that all historians must face. Yet the various codes of ethics and statements of professional standards produced by historical organizations, while they are a real contribution to the discipline, also reveal the historian's limited sense of professionalism. If we accept the sociologist's dictum that "ethics codes are the most concrete cultural form in which professions acknowledge their societal obligations," then the historical community's vision of this issue is seen to be narrow and rather self-serving.[17] Historians have focused on the "how" of ethical behavior, yet we have neglected the "why."

THE STRUGGLE FOR DEFINITION

Control over the definition of what is good history, of professional orthodoxy, is an important element of the ethics debate. Codes of ethics play a vital role in the process of definition. Other professions which have adopted codes of ethics can provide a useful comparison. In fields as diverse as medicine and engineering, codes have functioned to protect the public from the "social danger of uncontrolled expertise," to improve a profession's status, and/or to effect a professional monopoly. Of course, a code of ethics is only one formal mechanism, along with entry controls and informal behavioral controls, used to effect any or all of the above-mentioned goals. From this perspective, it is not at all surprising to see why public visibility was a major factor in prodding historians to deal with the question of professional ethics. The Loewenheim investigation, the Abraham affair, and the Sears case all had a direct impact on how the public perceived historians.[18]

For this reason, the suspicion with which many academic historians greeted public history, which by its very nature was involved in dialogue with the public, was logical and perhaps even beneficial. The social danger of unprofessional historical expertise loose in the public sector could be as menacing as George Orwell's image of the Ministry of Truth or as bland as a public relations "puff piece." Of course, the historical profession maintained mastery of the entry controls to public history through university-based graduate programs. But prior to issuing codes of ethics, the profession had no formal or informal means to mold the behavior of public historians once they left the campus. Academic historians, few of whom ever looked at the American Association of University Professors rather general 1966 ethics statement, were shaped instead by the peer pressure and traditions of their departments and institutions. In some cloisters, this pressure is great enough to supplant ethnicity or social background with "donnish refinement" in speech and appearance, as well as values and behavior.[19] Public historians—depending upon the nature of their work—interacted with fellow bureaucrats, lawyers, corporate executives, sometimes even ordinary people. Such environments exert influences other than the disinterested pursuit of knowledge. To function effectively, the historian working in a corporation or agency must, to some extent, be in harmony with the goals of that organization. Academic historians were initially uninterested in providing guidelines to reconcile this reality with the historical method. Pioneer public historians felt shunned by their former academic mentors. The head of one large cultural-resource consulting firm visited his alma mater only to be stung by the comment, "So you still can't find a teaching job?". For many years, the presumption that public history was low-status work, employment of last resort, further undermined the potential for engagement of the ethics issue and reinforced the presumption that since it was outside of the university's informal means of control, it was unethical.

The establishment of public history associations such as the National Council on Public History, the Society for History in the Federal Government, and the California Committee for the Promotion of History provided structures to informally control the development of the field. The leaderships of these organizations, in issuing formal ethical guidelines, reflected their reformist spirit. Not only did they seek to direct the expansion of public history, but they also set out to attack the traditional historian's "antivocational, antiutilitarian bias." Yet as Roy Lopata suggests in his essay, "Ethics in Public History: Clio Meets Ulasewicz," public historians' concern for ethics was not merely a function of their desire to protect the public or even to redeem their status within the profession. There was also the desire to protect territory. Larry Tise, then head of the North Carolina Division of History and Archives, said in 1979 at the first conference on public history: ". . . we need to determine that historians will permit only historians to do history work." He went on to call for "a certification program and code of ethics" in order to professionalize the field of history. For some public historians, a code of ethics became one of several mechanisms to assert the dominant position of history in the public sector.[20]

Concern with status, either by public historians in the marketplace or by academics within the profession as a whole, had much to do with the debate over ethics. "It seems a truism that claims of superior ethicality," wrote one student of professional ethics, ". . . are essentially claims of superior status or honor." Among historians, status is most commonly awarded through professional associations. Organizations such as the American Historical Association function on several levels. To young Oscar Handlin attending the 1936 AHA convention, the phrase "a community of investigators" seemed an apt description of the "company" of historians "laboriously inching the world toward truth." Historians were independent individual investigators whose work was part of ". . . a living stream of thought composed of the works that followed as well as those that preceded it." Yet the AHA was not merely an intellectual club, it was also a professional association made up of ". . . a small group of men and women, internally cohesive and held together by adherence to common standards and convictions." The association acted as an intermediary between individual historians and their responsibilities to Clio and to the public. Participation in the association showed one's solidarity with the goals and values of the group, and professional status was accordingly conferred.[21]

A code of ethics was undreamed of for historical associations because of their unified conviction that, as a community of scholars, they were providing a disinterested service to society. As long as there was faith in this vision of the profession, there was no demand for formal ethical guidelines. That historians were actually performing disinterested service seemed clear. Their work was generally not sullied by the client relationship of doctors or lawyers. That the profession performed a needed service was not doubted as long as most historians adhered to the Progressive synthesis, whose faith in American democracy related well to the citizen-training goals the educational system traditionally assigned to history.

After World War II when the Progressive synthesis began to unravel, the profession's service function became obscured to both society and many within the profession. For a time, the expansion of higher education, fueled by government spending and the baby boom, insulated the profession from public ambivalence over the value of its service to society. Within the profession, however, dissident voices were heard. The issues of the 1960s—racism, war, sexism, etc.—demanded, as Ronald J. Grele recalled, ". . . for professors to profess something and to make history relevant." New Left historians advocated a closer relationship between history and the public, but their politically-charged rhetoric alienated audiences within and without the profession. Their critique of history's relevance became associated with curriculum trends that reduced history to a fringe discipline.[22]

An additional legacy of "New Left" historiography was the profession's recent passion for social history and its rediscovery of social-science methods. While these trends did much to rectify the narrow political bias of past historians, they also helped to fractionalize the discipline. Like feudal kingdoms, subfields were carved out of the broader field of "the new social history": urban history, ethnic history, working-class history, and women's history. Like medieval society, subinfeudation became rife as historians pledged their allegiance to scores of specialized interest groups—many of which had their own journals, newsletters, and conferences. The lack of orthodoxy in basic subject matter, like the breakup of synthesis, left historians with little to bind them to one another. Membership in the national associations flagged as the old "community of investigators" became atomized.

Social changes within the profession further undermined the association's ability to confer status and provide leadership. During the 1960s and 1970s, a generation of historians more representative of the population both in terms of ethnicity and gender began to swell the ranks of the professoriate. There has in the recent past been what one historian calls a "'democratization' of the historical profession." The percentage of historians from lower-middle-class backgrounds has increased; but more significantly, because the absolute number of Ph.D's in history awarded during the 1970s skyrocketed, the total of lower-middle-class historians is very high. After all, 43% of all history Ph.D.'s granted since 1922 came between 1970 and 1978.[23]

Diversity has come to the history profession at the cost of cohesion. Intellectual and political as well as social cleavages have lessened the American Historical Association's ability to be an informal arbiter of who is "a good historian." The need for formal instruments of evaluation, codes of ethics, was inevitable.

SERVICE AND THE HISTORICAL PROFESSION

It is interesting to note that all of the recent codes of ethics in the historical profession have focused on individual action. Of course, most do not contain enforcement mechanisms or grievance procedures; rather, these guidelines attempt to apply whatever persuasive power prestige gives to their organization to ensure individual compliance. All of the recent codes assume the existence of something called "the historical profession," yet they speak only to individual historians. There has been no discussion of the profession's corporate duties and obligations.

The problem is that historians such as myself who have been involved in the ethics issue have tended to perceive the problem too narrowly. While focusing on the potential problems of practicing history, we forgot the critical role ethics play in defining a profession. Guidelines have been established which describe how a "good" historian will behave, but no concern has been shown for why it is necessary to observe those ethical restraints. We have called for "professional ethics" without grasping the essential redundancy in that phrase. Not every job is a profession. We may need stockbrokers or garbagemen, but there is no moral purpose in their work. Any true profession has a moral goal, the advancement of which is a social good. In history today, there is no consensus as to the moral goal of studying the past. We have been obsessed with refining our methods and techniques, yet we have neglected the whole point of doing history.[24]

Without launching into a debate on the philosophy of history—which, like most American historians, I am loath to do—let us consider the premise that the point of history is truth. "The historian's vocation," wrote Oscar Handlin, "depends on this minimal operational article of faith: truth is absolute; it is as absolute as the world is real. . . ." To accept this, we must embrace both the philosophical point that truth is knowable and the technical matter that, at least in some cases, the historical method can reveal what happened in the past. Of course, there are subjective factors arising from conceptualization, the narrative process, value judgments, and a host of idiosyncratic influences which complicate the analysis of the past. These factors, however, make the process of analysis more tortuous, not impossible.[25]

The moral purpose of history is to reveal the truth about the past. Yet is that a satisfactorily complete ethical foundation for a profession? Certainly truth or, to put it more humbly, the pursuit of truth about the past can serve as a base line for all historians. Without truth, there cannot be history. The past can be reassembled as propaganda, entertainment, or tradition; but unless such a process is guided by the pursuit of truth, it will never deserve the name "history." Of course, merely committing ourselves to the pursuit of truth does not guarantee us the acquisition of that prize. Errors of judgment will always mar our analysis, and few research projects are guiltless of omitting some relevant source. After all, most historians are wrong in one way or another. Being wrong, however, is not at all the same as being unethical. Although the pursuit of truth bonds all historians, it is only part of our professional ethic. Truth is not an abstract quality but a virtue vital in society. It strengthens the characters of individuals and empowers institutions to achieve their goals. History is not just a technical craft with a series of methods which lead to the truth. If it is a true profession, it not only pursues its moral goal, it must also be concerned with the use of that truth to produce a social good.

A profession owes service to society. "We are, after all, not a small group of clerks and mandarins guarding secret knowledge . . .," Gerda Lerner has observed, "but people with special skills, who translate to others the meaning of the lives and struggles of their ancestors, so that they may see meaning in their own lives." The utility of history is an inescapable part of our professional ethics. When we fulfill the fundamental human need to know about the past, we achieve our potential as a moral community of investigators. The greatest ethical challenge before the historical profession is to heighten consciousness of the ties of obligation that link the historian to the contemporary world. Of course, the public obligations incumbent upon historians vary with the specific niche or role they fill within the profession. The invention by Robert Kelley of the phrase "public history" has helped all historians become aware of the wide variety of professional roles performed by historians. Perhaps the field has even become too broad for a single, specific set of ethical guidelines to meet the diverse needs of historians; yet all historians must be made conscious of their responsibility to render service to the community, to use history for the public.[26]

To seek the truth about the past and serve society are the twin pillars of professional ethics for the historian. The academic-based historian has as much a responsibility to use the past for the public good as the cultural-resource consultant is bound by the obligation of truth. Academic historians serve when they teach, as well as through publication; but these activities, while important, do not absolve the historian from exploring other appropriate avenues of using history for the public good. In the end, ethical historians pursue their profession not because they are accustomed to the ambience of the academic milieu or because of the rewards of the marketplace or even because they have cultivated a refined sensibility about a part of the past. The "good historians" perfect their craft to create a usable past.

EXPLORING HISTORICAL ETHICS

Of course, service to society is not widely accepted as part of the historical profession's corporate responsibility. It has been speculated that this is because historians do not believe they have anything to contribute to the community. In 1964 English historian J. H. Plumb observed that "fewer and fewer historians believe that their art has any social purpose: any function as a coordinator of human endeavour or human thought." He went so far as to state that 90% of historians believe "that the subject they practice is meaningless in any ultimate sense." Nor is this belief restricted to historians. Theodore S. Hamerow recently observed that "To our society . . . the methodology of historical scholarship appears inadequate for an understanding of the world in which we live." For Hamerow, this widely-held sentiment constitutes a "crisis in history." But whether the problem is that historians have nothing to say or that society does not want to hear what historians are prepared to say, the fact remains that most historians at the center of the profession, in the university departments, make no attempt at dialogue with society.[27]

Because service has been ignored as a professional ethic for historians, the question of service has become a personal, subjective matter rather than an objective and professional concern. The question of whether a historian's work relates to the world is left as an individual choice to be confronted or, more often, ignored. Historical ethics, therefore, have been reduced to a single, narrow track best exemplified by the question: "How do I do honest work, consistent with history's quest for truth about the past?" While this question is an incomplete view of the historian's professional ethics, it is nonetheless a problem of considerable complexity in and of itself and one which is worthy of more detailed explanation. The essays in this volume largely focus on the challenge individual historians face in attempting to do honest, ethical history and at the same time serve the public.

Some historians, such as Roy Lopata, see codes of ethics not as an aid to the ethical historian but as, instead, part of the problem. For him, codes of ethics may yet prove to be a mechanism for creating more barriers between history and the public. Ronald C. Tobey accepts the utility of codes of ethics for historians but sees a fundamental division within the profession between academics and public historians. He stakes out the controversial position that the public historian is essentially an advocate. For Tobey, the cultural-resource consultant who prepares a National Register nomination or the expert witness in a legal dispute represents a specific interest. While honesty and fairness are vital, objectivity is neither cultivated nor desired. The public-policy setting within which public historians operate fashions truth out of competing interests. He calls for public historians to abandon the academic value of disinterested scholarship and adopt much more realistic and useful standards to guard against the real ethical challenge of conflict of interest. Tobey's contention that the public historian is an advocate is a bold statement of the central ethical issue of history.

Tobey draws heavily on the role of historians as expert witnesses to explicate his vision of public history ethics. Certainly this is among the most ethically challenging areas of public history. J. Morgan Kousser provocatively asks the question "Are Expert Witnesses Whores?" and answers it by scrutinizing the practice of history in both the judicial setting and the university. "Testifying and scholaring are about equally objective pursuits," he concludes. Joan Williams finds academic norms of objectivity quite at odds with the trial context. She agrees with Kousser that historians inside academia and inside the courtroom often pursue political ends through historical scholarship and that as long as this grows out of one's values as a citizen, such advocacy is quite ethical. Nor, she maintains, is such advocacy inconsistent with academic standards of objectivity so long as it observes "the methodological norms concerning treatment of evidence and counterevidence." But historians, as she demonstrates through a discussion of the Sears case, have not always been vigilant of their methodological norms and have pursued advocacy beyond the limits of qualification and counterevidence. Such actions are not only unethical, costing the historian credibility, but they risk hurting the very cause being advocated.

Historians working within bureaucracies, whether corporate or governmental, face a challenge similar to that of the expert witness. They work within institutions which are aided by history but whose basic mission is different from the goals of scholarship. Like expert witnesses, historians in the bureaucracy must be aware of the way this institutional context can influence their work. Donald Page and Carl Ryant both address this challenge in their essays. Ryant calls for historians in business to "realize that potential problems exist and attempt to design projects in a manner which both recognizes and minimizes these difficulties." While he decries institutional restraints, he does not feel they necessarily discredit the writing of business history within corporations so long as historians are "honest" to their readers about the nature of those restrictions. Donald Page, a veteran historian in the Canadian government, specifically addresses the problems of publishing commissioned history. Page, who has seen this issue from the historian's as well as the administrator's perspective, is sensitive to the natural desire of any institution to maintain a good public image. "While the public historian's interest in publication may be based on professional development or contributing to a body of scholarship or public debate," he writes, "the client or employing organization thinks primarily about its impact upon their future business operations." Page sees the reconciling of these differing interests through "mutually agreeable guidelines" before a public history project is started as essential to avoiding ethical problems associated with client censorship later in the project.

Martin Reuss of the Army Corps of Engineers addresses the dual responsibility faced by public historians working in government. They are professional historians often subject to peer review, yet they are also public servants working in agencies that must be answerable to the public. The conflict between the historian and civil-servant roles is seldom direct and clear-cut; rather, ethical challenges tend to be subtle. Factors such as heavy work loads, limited schedules, staff shortages, and changes in administrative priorities are more likely to create an atmosphere that challenges professional standards than the heavy-handed intervention of politicians. For Reuss, federal historians are faced with an ongoing challenge to demonstrate their flexibility as public employees yet also to educate their agencies that they are professionals. Reuss believes that the Society for History in the Federal Government's "Principles and Standards" "will help insure both qualities endure in the federal bureaucracy."

The desire to see history recognized as a field of professional practice, outside the halls of the academy, has been a powerful force in the emergence of the public history movement. Stanley Hordes, in his introduction to the National Council on Public History's "Ethical Guidelines for the Historian," and James C. Williams, in "Standards of Professional

Conduct in California," see ethical guidelines as a step in the growth of history as a profession. Neither Hordes nor Williams sees public history codes of ethics as a "panacea for all issues facing public historians," but they do believe such codes can arm historians "with the support of the professional community" and "assist both public historians and their clients in carrying out their . . . responsibilities."

The success of the public history movement's effort to carve out a nonacademic sphere of practice for history will not rest solely on the activities of the National Council on Public History or other public history associations; nor will the success of the movement, sadly, rest solely on the merits of what Clio has to offer the public. Greater public consciousness of history will take a commitment from the historical profession as a whole to the notion that a true profession owes service to the public. Certainly this ethic can be served in traditional ways as well as through public history; but without a dedication to history's relationship with the public on the part of the American Historical Association or, more importantly, on the part of collegiate departments of history, our collective development as a profession will be truncated and the public's basic human need to know where they came from will be an underserved target of opportunity for "sound-bite" journalists and other modern-day sophists.

REFERENCES

1. Marcus Tullius Cicero, *Cicero: De Oratore* (Cambridge: Harvard University Press, 1959), pp. 243–245; Polybius, *The Histories of Polybius* (Cambridge: Harvard University Press, 1957), p. 29.
2. Bob McKenzie, "Letter to the Editor," *The Public Historian,* Vol. I, No. 3 (Spring 1979), pp.4–5.
3. Oral History Association, "Oral History Evaluation Guidelines: The Wingspread Conference," *Oral History Review* 8 (1980), pp. 6–19.
4. American Association of Museums, *Museum Ethics* (Washington: American Association of Museums, 1978). Ullberg, Patricia, "What Happened in Greenville: The Need for More Museum Codes of Ethics," *Museum News* 60, No. 2, pp. 26–29. Weil, Stephen E., "Breaches of Trust: Museums, Ethics, and the Law," *Art News* 81, No. 10 (1982), pp. 44–55.
5. Society of American Archivists, "A Code of Ethics for Archivists," *The American Archivist* (Summer 1980), pp. 414–18.
6. David L. Browman, "Origins, Functions and Philosophy," *Directory of Professional Archaeologists* (n.p.: Society of Professional Archaeologists, 1981), pp. 1–3.
7. California Committee for the Promotion of History, "Standards of Professional Conduct" (Sacramento: California Committee for the Promotion of History, 1984). Reprinted in the Appendix to this volume.
8. James Williams, "How the CCPH Register of Professional Historians Works" (Sacramento: California Committee for the Promotion of History, 1984).
9. The NCPH's "Ethical Guidelines for the Historian" is reprinted in the Appendix to this volume.
10. The Society for History in the Federal Government's "Principles and Stan-

dards for Federal Historical Programs" is reprinted in the Appendix to this volume.

11. Edmund Pincoffs, "What Is Happening in Ethics?", *Federation Reports* (May 1984), pp. 28–31.

12. George M. Schurr, "Toward a Code of Ethics," *Journal of Higher Education* 53 (May/June 1982), pp. 318–34. For a contrary point of view, see Daniel Callahan, "Should There Be an Academic Code of Ethics?", *Journal of Higher Education* 53 (May/June 1982), pp. 335–44.

13. For a thorough discussion of the Loewenheim case, see Dewey W. Grantham and Richard Leopold, *Final Report of the Joint AHA/OAH Ad Hoc Committee to Investigate the Charges Against the Franklin D. Roosevelt Library and Related Matters* (Washington: American Historical Association and Organization of American Historians, 1970); and Francis L. Loewenheim, "A Statement in Rebuttal" (n.p.: December 1970).

14. Karen J. Winkler, "Brouhaha Over Historian's Use of Sources Renews Scholars' Interest in Ethics Codes," *Chronicle of Higher Education,* February 2, 1985, p. 1 and pp. 8–9.

15. James Joll, "Business As Usual," *New York Review of Books* 32, No. 14 (September 1985), pp. 5–10.

16. Joan Hoff-Wilson, "Access to Restricted Collections: The Responsibility of Professional Historical Organizations," *American Archivist* 46, No. 4 (Fall 1983), pp. 441–47.

17. Andrew Abbott, "Professional Ethics," *American Journal of Sociology,* Vol. 88, No. 5 (1983), p. 856.

18. *Ibid.,* pp. 860–61.

19. Theodore Hamerow, *Reflections on History and Historians.*

20. Roy Lopata, "Ethics in Public History: Clio Meets Ulasewizc," *The Public Historian,* Vol. 8, No. 1 (Winter 1986), pp. 39–46; Larry Tise, Comments on the "Future of Public History Symposium," *The Public Historian,* Vol. 2, No. 1 (Fall 1979), p. 60.

21. Oscar Handlin, *Truth in History* (Cambridge: The Belknap Press, 1979), pp. 3–5.

22. Ronald J. Grele, "Whose Public? Whose History? What Is the Goal of a Public Historian?", *The Public Historian,* Vol. 3, No. 1 (Winter 1981), p. 44.

23. Joan Hoff-Wilson, "Is the Historical Profession an Endangered Species?", *The Public Historian,* Vol. 2, No. 2 (Winter 1980), pp. 16–17.

24. Thomas F. Green, "On Seeing the Point and Knowing the Risks: Ethics and the Academic Community," *Journal of Thought,* Vol. 22, No. 3 (Fall 1987), pp. 12–13.

25. Oscar Handlin, *Truth in History,* p. 405.

26. Gerda Lerner, "The Necessity of History and the Professional Historian," *The Vital Past: Writings on the Use of History,* edited by Stephen Vaughn (Athens: University of Georgia Press, 1985), p. 113; Robert Kelley, "Public History: Its Origins, Nature, and Prospects," *The Public Historian,* Vol. 1, No. 1 (Fall 1978), pp. 16–28.

27. Hamerow, *Reflections on History and Historians;* pp. 21, 27.

This article is based on a paper presented at the sixth Annual Conference on Public History, Los Angeles, California, April 1984. It was presented as part of the joint OAH/NCPH session "Ethics and the Historian." I wish to thank the following individuals for their consultation and opinion on the concerns of this paper: Wes Chambers, Bary Freet, and Hazel Fuller of the Desert District Administrative Office of the Bureau of Land Management, Riverside, California; Joe Bosko, contract officer of the Forest Service's San Francisco District Headquarters; and Elisabeth Sichel, Attorney at Law, Corona, California. Of course, these persons do not necessarily share the thesis of this paper and certainly are not responsible for the tendentiousness of its presentation.

2

THE PUBLIC HISTORIAN AS ADVOCATE: IS SPECIAL ATTENTION TO PROFESSIONAL ETHICS NECESSARY?

Ronald C. Tobey

The rapid rise of public history and the concomitant entry of professional academic historians and academically trained historians into nonacademically sponsored research has repeatedly raised the question of whether the professional ethics that govern academic scholars adequately guide adjudication of ethical situations in the public arena. My original opinion on this question was that the differences between the academic and nonacademic scholarly enterprises were minor, and, consequently, any ethical problems deriving from these differences were adequately met by the ethical codes of the various public history associations, such as the Society of American Archivists and the American Association of Museums. Recently, however, my opinion has shifted. In this paper, I argue that academic scholarly ethics are inadequate in principle as well as in major practical ways for governing schol-

The Public Historian, Vol. 8, No. 1 (Winter 1986)
© 1986 by the Regents of the University of California

arship in the public arena. Driven by this conclusion, I present a program of ethical concerns for the profession to deliberate, and recommend special attention to professional ethics.

Academic ethics are codified in the American Association of University Professors' "Statement on Professional Ethics," of 1966. Standards of faculty conduct at the University of California, my own institution, for instance, are grounded in the AAUP statement. This statement addresses immediately the assumption upon which honesty by scholars and veracity in scholarship is based: that in pursuit of scholarship the professor is not in principle "seriously hampered" or "compromised" by "subsidiary interests." In other words, academic scholarship can in principle be conducted so that it is not influenced by nonscholarly interests, such as a pecuniary interest in the outcome of research or of publication.

The standard of disinterested scholarship is maintained, according to the AAUP Statement of Professional Ethics, by a community of free scholars, of which the professor is a member, whose evaluation and criticism test the veracity of scholarship. These principles of academic scholarly ethics also characterize the ethical conduct codes of federal research agencies. Federal researchers are similarly bound by the obligation to be free from financial interest in projects they are evaluating, and the evaluation process is built around a peer-review system.[1]

In examining whether these two principles of academic scholarship—disinterestedness and peer review—can adequately safeguard the truth of nonacademic scholarship, I will argue two points. First, the differences between the academic and the nonacademic arenas of scholarship are so fundamental that they can not. Second, in the public arena, scholarship will always have the appearance of interestedness and partiality, regardless of the reality, and the AAUP standards of professional ethics provide inadequate guidance in dealing with the problems of appearances. I shall not be arguing, however, that the appearance of interestedness in public history scholarship is only appearance; to the contrary, I think that in reality public history scholarship is interested, and implicitly represents an advocacy position.

How does public scholarship differ from academic scholarship, so that, if not by intent, then by default, public scholarship is interested scholarship? First, the scholarly program that generates academic scholarship is disciplinary, and within that framework, a matter of personal choice of the disciplinary scholar. In the public arena, the scholarly program that generates public scholarship is the public policy process. In scholarship in the corporate context, the profit-seeking strategy of the corporation generates the scholarship. By definition, and in practice, the public policy process and the profit-seeking strategy of the private corporation are interested enterprises. The public policy process is anchored in the politics of the interest-group state. Second, academic scholarship in principle is conducted without immediate reference to monetary interests; public scholarship is always implicated in ownership and income interests, because public policy process always refers to ownership of property and income. Third, academic scholarship is conducted without explicit analysis of the consequences in the distribution of political, social, and economic power that would be brought about by success of the scholarship. In the public arena, contrarily, public historical scholarship is part of a policy formation process that in turn is part of a political process where explicit analysis of the impact of policy on the distribution of power is always made. Such a political analysis directly implicates public history.

When the differences between the academic and public (referring to both public and private-corporate) arenas are so stated, the differences appear obvious. No scholar doubts that politics and law are constitutionally based and practiced on the basis of regularized representation of interest, that is, advocacy. Advocacy leads to statements that all parties recognize as claims of interest, rather than reports of truth. In the courts, legal representation is explicitly advocational. At the same time, while we recognize the advocative—even adversary—quality of the public arena, we do not think that truth and fairness are irrelevant. An extremely important clue as to how a professional ethics for public historians may be fashioned is that representation of truth and fairness emerge from the contest of competing interests in the public arena. We shall return to this clue below.

WATER AND DESERTS

Two cases of public historical scholarship illustrate the adversarial quality of public history scholarship. The first example is the legal struggle over the allocation of Colorado River water between California and Arizona. The second example is the federal policy struggle over conservation of the California desert. In 1955, the State of Arizona sued the State of California to break the Colorado River Compact of 1922 and to increase its draw of Colorado River water.[2] Arizona's stake in the contest was the growth of Central Arizona Valley agriculture and of the Phoenix metropolitan area. A problem of interpreting the wording of the 1922 compact quickly led to the specific question of whether the Gila River, which runs entirely within Arizona, was referenced by the compact, even though it was not named. Settlement of this question required, in turn, determining whether the Gila River waters were already fully appropriated for use at the beginning of the twentieth century. Arizona contended that the Gila River was naturally (in its virgin state) a low-volume river. California contended that the river ran with a low volume only because its water was already being used. This was a straightforward, historical issue, and the first witness in this long and monumental case was a historian, Dr. Russell Ewing, professor of history at the University of Arizona, Tucson. Dr. Ewing was introduced as a "quasi-expert" (I:189) on the history of the West, with special qualifications in the history of Arizona.

Arizona's direct examination of Professor Ewing sought to establish that during the period of Arizona history from the first European exploration in the sixteenth century to the railroad era in the nineteenth century, "there were no great changes in the character of the Gila River" (I:463-A). Ewing based his judgment on examination of original records of exploration and observation of the Gila over three hundred years. His opinion amounted to instant historical scholarship. Ewing's testimony clearly supported the argument of Arizona and in this sense must be considered as advocacy.

Counsel for California endeavored in cross-examination to tear apart Professor's Ewing's scholarly judgment, to show it to be partial and inadequately based. California introduced conflicting evidence on the extent of cultivation and of the cattle industry along the Gila River. As a result of this evidence, Professor Ewing was forced to withdraw the firmness of his conclusion and admit that his judgment was merely interpretive. Indeed, California eventually forced Professor Ewing to admit that he could not even answer the question of the virgin state of the Gila River. Let us join the cross-examination at this point:

Mr. Ely (California): Q (Question) I revert to my initial question, Professor. Are you able to select any historical period, any year or approximate period of years which would characterize the flow of the Gila River at a time when it had not been disturbed by the activities of man?
The Master (presiding judge): "Man," including red or white?
Mr. Ely: I intend to ask him that next.
The Witness (Ewing): Not as a historian, I couldn't do that.
Mr. Ely: Q Can you do it with the amendment that is implicit in the Master's inquiry? Can you name a period when the flow of the Gila River had not been depleted by the activities of the white man?
A No, Sir, I couldn't.
Q You are an expert historian. If you cannot do it, can anyone else?
A Yes, Sir. I should think geologists.
The Master: It is beyond the scope of the science of history?
The Witness: Yes, Sir. [I:487–488]

I did not present this cross-examination to reveal what must have seemed to Professor Ewing to have been the nightmare of a doctoral exam gone bad. I want to show that scholarship in this particular setting—what we might think of as the paradigm of the adversative proceedings—is necessarily advocative in character, and cannot prima facie be objective or disinterested. At the same time, the implicit bias of this advocacy is dealt with by rules and procedures. In other words, in the public setting, fairness in scholarship is not only substantial, but is also procedural. Advocacy is conducted according to rules of procedure that constitute a testing of substance. The cross-examination of Professor Ewing's testimony quickly demonstrated that it advocated Arizona's interest. The full meaning of public historical scholarship, in other words, does not end with the scholar's credentials and investigation, but must include also adversarial testing by opposing interests.

The second example I wish to develop concerns the preparation of the California Desert Plan from 1976 to 1980. The California desert conservation plan was mandated by the Federal Land Policy and Management Act (Section 601) of 1976. The Federal Land Policy and Management Act requires the management of federal lands on three basic principles: multiple use, sustained yield, and maintenance of environmental quality. Section 601 pertains to the federally owned and administered lands of the California desert, some 12 million acres in a total desert of 24 million acres. A special desert plan team of Bureau of Land Management (BLM) personnel assembled in the Riverside, California district headquarters for desert administration.

Public involvement in the preparation of the desert plan focused on two instruments: the California Desert Conservation Advisory Committee and the Draft Plan hearings. The advisory committee held a series of fifteen forums from 1977 to 1979 with desert residents and owners. Resource inventories by BLM staff were presented at these forums for discussion. After the Draft Plan had been prepared in February 1980, a public review including four major public hearings was held. Overall, in the three years of preparation of the plan, some 9,000 "separate inputs" were received by planning staff, constituting some 40,000 "separate comments." This entire process of public involvement was monitored and audited by the League of Women Voters "to insure that the public comments received on the Draft Plan alternatives were analyzed thoroughly and impartially and were fairly presented in a form that would provide the fullest opportunities for consideration in the decision-making process."[3]

Historical inventory and documentation of the desert was conducted both by BLM staff personnel and by contract. Typical products of such contracts include "Cultural Resources of the California Desert, 1776–1980: Historic Trails and Wagon Roads" by Elizabeth von Till Warren and Ralph J. Roske, associated with the University of Nevada, Las Vegas, and "Desert Fever: An Overview of Mining of the California Desert," by Larry M. Vredenburgh, Gary L. Shumway, and Russell D. Hartill, associated with California State University, Fullerton (this title references the privately printed book that developed out of the contract research). This historical research was not conducted within a neutral framework; rather, it was meant to provide the basis for protection of cultural values, that is, for restriction of public access. As Wes Chambers, assistant director of the Desert Plan staff, stated, "as a result of this planning program, sensitive and significant cultural values including wagon roads and trails will be assured greater protection through more intensive management."[4]

The power of planned protection and restriction of public access and use is revealed by the land classification categories imposed on the desert. The Desert Plan devises five classes of geographical use of the desert: controlled use or wilderness management, limited use, moderate use, intensive use, and unclassified. The controlled use category constitutes 17.3 percent of BLM lands and evoked great controversy, since it closed these lands to motorized access.

Within the category of controlled use are some forty-seven Areas of

Critical Environmental Concern (ACEC). The Areas of Critical Environmental Concern contain potential national register sites and other sites potentially eligible for listing on federal inventories, such as the Historic Buildings Survey and the Historic American Engineering Record. Historical research on such sites automatically becomes advocacy, because Executive Order 11593 (1971) requires that potential, federally owned National Register sites be protected as if they were already listed.

This example of public historical scholarship within the federal agency policy process reveals the same lesson as the example of legal testimony in a trial. Public historical scholarship is not disinterested or neutral, by reason of its imbeddedness in the public process. Fairness is maintained by the rules of procedure, which provide for testing of claims by advocates of opposing interests.

AN ETHICS AGENDA FOR PUBLIC HISTORIANS

In three major areas, the nature of public historical scholarship necessitates explicit instruction in professional ethics and codification of professional ethics for public historians. These areas are conflict of interest, fairness doctrine, and professionalization of status.

1. *Conflict of interest.* The Political Reform Act of 1974 and the Conflict of Interest Code of the University of California, for instance, require that University of California scholars disqualify themselves from making a decision concerning the academic merit of scholarly proposals of other scholars when that decision may foreseeably affect their own financial interests. This code statement is in line with the ethical posture of academic scholarship and federal agency contract review, which assume that such review and scholarship must be disinterested.

We must notice that public arena proceedings (not excluding governmental process), private sector enterprise, and legal proceedings are based upon the contrary notion, namely, that the pursuit of specific results—whether scholarly or remunerative—is conducted by parties interested in the results. Professional codes relating to such proceedings (of attorneys, for instance) establish conflict of interest ethics different from those established in an academic setting, on the principle that interested advocacy must represent only one interest, and represent it vigorously. In other words, academic conflict of interest codes require disinterestedness, whereas public arena codes require recognition of, and uncompromised and explicit representation of, interest.

From the point of view of the public arena, there is no ground of absolute disinterestedness on which the public scholar may stand. Other parties will perceive and respond to the public scholar as if that scholar represented an interest. The public process will force that perception; consequently it is necessary for the public scholar to adopt a conflict of interest ethical statement that will satisfy the expectations of the public arena. Such a statement would have, I believe, three elements. First, there must be formal disclosure of interest by the scholar. Second, there must be sufficient information about the scholar so that adversary parties may be reassured that the scholar does not unintentionally represent a covert interest. (A disclosure statement and biographical statement must be attached to each scholarly production of the public scholar. A by-line identification is not adequate.) Third, the public historian as advocate must claim to represent an interest, but only one interest.

2. *Fairness doctrine.* In academic scholarship, scholarly fairness depends upon the integrity of the scholar, and peer review. By fairness in scholarship, we mean, for instance, that originality is not falsely claimed, that evidence is not knowingly distorted, that presentation of evidence is not partial or biased, that opposing interpretations of evidence are accurately rendered and accounted for, and that research has been thorough. Given the enormity of a book-length scholarly enterprise, consistent fairness in practice depends primarily upon the integrity of the scholar, who will usually be the only person to have examined his or her own scholarship in detail. The scholar is presumed to have internalized the standards of academic scholarship in graduate training, and benefit of the doubt is given regarding the impartiality of the scholarship. Secondarily, fairness is maintained by peer review, i.e., the referee system of peer evaluation of funded research proposals, manuscripts submitted for publication, and peer criticism in other forums, such as scholarly conventions. .

In the public arena, fairness in public history scholarship cannot presumably be maintained in the same way as in academic scholarship. First, it is presumed that partiality in presentation and consequent distortion will be intrinsically part of the representation by advocacy. Second, peer review is not always a part of public history scholarship. This does not mean that public research proceedings are incapable of being fair. Rather, it means that safeguards of fairness are not implicit in public scholarship; instead, safeguards of fairness are procedural. Public hearings, court hearings with cross-examination, and possibility for legal redress of decisions when new material facts are presented provide a procedural context in which the fairness of a document may be tested. In addition, it is presumed that parties whose interest is opposed to that of the sponsors of the research will come forward and critique the scholarship or its implications. Fairness is therefore the result of the process, though each stage and each party in the process may not represent fairness in its entirety.

I believe that public history scholarship must make the leap from academic notions to public arena notions of fairness. I do not intend by such a leap, however, that academic notions of intrinsic or substantive fairness are left behind; rather, public arena notions of procedural fairness must be grafted onto academic notions of implicit fairness. Deliberation of proposals as to how this leap may be accomplished in practice should be a major part of the agenda of public historians in the years ahead.

3. *Professionalization of status.* There are a variety of reasons for

instruction in professional ethics and for a professional code of ethics for public historians, not least of which is protection of the enterprise itself, as well as of public historians. A professional code of ethics should provide a means by which responsibility and negligence in professional conduct may be distinguished. The public historian working as a publicly employed historical preservationist, for instance, may be sued for misuse of public agency procedures, such as not providing sufficient public notice of a hearing on a proposed building restriction. While such a suit would legally be addressed to the public laws that require such hearings, I believe that public history, as a scholarly profession, would be impugned by such a suit, as much as is the process of public conduct of governmental business, such as zoning law enactment.

One step in distinguishing between responsible practice and malpractice would be a statement of responsibility, to which public historians would ascribe. Such a statement would affirm, first, that public historians are responsible for scholarship conducted by themselves, regardless of the sponsorship of the scholarship and second, that public historians' highest responsibilities are to substantial *and procedural* fairness of scholarship. It should be accepted as adequate grounds for noncompliance of contracted research, that the public historian believes, for reasons made clear following initiation of research, that compliance would violate substantial as well as procedural fairness. For instance, if a public historian conducts research for a private corporation and that research is unacceptable to the corporation, leading to its suppression for practical purposes; then the historian should be legally capable of appealing to professional standards to break contract and not be compelled to complete the contract. Acceptance of this doctrine would mean that the historian would not have to return contract funds which were expended in performance of the contract up to the moment of disassociation. Lastly, formal instruction in professional ethics must be part of the training of public historians. The major public history professional associations, such as the American Association for State and Local History, the American Association of Museums, and the Society of American Archivists, already require graduate training programs to offer instruction in professional ethics if they desire these agencies' certification.

Ethical training, which we call "Professional Practice for the Public Historian" in the Program in Historic Resources Management at University of California, Riverside, would acquaint the public historian with the extensive ethical deliberation that has been conducted already by the mix of nonacademic historical professionals represented by archivists, museum curators, and anthropologists, for instance. It would acquaint public historians with the requirements of the public history process, exemplified, for instance, in federal contract research. The greatest possibility for the public historian to avoid ethically ambiguous research lies in the full knowledge of the character of public history proceedings.

REFERENCES

1. I am not addressing the question whether the AAUP Statement on Ethics accurately describes how scholars conduct scholarship, i.e., whether scholarship is actually disinterested. I separate the rules of ethics from normative description. This paper is not addressing a "straw man" in its characterization of academic ethics. The distinction between description and adjudication is precisely the distinction at the basis of the legal adjudication of legal responsibility in criminal proceedings. For instance, everyone agrees that biochemical states of the brain "cause" criminal behavior, but no one believes that description of such biochemical states enables adjudication of legal responsibility. Similarly, the AAUP statement does not need, and we do not need, for purposes of the argument in this paper, to describe the biochemical states of academic scholarship. For the AAUP ethics statement and University of California conduct code, see "Handbook for Faculty Members of the University of California" (1978). On the ethical statements and review policy of federal research agencies, see Department of Interior, administrative manual, section 1514 "Unsolicited Proposals," (1976) and section 1513 "Preparation and Administration of Negotiated Proposals" (1976).

2. Arizona v. California, Palo Verde Irrigation District, et. al., U. S. Supreme Court, October Term, 1956. All citations in the text are to the volumes reporting this case.

3. U. S. Department of Interior, Bureau of Land Management, Desert District, Riverside, California, *The California Desert Conservation Area Plan* (1980).

4. Elizabeth von Till Warren and Ralph J. Roske, "Cultural Resources of the California Desert, 1776–1980: Historic Trails and Wagon Roads," n.p., preface.

... Ulasewicz? He was the retired New York City cop who came out of Watergate with his "reputation" intact. The senators and the press thought he was funny. He knew better; he was telling it like it was. He had no delusions about his importance. He believed, and assumed everyone else knew, that paying hush money wasn't Kosher—but he did it, and probably would do it again, if the price was right.

3
ETHICS IN PUBLIC HISTORY: CLIO MEETS ULASEWICZ

Roy H. Lopata

Historians have served unnoticed outside the classroom for decades. Yet for reasons that remain obscure, more recent nonacademic historians, under the banner of public history, have asked, somewhat self-consciously, what we are—assayers of truth, or employees like everybody else? Thus, while academic historians have largely ignored the issue, public historians have begun to wrestle with the codification of ethical standards, canons of conduct, or similar commandments for their brethren. The code-makers have traveled along two parallel, and sometimes intersecting, paths. First, they hope to enshrine a special and complex methodology, taught in history graduate departments, available, by appointment only, from doctors of philosophy in history. A historian's guild, thereby established, would then serve as a bulwark against the invasion, real or imagined, of others into the historian's realm. That is, only those with appropriate training in history would be certified as "professional historians," able to subscribe to the tenets of the code. Historians would be assured that they alone would be responsible for guarding and interpreting the records, artifacts, and other relics of our nation's past. Governmental agencies, historical museums, libraries, and similar institutions would be comforted in the knowledge that when they hired a certified ethical historian they were getting the real thing.[1]

The second and perhaps more troublesome issue raised by historian

The Public Historian, Vol. 8, No. 1 (Winter 1986) © 1986 by the Regents of the University of California

code-makers involves the supposed tension between historical truth and
the requirements and goals of the institutions employing public historians. The code, here, would serve to protect, defend, and perhaps foster
historian whistle-blowers, hunting through institutional and corporate
archives for facts that would serve truth and justice. The code, so it is
said, would remind those who would hire historians that while they paid
the salaries, their historian employees would remain faithful to Clio
rather than Nixon.

Will it work? Will the twin goals of preserving history for the historians and protecting historians from themselves be served by a code of
ethics? Or are these goals inherently flawed within the context of the
public history idea?

Certainly, the historian's effort to limit access to historical agencies
and history-oriented employment follows the pattern of other professions. Doctors, lawyers, engineers, architects, psychiatric social workers,
surveyors, and so on have all tried, with varying degrees of success, to
erect barriers to keep outsiders from gaining employment traditionally
allocated to their respective fields. And in many of these cases, these
guilds protect both the professionals involved and the public. Who could
legitimately argue with licensing distinctions made between a brain sur-
geon and a chiropractor? But the question remains, can similar licensing
classifications be established for history-related positions to keep anthropologists or geographers out, for example, and keep historians in?

In the context of what public history has meant to those of us trained
in history and now working in the public sector, the answer is obvious.
From the outset, public historians have argued that historians cannot be
restricted to teaching alone; they can and should do other things. We
have repeatedly advocated an open-door policy for historians in business administration, research, planning, archival management, policy-
making, and analysis. The idea of an exclusive sector of the economy
reserved for historians, coupled with the notion that almost all other careers should be available for those with historical training, seems far-
fetched. The special qualifications historians bring to their tasks must
be real and valid and not based on artificially created restraints.

In my case, our local and more traditionally educated planners did not
exactly do handsprings when they learned, eight years ago, that a history
Ph.D. had been appointed to serve as Newark, Delaware's planning director. Eventually they learned, as I did, that a historian can survive as a
planner, but conversely does it not follow that planners with an interest
and knowledge of history might serve in history-related positions? For-
tunately, the artificial and academically generated barriers between professions have, to some extent, been eliminated in many governmental
institutional settings. As Melvin Levin, writing in *Planning* (the official
publication of the American Planning Association) notes, municipal
and management planning departments today tend to consist of "public
administrators, economists, MBAs, and the ubiquitous lawyers. Depending on the type of operation, there may be a good many engineers
and scientists, statisticians, accountants, educators, or even exotic clas-

sicists and historians."[2] Thus, any effort to certify historians will surely prove counterproductive and, beyond that, blatantly contradicts public history's essential multidisciplinary and multivocational approach. A movement that encourages the use of history outside the classroom cannot erect barriers to keep other professionals from doing the things historians wish to reserve for themselves.

On the other hand, while we might reject using the code to validate some form of historian's guild, we might at a minimum accept the idea of a code to help historians struggle with their consciences when truth conflicts with duty. This issue, the question of historian as institutional advocate versus historian as objective and neutral scholar, has stimulated the most debate and concern, especially amongst those who imagine that such tensions are inherent in nonacademic careers.[3]

Obviously, just as governmental agencies, businesses, or organizations employing English Ph.D.s would expect good writing, such institutions should anticipate good history from historians. A client who hires a historian for historiographical tasks is obviously interested in a real past, not fiction—a usable past perhaps, but at a minimum the historian's best judgment as to what happened and why. But at the same time, historians for hire cannot remain employable for long if their personal needs or curiosities override their employer's legitimate interest in the product. The tug-of-war between, on one extreme, the objective historian let loose to work his will in the archives and, on the other, the hired gun writing institutional public relations, remains to be fought out on a case-by-case basis. It seems more useful and practical for all parties to agree upon the specific ground rules at the start—including arrangements for mediating disputes—than for historians to establish a generalized code of behavior.

Moreover, public history does not refer solely to historians undertaking clearly history-related employment in nonacademic settings. Indeed the public history idea, as it has evolved through the pages of *The Public Historian* and the classroom, has explicitly endorsed the notion that the historian belongs just about everywhere in society outside medicine, mathematics, and the sciences. Thus, public history implies that historians can do more than write history for hire—after all, how many opportunities of this type can possibly exist; they can, in fact, work as employees for labor unions, for federal, state, or local governments, for nonprofit organizations, and for every other institution imaginable. This is not to say that the tools of the trade, or the historian's habit of seeing the present through precedent, do not come to bear at times, but rather that these things, wonderful though they may be, are not the work itself. Employees with graduate training in history will not be hurt by a historian's code, but they will be much better served through their relevant professional organization codes, internal institutional standards, and, of course, personal integrity. Perhaps these are not historians at all—yet, the more there are of them the more there are of the other kind, those who teach history and do so without a code.

In any case, the code-makers can rest easy. The imagined moral and ethical dilemmas seldom arise for the historian employee, and those that do either could have been avoided from the outset, or can be resolved through existing mechanisms or personal choice. And because my municipal experience has to a considerable extent involved land use and development—a field rife with unethical, not to mention corrupt, possibilities—I think I can speak with some authority on the matter.

From the beginning of my work with the City of Newark, I understood that I served at the pleasure of Newark's city manager (who hired a historian at some, albeit minor, risk), and with the support of the representatives of our citizens—Newark's city council. Before taking office, I took an oath to support the Constitution of the State of Delaware and the Constitution of the United States of America. I had no reservations about taking these oaths; I needed the work and, as I understand these documents, they are worth supporting. I also assumed that if the citizens of Newark ever asked me to ignore either the United States or the State of Delaware constitutions, to violate any state or city laws, or, and this remains paramount, to disregard my own understanding of how cities function, grow, and prosper, I would leave. Like almost everyone I have come to know in public service, I understand that my crusades had to coincide with those of the community that I had been hired to serve. Ethics, morality, right or wrong—all come into play (outside of the obvious area of bribery) if I cross the line and begin to follow my own agenda, rather than that of the citizens of Newark. And this point of view is not unique; rather it is the norm for staff members in public service.

For example, in the published results of a recent survey of over 600 publicly employed planners and members of the American Institute of Planners (now known as the American Institute of Certified Planners), the authors conclude that "ethical standards in planning are relative. It is certainly true that some kinds of behavior, such as distorting information, are considered unacceptable by the vast majority of all planners. *But even for these behaviors, there remain some planners who still consider them ethical* [my italics]. . . . This variability in ethical judgment means that it is very difficult to establish any single ethical standard that is meaningful to the whole profession".[4] Planners, like historians, find their values shifting in response to changing circumstances despite the existence of a detailed American Institute of Planner's Code of Ethics and Professional Conduct, originally adopted in 1948, and subsequently revised and expanded in 1959, 1970, and 1981.

Yes, but what about truth? Suppose no matter how carefully arrangements are made prior to undertaking a task, the historian or the employee comes across some earthshaking fact that must be exposed. Well, here again, subjective judgment comes into play; that is, how important is the issue and, if it is crucial, is the institutional explanation plausible. After all, daily events are subject to numerous, often conflicting interpretations, putting historians under considerable strain when attempting to assess matters that have receded in time

And, as luck would have it, literally the day I began this essay, a small example of the limitations of historical evidence occurred which might be relevant here. In my position as planning director, I have had the dubious honor of being one of those who, in effect, "create" the facts that historians might sift through in their quest for truth. A future University of Delaware graduate student, for example, doing research on the history of land-use regulation in Delaware, might come across the following headline in the Wilmington *Morning News:* "Newark Stiffens Requirements for Occupancy of Developments." Then he or she would read that the "Newark City Council has voted to issue certificates of occupancy for up to fifty percent of a development, if the developers meet certain stiffer requirements. . . . Roy H. Lopata, Director of Planning, told the council that while the flexibility in regard to bonding would allow builders to sell homes faster, the fact that no more than fifty percent of the homes in a new subdivision can be sold under this arrangement stiffens the old requirement." Further on, the historian would note that Lopata told a reporter, "Sometimes developers go broke. We needed to find different ways of bonding so no one skips town and doesn't finish a subdivision."[5] Not surprisingly, nothing in this article is correct. The ordinance that I drafted and that our city council approved *relaxed* requirements for occupancy of developments. In any case, the point here is that historians often find the meagerist of records of the events they wish to describe—in this instance a straightforward news article would tell the historian the opposite of the truth. Could the historian find it by reading the new ordinance? It is not likely. Without experience in subdivision regulation or land-use law, the ordinance would appear meaningless. Obviously, reading history's first drafts in the press, when you know what really happened, tends to foster a somewhat jaundiced—perhaps cynical—attitude toward the historian's efforts, years later, to reconstruct events as they really occurred.

Beyond that, it is because historians understand, in theory at least, that our societal problems have complex and multi-faceted roots, that historians have the potential to help solve them. Presumably, we are not wedded to preconceived notions, caught up in fads, nor easily swept off our feet by new panaceas. We do not offer some special methodological mumbo-jumbo. What we offer instead is the very opposite—history tells us that making things work is hard work; simple truths will not do when our cities and communities face mounting financial and physical problems. As Marc Pachter has said, "public history is awkwardly defined as a field, but it may deserve to be described as an attitude."[6] And it is that attitude, the combination of the pragmatic with a philosophy based upon and tempered by historical perspective, that stands in stark contrast to the typical description of many of my planning colleagues:

A number of planners (often, but by no means always, recent graduates) tend to scatter moral preachments about like confetti. Full of instant judgments on the ethical failures of their superiors or on the inequities of a system that rewards establishment toadies, oppresses the poor, and promotes senile incompetence, they display a morbid suspicion of the system bordering on paranoia. Another, less blatantly obnoxious breed of planners behaves like a stuffy priesthood. They issue edicts. Conscious of their special training, their chosen mission, and their unique skills, these planners present their superiors with The Plan, correct and therefore unassailable. If in the normal course of events The Plan is modified and compromised, they refuse to acknowledge paternity for the bastard, let alone take responsibility for implementation. Once again they have cast their pearls before the swine and the porkers have won."[7]

Interestingly, when I came into planning I seem to have understood implicitly that nothing is forever, that plans change, that we cannot look forward with any real sense of purpose or chance of success without standing on the firm ground of what has come before. This is not to imply that public history results in crude historical determinism or municipal planning and management by historical analogy. But rather, that historical perspective helps insure that public servants, with or without graduate training in history, will better understand the relationship of the past events to the tasks at hand.

Of course public historians have feelings and, perhaps, passionate points of view. Of course public historians have a sense of right and wrong. And our morality is shaped by the study of history. Yet our sense of morality or ethics is much like the history that each of us writes alone. We build book upon book on the work that comes before us. We learn and borrow from one another. The result—the collective story we tell—becomes written history. In the end, however, what we write and what we do must stand on their own merits. History remains a solitary task; we seldom write or research by committee. So, too, the ethical and moral considerations we bring to our scholarship, our research, and our service; we can no more write codes for each other than we can write each other's books, articles, reports, or memoranda. In my case, I will do my work as before, and let the citizens I serve judge me.

REFERENCES

1. I first heard this idea suggested (but not necessarily advocated) in a public history context by G. Wesley Johnson at the Third Annual Conference on Public History session "The Professionalization of History," Raleigh, North Carolina, April 25, 1981.
2. Melvin R. Levin, "Bumpy Roads Ahead," *Planning*, July 14, 1984, p. 30.
3. See especially Terence O'Donnell, "Pitfalls Along the Path of Public History," *The Public Historian* 4, no. 1 (Winter 1982), 65–72.
4. Elizabeth Howe and Jerome Kaufman, "The Ethics of Contemporary American Planners," *Journal of the American Planning Association* 45 (July 1979), 253.
5. *Wilmington Morning News,* July 14, 1984.
6. Marc Pachter, "A Historian . . . is a Historian . . . is a Historian," *Humanities,* October, 1981, p. 10.
7. Levin, "Bumpy Roads Ahead," 31.

Previous versions of this paper were given at the Social Science History Association Convention in 1981, at the Association of American Law Schools Convention in 1983, and at the Caltech History Colloquium in 1983. One of the special joys of writing and giving this paper has been the chance to learn from people whose attention I would not usually be able to demand. I particularly want to thank for their comments Brian Barry, Derrick Bell, John Benton, Armand Derfner, Jim O'Fallon, Phil Hoffman, Will Jones, Dan Kevles, Steve Morse, and Ed Still. Since it seems likely that all of them retain some reservations about the paper, none should be held responsible for its remaining flaws.

4
ARE EXPERT WITNESSES WHORES? REFLECTIONS ON OBJECTIVITY IN SCHOLARSHIP AND EXPERT WITNESSING

J. Morgan Kousser

Expert Witnesses' general reputation for veracity is not untainted. In the elegant and tasteful expression of Harold Green, director of the Law, Science, and Technology Program at George Washington University, "Expert witnesses are whores. . . ." Others interviewed for a newspaper article on science and public policy, in which Green's statement appears, were somewhat more charitable in their diction, but affirmed that expert witnesses were "chosen not for their wisdom or sagacity but for their willingness to say in the simplest, clearest, least tentative way what a particular side wants said."[1]

On the other hand, some scholars who have served as experts, who are not, perhaps, entirely unbiased witnesses on the topic, claim to have retained their virtue. James Rosse, a Stanford economist who was reportedly paid $240,000 by American Telephone and Telegraph in 1981 to

The Public Historian, Vol. 6, No. 1 (Winter 1984)
© 1984 by the Regents of the University of California

perform studies in support of that corporation's position in its antitrust case, contended that "the legal process would tear to shreds any person who altered his views for a trial," and asserted that he informed the company that "there are things I will not testify to." Dean Henry Rossovsky of Harvard, an economist who testified for IBM during its antitrust case, insisted that scholars who do this type of consulting have a strong incentive not to distort their views or to dissimulate, because they must protect their professional reputations. "They don't have any other assets of significance," Rossovsky told a *New York Times* reporter. "If you get the reputation of being a hired gun, it won't help you."[2]

The question of the possible tensions between advocacy and objectivity presents somewhat different facets to the three groups most directly concerned with expert witnessing: scholars, lawyers, and judges. Responding to historian Lee Benson's 1977 Social Science History Association presidential address, which had the provocative title "Changing Social Science to Change the World," political scientist Warren Miller distinguished between pure and applied science and commented that "the motivation to do good—or bad—is simply different from the motivation to find out how things work, and it is the transformation of the latter motivation into action that is science."[3] For historians, more particularly, the crux of the problem is not the old epistemological chestnut, "Can the study of history be objective?" but a simpler and less absolute, if longer, question: "Assuming that it makes sense to say that some analyses are more objective than others, are historians who serve as expert witnesses likely to be less objective, either because of their own commitments or because of some aspects of the legal process, than other historians are, or than the witnesses themselves are when they are doing their normal scholarship?"

Lawyers see the topic from a different vantage point. If my experience with them is at all representative, attorneys tend to believe that their own experts are pure, even to the point of being too prissy to agree to state their own conclusions in a way which would be most helpful to the lawyers' clients—while the other side's are merely lying for money. Should lawyers treat expert witnesses—for either side or both—as analogues to celebrity endorsers of products? Is Dr. K's analysis of the reasons for the adoption of the Mobile city government act in the 1870s worthy of more deference than Dr. J's endorsement of a basketball sneaker?

Judges, whose distorted "law office" versions of history written to serve their own points of view reverberate from *Dred Scott* through *Wesberry v. Sanders* (the Georgia legislative reapportionment case) to *Mobile v. Bolden,* may see the problem of experts' objectivity in yet another guise.[4] Have expert witnesses, to paraphrase Chief Justice Taney's famous phrase in *Dred Scott,* any opinions that judges are bound to respect? Is the view of a credentialed historian or other social scientist entitled to any more weight than that of a man on the street or a random law clerk, or than the judge's own "common sense"? (In two of the cases in which I've been involved—not, let it be noted, ones in which the side which I was testifying for won—the judges' answers, as implied by their opinions, have been "Yes, if the witnesses agree with my preconceived, seat-of-the-pants opinion; otherwise, no.")

My own experience as an expert witness in six voting rights cases causes me to doubt the soundness of Warren Miller's observation, quoted above. Changing the world and doing normal social science or history are not such different pursuits after all. Perhaps I am blinded by good intentions or the heat of battle, but it seems to me that cases from Birmingham; Mobile; Selma; Brownsville, Tennessee; and Sumter, South Carolina; as well as an appearance before a House Judiciary Subcommittee hearing on renewing the Voting Rights Act, afforded me opportunities *to tell the truth and do good at the same time.*

Those of us who desire to bring scholarship to bear on current policy problems, moreover, need no new institutional arrangement to make our advocacy more effective. Indeed, the organization of a group of progressive scholars to produce policy-relevant studies, such as Lee Benson has proposed, might well reduce, rather than increase, its members' ability to influence policy.[5] For not only would it call into question the scholars' *reputation* for objectivity—which my experience has taught me is a necessary condition for them to exert any influence at all—but by removing some of the usual professional checks on slipshod scholarship, it might also undermine their objectivity in *reality* as well. Changing social science might therefore leave the disciplines worse off, and the world unchanged.

Before discussing the more general question, let me explain how I got involved in testifying. Since, as a historian, I have an occupational susceptibility to genetic explanations, my story will require a detour into the history of civil rights law. It may not be straining words too much to assert that the Fifteenth Amendment contains an explicit reference to intent. The right to vote, it declares, shall not be "denied or abridged *on account of* race, color, or previous condition of servitude" (emphasis added). One reading of the phrase is that any law or practice adopted with a racially discriminatory intent ("on account of race") is by that fact alone unconstitutional. Despite the fact that the Fourteenth Amendment contains no language which even this clearly refers to intent, the courts have read an intent criterion into it. In fact, they have intermingled the standards of proof and lines of cases under each of the two amendments, which would no doubt be confusing enough if separated, to such a degree that the whole area of the law has become covered with a sort of constitutional kudzu, a mass of pullulating, ever more tangled, parasitic vines which have long since grown over and hidden the original constitutional saplings.

Thus, in *Plessy v. Ferguson* in 1896, the Supreme Court was content to assume that racially separate railroad cars were in fact equally comfortable and convenient, while it concentrated on denying that whites who imposed segregation *intended* it to be racially discriminatory. In *Williams v. Mississippi* in 1898, the Court admitted that the framers of the 1890 Mississippi Constitution intended to deny blacks the right to vote, but held that since the plaintiff had not shown that their intent was carried out, he had not proved a constitutional violation. The next year, in *Cumming v. Richmond County,* the justices shunted aside the obvious fact that the Augusta, Georgia school board discriminated when it provided two public high schools for whites, but closed the only one it had run for blacks, and focused on what Justice John Marshall Harlan took to be the crucial question—whether the school board had behaved "reasonably," or, in other words, without an *intent* to discriminate. Presented with evidence of both intent and effect in *Giles v. Harris,* a 1903 voting case, that great liberal Justice Oliver Wendell Holmes threw up his hands and declared disfranchisement a "political question."[6]

More recent courts have hacked no clearer path through the judicial thicket of intent and effect. In *Brown v. Board,* the Supreme Court appears to have assumed that if the National Association for the Advancement of Colored People's (NAACP's) lawyers and expert witnesses could show that segregation had bad effects on black children, then they need not prove that school officials acted intentionally to bring about those consequences, but only that they had meant to segregate the schools, which of course all admitted. Where segregation was not formally established, however, the focus shifted to the school board's actions, such moves as gerrymandering attendance zones and siting new schools only in safely segregated areas being taken as evidence of the authorities' segregative intent. Segregation because of housing patterns (patterns which were no doubt partly produced by the actions of other governmental agencies, if not by the school boards), may have been indistinguishable in its effects from so-called *de jure* segregation, but since it was allegedly not intended, it was ruled constitutional, for example, in the Detroit school case, *Milliken v. Bradley.*[7]

That there were close parallels between the school cases and those in the voting rights and other areas is hardly surprising. Tuskegee, Alabama gerrymandered its town boundaries so blatantly as to leave no question as to its racially discriminatory intent; therefore, the Supreme Court could finesse the issue.[8] In the initial reapportionment opinions, too, intent played little role, and attempts to achieve legislative ends which would in other cases have induced judicial obsequiousness were blithely shunted aside in the drive for a population equality effect.[9] Yet in the Indianapolis at-large voting case, *Whitcomb v. Chavis,* the Court ruled that evidence of a racially unequal impact, by itself, was not enough; whereas, a week later in the Jackson, Mississippi municipal swimming pool closing case, *Palmer v. Thompson,* it concluded that an overwhelming case based on intent was insufficient.[10]

The lines between intent and effect crossed and re-crossed in what now seems to be the leading Supreme Court case on at-large voting in multi-member districts, *White v. Regester.* Since the Voting Rights Act and the Twenty-fourth Amendment suspended literacy tests and poll taxes, at-large elections have been perhaps the major device for abridging or "diluting" minority political power. In *White,* a 1973 case from Dallas, the Supreme Court held that there is no constitutional right to proportional representation, and that at-large systems are not, *per se,* unconstitutional. They are illegal, however, if combined with other electoral devices which reduce the chances of minorities to elect persons of their choice, and if they occur in areas with a history of racial discrimination which is currently manifested in racially discriminatory slating groups, racial bloc voting, and a lack of responsiveness by officials to minority desires, or at least some of these. Further, direct evidence that the system had been established or maintained for a racial purpose, if such evidence were available, would, insofar as one can be sure of any doctrinal consistency in this area of the law, be held to be probative. In the leading Appeals Court decision, *Zimmer v. McKeithen,* the *White* indicia were restated and refined, while in a series of mid- to late-1970s Supreme Court cases not directly related to multimember districts, the Court emphasized with increasing insistence that intent was central to all racial discrimination cases.[11]

White and *Zimmer* made clear that expert testimony by historians might be useful to paint a general picture of the history of racism, in order, at the least, to educate judges or to remind them of social facts which they might otherwise prefer to forget.[12] And such testimony might be determinative if the historian could produce credible circumstantial or direct evidence that the intent of the framers of laws passed some time ago, now under challenge, was discriminatory. But whereas civil rights lawyers seem to have been well connected to a network of sociologists and political scientists who did research on voting rights, neither they nor the social scientists knew many historians, and historians were almost wholly ignorant of the relevant developments in the law. I was "discovered," if that is the correct word, by Edward Still, a particularly assiduous Birmingham lawyer with a pronounced historical bent (who has since gone on to do graduate work in history as a sideline) who read my book, called and recruited me, and mentioned my name to others. Thus, by the fateful day of April 22, 1980, I had been engaged as an expert witness in two cases, in one of which I was to serve mainly the "educational" purpose of recounting the history of racism in South Carolina politics, and in the other of which my role was to show the discriminatory intent behind a particular provision of the 1901 Alabama Constitution.

The event of April 22, 1980, which threw the civil rights forces into what turned out to be a productive tizzy and which made historians, temporarily at least, not only window-dressing but necessary participants in voting right cases, was the Supreme Court's decision in *Mobile v. Bolden.*[13] Writing for a four-man plurality, Justice Potter Stewart, without explicitly overruling *White v. Regester,* reinterpreted its holding as requiring proof of discriminatory intent and denied that the so-called "*Zimmer* factors," which had been derived chiefly from *White,* added up to evidence of intent. To some observers, it appeared that the Court, or at least the prevailing opinion, was demanding production of a gun still smoking after fifty years or more; that is, that plaintiffs had to prove that legislators who passed laws, often as long as a half-century ago, were actuated by racially discriminatory motives.[14] If this interpretation stuck, the Justice Department, the NAACP Legal Defense Fund, the Mexican-American Legal Defense Fund, the American Civil Liberties Union, and private attorneys for minority groups had little choice but to *call in the historians.* The facts of Reconstruction, Redemption, and the Progressive Era became as relevant in the courtroom as regression analyses of racial bloc voting had been since 1973.

At the time the Supreme Court heard *Bolden* and a companion school board case from Mobile, *Brown v. Board,* the lawyers for neither side had done all their historical homework. They traced the at-large systems back to 1911 and 1919, respectively, and stopped there. When the Supreme Court remanded *Bolden* and *Brown* back to the federal district court, the Justice Department and the Mobile counsel who had handled the case for the NAACP-LDF, assisted by a historian located in Mobile, Peyton McCrary, discovered that the at-large features of the election systems dated not from the teens, after most blacks had been disfranchised in Alabama, but from the 1870s, when the threat of black political power was much more palpable.[15] I was brought in principally to provide "full period coverage," as one would say in the history job market, since McCrary's scholarly research had been on the Civil War and Reconstruction, while my specialty has been the post-Reconstruction and "Progressive" eras.

Researching the cases felt familiar. I started with some general but not unshakable beliefs about how the world works and how historians should seek to explain things, a hypothesis to test, and some prior knowledge of election laws and of the place and period. After culling through the evidence, I tried to organize it to bring it to bear on the question of why the Alabama legislature passed a law providing for at-large elections for Mobile in a certain year. It was only in preparing for and going through cross-examination and watching others be cross-examined that the question of biases different from those encountered in more traditional scholarly pursuits arose. (How *dare* opposing counsel imply that I would shade the truth to make a point for the sake of money or ideology!) But once opened, the question of objectivity would not—will not—recede entirely from my consciousness. Somewhat different research experiences in three other cases, in which I worked with and against different lawyers and before different judges, expanded my experience, but did not change the nature of the questions or answers about objectivity.

What does scholarly objectivity in history consist in, how do one's values enter into one's normal scholarship, and is the situation any different for one preparing to testify as an expert witness? First, values, tastes, talents, and circumstances guide one's initial choice of topic. What seems interesting to one person may bore another—I like tables and equations, and narrative puts me to sleep, but I recognize that other people's views differ, though I cannot account for their egregious preferences. As a southern white liberal with a life-long interest in politics, I naturally gravitated toward political history, more specifically southern political history, and even more particularly the politics of race and class in the South. Others with different burdens or penchants would consider such topics dull, but sex or death or women fascinating. I find all three subjects absorbing—but not to read about. Much good history, too, is written by people caught up in special circumstances or surroundings. Local history examples too numerous to detail spring to mind, but other cases would include Trevor-Roper's work on Hitler's last days, occasioned by his participation in a British intelligence task force, and C. Vann Woodward's *Battle for Leyte Gulf,* a product of his wartime Washington navy job of consolidating and making sense of battle reports.[16]

The prevailing research agenda determines other choices of topics. A subject closely related to a currently "hot" topic in a field may get a scholar a grant, and will nearly guarantee a longer vita, perhaps a prize, and maybe even tenure. Equally good work far from conventional interests will saddle one with a reputation (if any) as a person who may be "solid," but who works on dull or strange topics, or (if one is very lucky or insightful) eventual, possibly posthumous recognition as a "pioneer." Similarly, the whims of funding agencies are not entirely irrelevant to the activities of academics or at least to the packaging of those endeavors. It was no coincidence that when the Nixon administration began pouring money into the National Cancer Institute, cancer research became a growth area in biology. As all these examples show, value-laden or self-interested reasons for choosing research topics are so omnipresent that it is difficult to imagine someone who could not be faulted for having a bias in choice of topics. Indeed, it is hard to understand what it would mean to say that someone had chosen his topic "objectively." As a consequence, any charge on this ground of a lack of objectivity for a historian doing legal casework must be *nol-prossed.*

A second consideration related to objectivity is in the assumptions a historian or any other social scientist makes and in the ways in which he or she formulates the chief questions. Here, I must confess to bias. I believe in making assumptions, reasoning processes, and conclusions as clear and explicit as possible. Some historians practice and even preach obfuscation for art's sake, and many social scientists purvey muddledness in the name of science. I intend otherwise, even if I do not always attain the desired result.[17] Furthermore, I am an unabashed Ockhamite (that is, I have a strong preference for parsimonious explanations); a confirmed believer in rational, maximizing behavior, especially by those calculating persons, politicians; and a person with very low Bayesian priors about unintended consequences. If I find blacks—or poor whites—shut out of politics, I immediately suspect that it didn't just happen to turn out that way, and I have faith that if I find the means employed and the wills involved in perpetrating the causal act or acts, the protagonists and their weapons in one geographical area will closely resemble those in other places, and the basic reasons for their activities will be simple.

Yet in speaking of this as a "bias," I mean "predisposition" or "proclivity" rather than "unalterable presupposition." All scholars begin with some proclivities such as these, and nearly all scholars alter their predispositions little by little as they accumulate more experience. Some, either as neophytes or at some stage in their lives before (or after) senility, prefer complexity, assume irrationality, and deny intent aprioristically. It is to be hoped, however, that both forest people and trees people, while they might be attracted to different facets of the scenery, would at least be able to agree roughly on what trail to follow through a particular wood. Less metaphorically, a modeler might admit the inadequacies of his schema in representing a certain situation, while a person of idiographic propensity might agree that uncomplicated explanations are sometimes correct. In any event, differences in such assumptions color scholarly and contracted work equally. If I sin, it is in monographs as well as in testimony. Yet since one inevitably must make some such leaps of faith, since one cannot escape these fundamental epistemological issues even by ignoring them, making them cannot rob one of objectivity unless objectivity is never possible. The directed verdict on count two must therefore be acquittal.

Third, did the procedure for examining evidence, which admittedly differs from that I would normally adopt, bias my conclusions, therefore robbing the project of objectivity? Generally, after deciding what to study, picking out, in a preliminary fashion at least, what principal questions to ask, and ransacking the secondary literature, I would go through as many primary documents as are available—newspapers, manuscripts (if any), official documents, voting returns. This procedure reflects a professional tradition in history which stretches back at least to the establishment of the first American graduate programs a hundred years ago. The image of the lonely scholar, or perhaps, to modernize it a bit, of the lonely research team, seeking truth by applying their open but careful minds to the appropriate evidence, is pervasive among social scientists and humanists. Scholars may make mistakes, study uninteresting topics, fail to express themselves well, or even reflect unconsciously the popular world view or disciplinary paradigm dominant at the time they're working, but they don't, in this standard stereotype, purposely distort. Truth is produced by what might be called a "linear" process.

In the adversary tradition, on the other hand, truth is assumed to emerge, if at all, as part of a dialectical process. The lawyer's ideal world is, in this respect, rather like Adam Smith's: when every lawyer seeks simultaneously to maximize the chances of his or her own client, assuming that each abides by some fundamental rules of fairness, an Invisible Hand guides the process toward the maximum production of truth. Lawyers are supposed to be advocates, to represent their clients. They are not to pursue some abstract "truth" or "social good," but only the very relative interests of the people who hire their services. Graduate schools and law schools may often cohabit on the same campus, but in their self-conceptions, they have long since divorced. This separation breeds deep suspicion on each side of the other's pretensions and processes.

Despite suspicions, I have had to accept the fact that in the cases I

have worked on, others—the Justice Department, the LDF or other lawyers for the plaintiffs, and the lawyers and experts for the localities
whose electoral systems are being challenged—perform most of the culling of primary sources. I read what they send me and what I specifically
ask for. This would worry me more if the documents were secret or private, or if the lawyers with whom I've worked denied requests for papers
or documents I asked them to look for, or if the lawyers on each side
didn't have a strong interest in confronting the court with all the evidence which could possibly buttress their positions. In fact, none of the
material is private; and every request I've made for information—and
I've been bothersome, in order to insure that I look at everything which
might be relevant—has been complied with. Moreover, it appears to be
in the nature of research for such litigation that the lawyers (exactly like
scholars in this respect) don't know just how to put together the facts or
which facts will turn out to be of relevance until very close to the last
moment. They do the research when they can, drib and drab it out to
prospective experts, put it all together the last night. Thus, time pressures and lack of complete foresight guard against their stacking any but
the most obvious evidence.

Only two things about the process are bothersome. In the first place,
even if the adversary process leads to truth, it's less likely to if the legal
talent on each side is unequal. And I'm afraid that the acumen of counsel on the side of those charging discrimination has almost always been
superior, in the cases I've been in, to that of the defenders of at-large voting. In other words, I can't be sure that the other side would recognize
evidence for their cases if it jumped off the page at them. In the second
place, despite the extensive discovery procedures which drag out modern litigation, lawyers have a gaming tendency which leads them to hold
back evidence until cross-examination. And there is a natural contrary
tendency for a witness to stick to his guns when challenged, to consider
cross-questioning a combat, and therefore to disregard evidence offered
at this time against his case. No one wants to look foolish or contradictory, or to conclude that he wasted his time.

These doubts are connected with a fourth consideration, that of advocacy. Does the fact that one is making a case, is part of a team with a particular value-laden objective, by itself undermine the usual standards of
scholarly objectivity? In all but one respect, I think it doesn't. After all,
scholars do get committed to particular arguments—the Civil War was
or was not irrepressible, the living standard of the working class in England rose or fell in the nineteenth century, the American Revolution
was primarily an intellectual or alternatively a social movement—and
they rarely change their minds. (One might note, parenthetically, that
the same state of affairs characterizes the physical sciences, for as
Thomas Kuhn has pointed out, defenders of old paradigms rarely
switch, they just retire.)[18] Nonetheless, scholars sometimes modify their
stands, particularly on relatively minor points. They circulate papers
and accept criticisms, alter some treatments in subsequent editions of
books, at times even confess error. The trouble with a trial is that it's a

one-shot affair, that one goes from expression to publication without circulation, copy editing, or galley proofs. Since one can hardly call up the judge six months later and say "I've changed my mind; I was wrong," the process of lengthy contemplation of one's interpretation, a usual part of scholarship, is necessarily private and naturally truncated for an expert witness.

A fifth point follows closely in train. It is the core of the objectivity question. Did one pick only those pieces of evidence which fit one's case, and did one twist the story to bypass evidence which could not be ignored? Here, the adversary process seems to provide a safeguard at least equal to those in academia. To most judges, the most credible expert witnesses are persons who have published fairly widely on the topic or on kindred ones. To most lawyers, risk-averse souls who prefer not to be surprised during trials, the best witnesses are experienced ones. Since books, articles, and previous testimony, affidavits, and depositions are matters of public record, an expert who takes contradictory positions on two similar pieces of evidence or similar positions on two contradictory pieces of evidence is placing his reputation at risk in a bet not only on the stupidity of opposing counsel in the instant case, but in every other case to come.

Furthermore, it is somewhat easier, indeed, it is unavoidable in witnessing, to make oneself conscious of contrary cases. Even if the other side's barristers are inferior, at least in this rather specialized area of the law, one always overprepares for cross-examination, and one is pressed in the moot court tradition by one's own side. No doubt lawyers might pull their punches to avoid unsettling their own witnesses, but that's a dangerous course, because the witness might sense duplicity or the contending lawyers might pull off lucky shots. Moreover, the witness, more frightened of a courtroom than the lawyers are, naturally tries to think of every possible question. The whole process, therefore, encourages the questioning and testing of interpretations much more than do normal scholarly procedures.

The sixth and final question breaks the analogy with regular scholarship, and rests on a counterfactual thought experiment. If I were testifying for the other side, would my conclusions differ? I feel certain that, at least in the cases in which I have been involved, they would not: I would find evidence of an intent to discriminate in the passage or maintenance of the system. I also recognize that if my analysis did vary depending on whom I was working with, my days as a credible expert witness would be over. I even half wish that some local government would retain me—they seem to pay better than the LDF or Legal Services or even the Justice Department, and it would be satisfying to take their money and then upset their case. Still, one aspect of the question bothers me: assuming that if I did appear I would speak truthfully and fully, *would* I testify for the other side?

The difficulty is that expert witnesses generally do more than testify. Unless they are brought in at the very last moment or are working with extremely overbearing, absurdly self-confident lawyers, witnesses usually have some role in organizing cases and especially in planning research on the facts. For if they do not understand their case, they cannot know what is relevant, and if they don't assist in and partly direct the gathering of the facts, they cannot be sure they have seen all the important evidence. Even if, as "educational" witnesses, experts are chiefly used to report on the state of research in some academic field, they will have to know enough to know when to stop talking—a difficult thing for professors in the best of circumstances—and they will probably be asked for advice on other aspects of the case, on other witnesses' reputations, on how to rebut their testimony, and so on. Expert witnesses do not merely give opinions; they join a company.

Since, as a person, I believe strongly in racial equality, and since, as a social scientist, I find the empirical and theoretical evidence of the racially discriminatory impact of at-large systems overwhelming, could I work with lawyers who were attempting to preserve an at-large system in a jurisdiction which included a large and geographically separate minority group? (Other, analogous questions would occur to other potential expert witnesses or to me in other contexts.) Should the answer depend on the degree of oppression in each individual case, and how can that be gauged, especially before one knows much about the particular facts? Or should every situation be analogized to that of a chemical engineer in Nazi Germany being asked to perform experiments to determine the least costly but most efficient combination of gases lethal to humans—an objective, value-free scientific question in a sense, but a request which few, in hindsight at least, would agree to honor.

This last question is but a variation on the Faustian quandary: should one compromise with evil, and, if so, how far? While I am not pretentious enough to hazard a general answer, I do have some observations. First, the learned alchemist's dilemma was one-sided. It wasn't the Lord, but the Devil who offered him fame and fortune in exchange for his soul. Presumably, if the proposition had originated in the upper, instead of in the nether regions, the good doctor would have had no second thoughts. Likewise, an expert who bears witness truthfully and for the side he or she favors as a citizen does not, on this count, jeopardize his or her virtue. Second, to the extent that scholarship, however intended, is ever usable, either as a direct influence on current policy or by providing a general background, a context, or a part of the learning experience of the makers of present or future policy, the dilemma is inescapable. The scholar publishes, and, having done so, loses control over the uses to which his or her material can be put.

Let me illustrate this last point with a personal anecdote. For a congeries of empirical and value-laden reasons, I favor abolition of the electoral college. This age-old question was debated seriously and actually voted on by the U.S. Senate in July of 1979. In an extension of remarks section of the *Congressional Record* which dates from that time, I had the honor, if that is the proper phrase, to be cited a dozen times in a report prepared by the Congressional Research Service which was inserted into the record by a senator.[19] This was the first time that my name appeared in the *Congressional Record,* and it may well be the last. Although I am not a daily devotee of that publication, a friend who noticed it was kind enough to send it to me. The trouble was, I was cited to support the case *against* abolishing the electoral college, and, as if to heap on the insults, the senator who requested the study and had it put into the *Record* was one whose actions rarely fail to outrage me, Orrin Hatch. To top it off, shortly after I had posted a response to a sympathetic senator, in which I tried to show that my work and other evidence, while cited correctly, had been employed superficially, and that a deeper analysis of southern voting patterns in the nineteenth and twentieth centuries really supported the case for abolition, rather than the converse, I learned that the vote on the electoral college had just taken place, and that my small contribution could no longer even add a historical grace note to the debate. Although I had hatched no Faustian bargain, and gained neither glory nor remuneration from this episode of scholarly "influence" on public policy, my words had done the Devil's work just as surely.

The process by which a fundamentally honest expert witness arrives at conclusions, I have tried to argue, differs less from that which honest scholars employ in their everyday work than is sometimes charged. Insofar as they do diverge, moreover, it is by no means clear that the normal procedures guarantee more objective results than those a witness uses. Warren Miller's statement about the different motivations involved in trying to "do good" and to "find out how things work," quoted at the beginning of this paper, is not in accord with my experience. For potential assaults on a scholar's objectivity are possible anywhere. Social scientists' virtue is no more at stake as they walk down the dark alleys of policy relevance than it is on the brightly-lit streets of the campus. Further, if, instead of confining themselves closely in their ivory towers, they broadcast their thoughts, like paper airplanes, down into the popular mists, they can no longer control whether their fragile crafts are wafted on winds of change or on counter-currents of reaction. To return to the metaphor with which I began, historians should regard themselves, and should be regarded by lawyers and judges, neither as virgins nor as members of that other ancient profession. Testifying and scholaring are about equally objective pursuits.

REFERENCES

1. Lee Dembart, "Science and Public Policy—Who Is Served?" *Los Angeles Times,* November 9, 1981.
2. Fox Butterfield, "Faculty Consultants: Higher Educators Getting Higher Fees," *Los Angeles Herald Examiner,* June 16, 1982. Since historians' fees for a case are on the order of 1 percent of Rosse's, their incentives to play paladin are considerably less.
3. Benson's address and Miller's response are both in *Social Science History* 2 (1978), 427–48. The Miller quotation appears on p. 444.
4. See Alfred H. Kelly, "Clio and the Court: An Illicit Love Affair," *Supreme*

Court Review (1965), 119–58; and, on *Bolden,* J. Morgan Kousser, "The Undermining of the First Reconstruction: Lessons for the Second," in *Extension of the Voting Rights Act: Hearings Before the Subcommittee on the Judiciary, House of Representatives,* 97th Congress, 1st Session (Washington: Government Printing Office, 1982), 2017–20.

5. Lee Benson, "Doing History as Moral Philosophy and Public Advocacy: A Practical Strategy to Lessen the Crisis in American History," paper delivered at the Organization of American Historians' Convention, April 1, 1981.

6. The citations are: Plessy, 163 U.S. 537 (1896); Williams, 170 U.S. 213 (1898); Cumming, 175 U.S. 528 (1899); Giles, 189 U.S. 475 (1903). On these cases, see J. Morgan Kousser, "Undermining of the First Reconstruction," 2020–21, and "Separate But Not Equal: The Supreme Court's First Decision on Racial Discrimination in Schools," *Journal of Southern History* 46 (1980), 17–44.

7. Brown v. Board of Education, 347 U.S. 483 (1954); Milliken v. Bradley, 418 U.S. 717 (1974).

8. Gomillion v. Lightfoot, 364 U.S. 339 (1960). Justice Stevens apparently yearns for those earlier, simpler days when discrimination stood out like a crudely drawn twenty-eight-sided figure. See his dissents in Mobile v. Bolden, 446 U.S. 55 (1980), and Rogers v. Lodge, 50 U.S.L.W. 5041 (U.S. July 1, 1982).

9. Baker v. Carr, 369 U.S. 186 (1962); Gray v. Sanders, 372 U.S. 368 (1963); Wesberry v. Sanders, 376 U.S. 1 (1964). In some more recent reapportionment cases, such as the 1982 Georgia Congressional redistricting case, Busbee v. Smith, 549 F. Supp. 494 (D.D.C., 1982), the question of racially discriminatory intent has received central attention. On the contradictions between the Court's stance in reapportionment and racial vote dilution cases see James U. Blacksher and Larry T. Menefee, "From *Reynolds v. Sims* to *City of Mobile v. Bolden:* Have the White Suburbs Commandeered the Fifteenth Amendment?" *Hastings Law Journal* 34 (1982), 1–64.

10. Whitcomb v. Chavis, 403 U.S. 124 (1971); Palmer v. Thompson, 403 U.S. 217 (1971).

11. White v. Regester, 412 U.S. 755 (1973); Zimmer v. McKeithen, 485 F. 2d 1297 (1973). The other leading relevant cases were Washington v. Davis, 426 U.S. 229 (1976); Village of Arlington Heights v. Metropolitan Housing Development Corp., 97 S. Ct. 555 (1977); and Personnel Administrator of Massachusetts v. Feeney, 442 U.S. 256 (1979). The best discussion I have read on the topic is Larry G. Simon, "Racially Prejudiced Governmental Actions: A Motivation Theory of the Constitutional Ban Against Racial Discrimination," *San Diego Law Review* 15 (1978), 1041–1130.

12. That social science expert witness testimony is often used to "educate" judges is shown in Joseph Sanders *et al.,* "The Relevance of 'Irrelevant' Testimony: Why Lawyers Use Social Science Experts in School Desegregation Cases," *Law and Society Review* 16 (1981–82), 403–28.

13. The chief danger for the 1982 renewal of the Voting Rights Act (VRA) was apathy. Since it represented a clear and present danger, and not just a potential threat to minority voting rights, particularly in the classic center of racism, the small-town South, *Bolden* made it much easier for the civil rights forces to work up enthusiasm for the VRA among the membership of their

organizations as well as among editorial writers. Thus, Justice Stewart was for the VRA what Interior Secretary James Watt was for the Clean Air Act.

14. The Fifth Circuit Court of Appeals, in Nevett v. Sides, 571 F. 2d 209 (5th Circuit 1978) had tried, by combining some of the language and reasoning from Washington v. Davis and Arlington Heights with the *Zimmer* list, to bring the two approaches into conformity with each other. The *"Zimmer* factors" could be read as indicative, if not of the motives of the framers of the law, then of those of the ethnic majority and the elite leaders who maintained the political system at the time. It now appears that *Nevett* was a better predictor of the Court's eventual position (in Rogers v. Lodge) than was Stewart's *Bolden* opinion. For a "smoking gun" reading of *Bolden,* see Aviam Soifer, "Complacency and Constitutional Law," *Ohio State Law Journal* 42 (1981), 404.

15. The opinion on remand is Bolden v. City of Mobile, 542 F. Supp. 1050 (S.D. Alabama 1982). In his first *Bolden* opinion (Bolden v. City of Mobile, 423 F. Supp. 384, 397 (S.D. Ala. 1976)), Federal District Court Judge Virgil Pittman, who decided in favor of the black plaintiffs, characterized the situation after passage of the Alabama Constitution as "race-proof," by which he meant that race could not have been a motive for legislative action in 1911 because most blacks were disfranchised then. In the remand, the plaintiffs produced evidence, put together primarily by McCrary, which showed that enough blacks were registered to vote in the years following 1908 in Mobile to pose a threat to carry or seriously influence at least one ward, had a ward system been adopted. Even if this had not been so, however, the "race-proof situation" argument has always struck me as curious. If blacks were excluded for reasons of race from participating in a decision which even eventually affected them, why wasn't the process itself so tainted that the system should be thrown out? If it be feared that this would result in the overturning of all laws passed during the whole period, the answer is that those which have no present discriminatory effect are therefore not unconstitutional.

16. Hugh R. Trevor-Roper, *The Last Days of Hitler* (London: Macmillan and Company, 1947); C. Vann Woodward, *The Battle for Leyte Gulf* (New York: Macmillan and Company, 1947).

17. Caltech colleagues have pointed out to me that this set of beliefs may partially account for my being chosen as an expert witness, that if I were less inclined to generalize and to state conclusions baldly, or, conversely, felt less compelled to spell out the steps in my arguments, lawyers would not have chosen me. This observation does not, however, reflect adversely on the case for comparative objectivity in expert witnessing. It merely suggests that the decision rule for lawyers choosing experts should be to pick those experts who, in their scholarly work, openly state their results and the process by which they arrived at them. It implies nothing about the further remark, quoted at the beginning of this paper, about choosing witnesses who will say "what a particular side wants said."

18. Thomas Kuhn, *The Structure of Scientific Revolutions* (Chicago: University of Chicago Press, 1970).

19. *Congressional Record-Senate* (June 13, 1979), S7604–S7615.

5

CLIO MEETS PORTIA: OBJECTIVITY IN THE COURTROOM AND THE CLASSROOM

Joan C. Williams

The controversy other ethics when historians testify as expert witnesses focuses on objectivity. Commentators disagree as to whether participating in a trial jeopardizes a historian's objectivity. While J. Morgan Kousser concluded in 1984 that "Testifying and scholaring are about equally objective pursuits," others have offered the more traditional analysis that expert witnesses are "whores" (though usually in politer language).[1]

While both sides of the debate have shied away from theoretical questions as to whether objectivity is possible, a more theoretical approach is helpful in disaggregating what historians mean by objectivity. Sometimes commentators who argue that expert witnesses face potential ethical problems contrast the advocacy role of historians in public forums with "disinterested," "neutral," "objective, historical truth." This view of history as a nonpartisan search for objective truth is part of a long historiographical tradition, but it is inconsistent with the vast contemporary theoretical literature that suggests that scholarship by its nature is political. Kousser is right in this sense when he claims that "scholarship and testifying are equally objective: neither does or should attain this kind of objectivity."[2]

Yet commentators also mean something quite different when they speak of "objectivity," namely that responsible history observes certain methodological norms. Because of needs that arise from the trial context, historians as expert witnesses will ordinarily be under intense pressure to deviate from these methodological norms. I develop my analysis of these two kinds of objectivity by discussing the testimony of two of the best-known expert witnesses in recent history, Rosalind Rosenberg and Alice Kessler-Harris, each of whom testified in *Equal Employment Opportunity Commission v. Sears, Roebuck & Co.*

* * * *

At times commentators who argue that expert witnesses face potential ethical problems contrast the advocacy role with a vision of scholarship that on closer examination appears outdated. Stanley M. Hordes, for example, in decrying "the advocacy approach to history" contrasts "One group of historians [who] feels strongly that . . . merely by their presence in the public arena their role as advocates is natural, open, honest, and even desirable" with another group (in which he clearly includes himself) that believes that historians should advocate political interests "only when such a position is consistent with objective, historical truth." Hordes is clearly reacting to a vision of the historian as captured corporate mouthpiece, yet he fails to separate his concerns for rigorous historical methodology from an assumption that historians in public forums are somehow tainted by their involvement in situations with explicit political stakes. Ronald C. Tobey, in arguing that "scholarly ethics are inadequate . . . in the public arena" also expresses uneasiness with a context in which scholarship is part of an explicitly political process.[3]

Underlying both these views is the assumption that historical scholarship reflects objective truth. This is a long-standing assumption, recently documented (and questioned) by Peter Novick in *That Noble Dream: The "Objectivity Question" and the American Historical Profession.* Historians' long-standing claims for objectivity, however, conflict with recent scholarship in several ways. First, the assumption that respectable scholarship presents objective truth unsullied by "extraneous" political concerns rests on a view of the professional as a nonpartisan expert that has been definitively challenged in historical as well as sociological literature. The Progressive image of the professional as an impartial, apolitical expert solving problems through privileged access to objective truth is widely regarded today as reflecting professional ideology more than it does professional practice.[4]

The assumption that respectable scholarship is "objective" in the sense of being apolitical is also inconsistent with the widespread acknowledgment among historians that their values affect their scholarship. Kousser's image of the professional as an expert who, though bound to some extent by professional norms, is nonetheless a political actor is closer to current thinking. Kousser presents his conclusion in an intuitive, nontheoretical manner, by describing the indubitably political influences on scholars' choice of topics—ranging from the scholars' political preferences to the "whims of funding agencies."[5]

There is, of course, a vast theoretical literature that analyzes how liberal arts scholarship is political in nature. This scholarship is part of the intellectual movement I have elsewhere called the new epistemology, which includes Anglo-American philosophers, French post-structuralists, neo-Marxist critical theorists, and American literary critics. Its tenets have most often entered history in an intuitive, nontheoretical way, as in Kousser's piece, though historians have at last begun to approach this literature from its original sources in a tentative and highly selective way.[6]

A central insight of the new epistemology is that all interpretation implies a viewpoint, and that one's choice of viewpoint is necessarily a political act. This principle has immediate implications for the expert witness. It implies that the attraction of some historians to litigation in which they can further their political values does not necessarily jeopardize their professional "objectivity." It also implies the opinion espoused by Kousser, among many others, that ethical scholarship inside academia or out is scholarship that reflects one's values as a citizen. So long as historians observe the methodological norms concerning treatment of evidence and counterevidence, their decision to play an explicitly political role is, as Kousser suggests, not a deviation from the role they play as scholars, but rather a continuation of it. But—a fact often ignored in the theoretical literature—this does not obviate the second, methodological type of objectivity.[7]

Historians' methodological norms are primarily an oral tradition, passed on to successive generations of students in graduate seminars, but Ronald Tobey offers a fair articulation of those norms. Historians should do thorough research and should avoid both false claims of originality and conscious distortions of the evidence, he notes. I suspect these standards are supported by wide consensus among historians. The norms that present the greatest problems for historians acting as expert witnesses are those concerning treatment of supporting evidence and of counterevidence.[8]

The norms concerning treatment of supporting evidence encourage historians carefully to qualify the data that supports their interpretations. I find historians generally unconscious of the extent to which they are taught to qualify their statements. The criticism "it's more complicated than that" is almost invariably a safe one in historical circles, while overly aggressive bonding of materials into a seamless thematic whole can easily raise eyebrows. The most successful historians, of course, manage to imbue material with the interpretation they advocate in a cohesive and persuasive way, but even they often nod to the norms against oversimplification by highlighting the limitations of their evidence. Thus, Nancy Cott, in both of her widely influential books, carefully notes in her introduction that she depended primarily on evidence from middle-class white women. She at once justifies her decision and admits its limitations, in a highly savvy preemptive strike.[9]

For a historian to acknowledge the existence of counter-evidence is a somewhat riskier endeavor. This occurs primarily in historiographical studies that highlight the strengths and weaknesses of competing interpretations. For articulation of this norm in day-to-day historical work, one must turn to unfavorable reviews. One recent example was a review of Anne Norton's *Alternative America: A Reading of Antebellum Political Culture* in *Reviews in American History.* Norton came in for some particularly harsh criticism for an ambitious book that attempted to crystallize an analysis of nineteenth century culture using techniques from works in literary criticism, political science and philosophy influenced by the new epistemology. In the process, she was criticized severely not only for inaccuracies but for ignoring counterevidence. One senses that the sweeping nature of her enterprise set her up, a sense many young historians may well share, for few have attempted such ambitious studies in recent years.[10]

Both the norm favoring qualification of one's evidence and that favoring fastidious disclosure of counterevidence are in sharp contrast to the norms of trial advocacy. The law places a much higher premium than does history on a seamless interpretation that is sweeping in its scope and carries with it a sense of rigorous and inexorable logic. In legal briefs, lawyers may choose to disclose limitations in their evidence in a preemptive strike, but an equally respectable alternative is to try to hide the limitations of one's argument. The sharp contrast between historical norms and legal ones emerges clearly when one recognizes that it is only in a narrow, criminal context that litigants are under an ethical obligation to disclose to opposing counsel factual information relevant to his case. (Such information would necessarily be counterevidence that cut against the interpretation of the disclosing party.) Even judicial opinions, which are more open-textured than lawyers' briefs, often simply ignore evidence that cuts against the party whose side they have chosen. Moreover, when judges do address counterevidence, it is often to discount its importance at virtually any price.[11]

Lawyers are, of course, aware that these norms yield interpretations that are not as objective as human interpretations can be. Their traditional explanation was to offer a process vision of truth: the clash of views would ensure that the truth would out. Some public historians recently have taken up this rationale for adopting advocacy ethics, an ironic development since this somewhat complacent view has been under severe challenge in legal circles for decades.[12]

Despite such challenges, the slash-and-burn style of advocacy persists and probably predominates. Why? The answer may well be in the social dynamics of litigation. Keep in mind that judges are forced into an either/or decision. This means that any judge, in any lawsuit, is going to disappoint a litigant in a matter the litigant cares about intensely. As all parents know, the most natural reaction in the world is for a decision-maker in this situation to act as if any decision other than the one he has chosen borders on the irrational. Lawyers' tolerance of interpretations that both fail to qualify evidence and that avoid counterevidence in a brazen fashion stems from a similar social dynamic.

In summary, then, public historians' discussion of whether expert witnesses can be objective fails to distinguish between two quite different types of objectivity. Historians never have been objective in the sense of being apolitical. Thus the explicit political stakes involved in many courtrooms does not threaten their tradition of professionalism. In another way, though, historians testifying as experts need to be aware of the different norms of the classroom and the courtroom, for each context has quite different methodological norms.

I will proceed by applying this analysis to the historians whose expert testimony has become a *cause célèbre:* Rosalind Rosenberg and Alice Kessler-Harris in the case of *EEOC v. Sears.*

First, some background. The EEOC charged Sears, Roebuck and

Company with discrimination against women in hiring and promotion. The EEOC case was based on statistical evidence showing a disparity between the proportion of women in the commission sales jobs at issue and the proportion in the relevant labor market. Instead of doing what most defendants do—challenging the plaintiffs' definition of the relevant labor market—Sears took an innovative approach.[13] It argued that relatively few women took commission sales positions because many women lacked interest in the positions. Sears argued that these jobs did not appeal to women because the job requirements clashed with values peculiar to women, who disliked the competition and risk the jobs entailed, felt uncomfortable with the products involved such as hardware and automotive parts, and did not want to work the hours the jobs required.[14]

Two historians testified at the trial: Rosalind Rosenberg for Sears and Alice Kessler-Harris for the EEOC. Rosenberg immediately found herself in the center of a bitter controversy, in which other historians of women charged her with using her expertise in an unethical way that hurt equal employment opportunity for women. Rosenberg, in what became an increasingly bitter battle, responded that she was just following out her feminism to its logical conclusions, and that her opponents were demanding that she suppress the truth for political reasons.[15]

One aspect of the controversy concerns the first kind of objectivity: the relationship of a scholar's testimony to her politics. I suggest each side has oversimplified the issue. What was involved in *Sears* was less an ethical problem than an intellectual one. Both Rosenberg and Kessler-Harris were placed in a difficult position by a central intellectual problem in women's history and feminist theory only now beginning to be addressed: how and why can the enormously influential literature on women's culture be used against women? I have argued elsewhere that historians' love affair with nineteenth century women's culture was part and parcel of the romance with gender led by feminists of difference, notably Carol Gilligan. Gilligan reframed the cult of domesticity, and in doing so ignored the extent to which domesticity functions as hegemony, as an ideological structure designed to ensure that the oppressed freely choose their oppression. Domesticity's compliments have urged women from the nineteenth century until today to choose social and economic marginalization and celebrate that choice as a badge of virtue.[16]

This analysis of domesticity as hegemony explains why Sears found it so easy to use against women the recent work of feminists of difference ranging from that of Gilligan herself to historical studies such as Katherine Kish Sklar's biography of Catherine Beecher. Sears used the literature of difference to argue that women as a group "choose" to observe gender roles. It mobilized Victorian compliments to explain why: women are too focused on higher things, notably their relationships at home and at work, to be suitable for hard-driving commission sales positions.[17]

Both Rosenberg and Kessler-Harris were thrown off guard by Sears's approach. Kessler-Harris was convinced that something was amiss, per-

haps influenced by her background in labor economics, where conserva-
tive human capital theorists have long argued that the wage gap between
men and women results in large part from women's choice to invest
more heavily in their husbands than in themselves. Rosenberg, whose
studies had concentrated on ideology, not economics, made two somewhat inconsistent arguments for Sears. At times she argued she was fear-
lessly following through her feminism to its logical conclusions—an
argument that appeared to acknowledge that her testimony would hurt
women. In other contexts Rosenberg argued that her approach would
help women because, by acknowledging women's different interests, she
could highlight women's special needs, notably for child care. Kessler-
Harris's response emphasized the diversity of women and downplayed
the impact of gender roles on women's work.[18]

Ultimately, then, these two late twentieth century historians replayed
the special treatment-equal treatment debate that has divided American
feminists for well over a century. In one sense, perhaps a perverse one,
Rosenberg performed an important service by bringing historians face
to face in an urgent way with the pressing need for a reevaluation of this
literature. *Sears* certainly highlights the risks presented by contemporary authors' insistence that women are different, and perhaps better,
than men. Indeed, the *Sears* controversy has fueled a swing away from
"women's culture" to an examination of diversity within women's history, as well as a theoretical literature exploring the landscape "beyond
sameness and difference."[19]

While I fault neither Rosenberg nor Kessler-Harris for the relationship of her testimony to her politics, both to some extent violated methodological norms of objectivity. Presumably under pressure from their
lawyers, both historians—although Rosenberg far more than Kessler-
Harris—violated historical norms concerning treatment of counterevidence and inclusion of adequate qualifications.

Rosenberg's testimony shows most clearly the influence of the Sears
lawyers, who used her testimony to make their argument that men and
women "have [different] interests and aspirations regarding work" in an
ahistorical and universalistic fashion. "The distinction between male
and female serves as a basic organizing principle for every human culture," the testimony begins, citing Michelle Rosaldo and Louise
Lamphert's *Women, Culture and Society* without mentioning that its authors are careful to point out that though gender exists across societies,
gender stereotypes vary widely among different societies.[20]

The testimony continues in a decidedly ahistorical vein. "Throughout
American history there has been a consensus, shared by women, that, for
women, work outside the home is subordinate to family needs."[21] This
sentence reaches back as far as the seventeenth century the work patterns created by the industrial revolution, when work was isolated tem-
porally and geographically from family life. Modern work patterns
assume an ideal worker with no child care or housekeeping responsibilities, and so made "work" (redefined as wage labor) inconsistent with
"family needs." The ideology of domesticity stepped in to provide the

gendered allocation of wage labor and family responsibilities the testi-mony refers to, but only in the nineteenth century.[22]

As if anticipating the charge of anachronism, Rosenberg notes in her next paragraph that even in the seventeenth century:

> . . . America divided work according to sex. Women cared for the children, prepared the food, nursed the sick, made the clothes, and tended the gar-den. Men worked the fields, cared for the livestock, and represented the family in the outside world. Many of the jobs that men and women perform in the labor force today are the modern equivalents of traditional male and female tasks.[23]

Although the testimony cites Laurel Ulrich's *Good Wives,* it ignores the contrasts Ulrich draws between seventeenth century womanhood and the nineteenth century ideology of separate spheres. The testimony ig-nores the differences between gender roles in a traditional society and those that evolved after the industrial revolution—although Ulrich's book contributes to a large literature that contrasts the nineteenth cen-tury with colonial conditions. Note, for example, how the testimony ad-mits that women were engaged in household production in the seventeenth century, but ignores this striking difference between colo-nial and modern times.[24]

But the most basic question is why women's activities in seventeenth century semi-subsistence society are relevant at all to the wage labor preferences of late twentieth century women. They are only if one posits eternal, unchanging gender roles closely tied with women's nature. Further analysis of the testimony shows that this is exactly what Rosenberg's testimony does, as she shifts from her historical data to psy-chological data from Gilligan and others who posit a "different voice" that attributes to women characteristics derived from domesticity. "Through American history women have been trained from earliest childhood to develop the humane and nurturing values expected of the American mother," Rosenberg testifies, evidently forgetting that this image of motherhood is a relatively modern invention. Rosenberg's tes-timony consistently functions to transform nineteenth century ideology into eternal truths about women's behavior.[25]

The net result of Rosenberg's testimony was to paint a view of women highly useful to Sears but in gross violation of norms of historical analy-sis. Moreover, the only time Rosenberg's testimony acknowledges that all women do not fit the stereotype she advocates is when she appeals to the standard sexist argument that the only women who have abandoned "traditional values" are (uppity?) college women.[26]

A consistent blurring between ideology and behavior helps Rosenberg establish a universalistic tone to her description of women. She testified:

> Historically, the emphasis on independence and competition among men and on dependence and cooperation among women has been especially marked in American society. The rapid expansion of capitalism in America led to a heavy emphasis on such qualities as political liberty, economic mo-

bility, and competitive individualism for men. Women, on the other hand, were exhorted to be nurturant and selfless, to serve as a stabilizing force in an otherwise unstable society.[27]

Rosenberg cites Barbara Welter's famous article on "The Cult of True Womanhood," but blurs the fact that Welter was discussing ideology, not behavior. The testimony continues in a universalistic vein, referring to a consensus that attached a stigma to wage labor by married women, ignoring completely the established literature that documents that (even in the nineteenth and twentieth centuries) this stigma did not prevent wage labor from being an accepted part of the lives of black and working class women.[28] About the time Rosenberg testified, Nancy Hewitt published her influential article crystallizing the critique of "women's culture" as focusing excessively on the experience of middle-class white women. Even if Hewitt's article was not available to Rosenberg, the monographic studies of blacks and working class women upon which Hewitt bases her critique were.[29]

The universalism and ahistorical quality of Rosenberg's testimony violate norms that require a historian to carefully qualify her generalizations and to take counterevidence into account. Kessler-Harris's testimony, while it presents fewer problems than Rosenberg's, also fails to observe methodological norms.

Rosenberg's testimony left the EEOC with two basic choices as to how to respond: either they could counter Sears's universalism with evidence of diversity, or they could present an alternative, but equally universalistic vision of women. To the extent that Kessler-Harris does the first, her testimony is on safe ground, because she is making the historian's standard "it's more complicated than that" argument. On occasion, however, Kessler-Harris slips into statements as universalistic as Rosenberg's. The best example was her statement that "Where opportunity has existed, women have *never failed* to take the jobs offered." (emphasis added) This statement is as brazenly unqualified (and, therefore, as indubitably untrue) as much of Rosenberg's testimony.[30]

On the whole, however, Kessler-Harris avoids such overstatement and so adheres much better than Rosenberg to historians' norm of respecting the complexity of life. Kessler-Harris was less successful in her treatment of counterevidence. Kessler-Harris entered the case because she discovered that Rosenberg had used her (Kessler-Harris's) work in support of Sears, in particular her analysis in *Out to Work* of the complex interaction between the mandates of domestic ideology and the desire of all workers for high-paying, prestigious work. While Rosenberg gave a largely one-sided view, stressing only the domesticity side of the equation, Kessler-Harris in her testimony gave an equally one-sided view, characterizing women as rational economic actors and severely underplaying the role of domesticity in women's choice of work. This position is in marked contrast to the analysis in *Out to Work* itself, where Kessler-Harris freely admitted that domesticity influenced the job preferences of women as a group (not of each individual woman, an important legal point). Kessler-Harris's denial of the influence of domesticity opened her up to Sears's rebuttal testimony, which highlighted the inconsistency between her testimony and her book.[31]

Unlike Rosenberg, Kessler-Harris paid dearly for her slips from objectivity. The trial judge, a Reagan appointee not predisposed to the EEOC, referred to her "women have never failed" statement to undermine the credibility of EEOC witnesses in general. Since Rosenberg's universalism comported with the judge's own views, Rosenberg's methodological failings did not hurt Sears's case. But the experience of Kessler-Harris highlights the fact that historians who violate methodological norms may end up hurting the side they wish to help.[32]

To summarize, the focus in public history on the objectivity of expert witnesses lumps together two very different types of issues. The first concerns the relationship between the witness's testimony and her politics. I argue that neither scholarship nor testimony is, nor should be, value-free: the ethical question is whether the testimony comports with the values of the witness as a citizen. The historian as expert witness does have to concern herself with *methodological* objectivity. Historians' norms regarding treatment of counterevidence and careful qualification of supporting evidence are an important asset, which historians should be vigilant to observe in public forums as well as academic scholarship. Not only is this path intellectually more honest, the *Sears* case shows that overstatement can lead to legal as well as scholarly difficulties.

REFERENCES

1. J. Morgan Kousser, "Are Expert Witnesses Whores? Reflections on Objectivity in Scholarship and Expert Witnessing," *The Public Historian* 6, no. 1 (Winter 1984): 5–6, 19; Stanley M. Hordes, "Does He Who Pays the Piper Call the Tune? Historians, Ethics, and the Community," *The Public Historian* 8, no. 1 (Winter 1986); Ronald C. Tobey, "The Public Historian as Advocate: Is Special Attention to Professional Ethics Necessary?," *The Public Historian* 8, no. 1 (Winter 1986).

2. Quotes are from Tobey, op. cit., p. 27; Hordes, op. cit., p. 55. For a discussion of objectivity in historical studies, see Peter Novick, *That Noble Dream: The "Objectivity Question" and the American Historical Profession* (New York: Cambridge Univ. Press, 1988).

3. Hordes, op. cit., p. 55; Tobey, op. cit., p. 21, 23.

4. Hordes begins, "While none of us can be totally objective and free from cultural biases . . .," the remainder of his piece fails to follow through the implications of this insight. Hordes, op. cit., p. 53. An apt cite for the links between power and professionalism is Michel Foucault's, *Discipline and Punish: The Birth of the Prison* (New York: Pantheon; tr. Alan Sheridan, 1977). For an application to sociology, see Eliot Friedson, *Professional Powers: A Study of the Institutionalization of Formal Knowledge* (Chicago: The University of Chicago Press, 1986). For reviews of the historical literature, see Laurence Veysey, "*Who's a Professional? Who Cares?*," *Reviews in Amer-*

ican History 3 (1975): 419; Thomas L. Haskell, "Power to the Experts," *New York Review of Books,* October 13, 1977, p. 28.

5. Kousser, op. cit., p. 12–13.
6. Joan C. Williams, "The Death of Transcendence and the Rise of the New Langdells," *New York University Law Review* 62 (June 1987): 429. For notable recent examples of historians' use of the new epistemology, see Joan W. Scott, "Gender: A Useful Category of Historical Analysis," *American Historical Review* 91, no. 5 (December 1986): 1053; Thomas L. Haskell, "The Curious Persistence of Rights Talk in the 'Age of Interpretation,'" *Journal of American History* 74 (December 1987): 984.
7. Kousser, op. cit., p. 18. A sophisticated discussion of methodological objectivity is Lawrence Rosen, "The Anthropologist as Expert Witness," *American Anthropologist* 79 (1977): 555.
8. Tobey, op. cit., p. 28.
9. Nancy F. Cott, *The Bonds of Womanhood: "Woman's Sphere" in New England, 1780–1835* (New Haven: Yale University Press, 1977): 10–12; *The Grounding of Modern Feminism* (New Haven: Yale University Press: 1987): 9–10.
10. *Reviews in American History* 15 (December 1987): 63.
11. Section on Criminal Justice of the American Bar Association, American Bar Association Standards Relating to the Administration of Criminal Justice 2d edition, Tentative Draft Approved February 12, 1979: Standard 3–3.11 (Disclosure of Evidence by the Prosecutor.) In civil trials a lawyer need disclose facts that cut against him only if failure to do so would constitute assisting a criminal or fraudulent act, American Bar Association, Model Rules of Professional Conduct, Rule 3.3(a)(2). Both reprinted in Thomas D. Morgan & Ronald D. Rotunda, *Professional Responsibility* (Mineola, N.Y.: The Foundation Press Inc., 1988): 250, 140.
12. Tobey, op. cit., p. 27. For an example, see Jerome Frank, *Courts on Trial— Myth and Reality in American Justice* (Princeton, N.J.: Princeton Univ. Press, 1949): 80–102.
13. Equal Opportunity Commission v. Sears, Roebuck and Co., 428 F. Supp 1264, 1308–1312 (N.D. Ill., 1986) (hereafter cited as *EEOC v. Sears*); affirmed by the United States Court of Appeals for the Seventh Circuit, 839 F.2d 302 (1988) (hereafter cited as *EEOC v. Sears*, 839 F.2d 302). The EEOC has decided not to appeal the case. Conversation with James P. Scanlan, June 1, 1989. The court documents cited are filed in the Federal District Court for the Northern District of Illinois and the Seventh Circuit Court of Appeals respectively. The Sears case involved allegations of discrimination concerning not only hiring but also promotion. In addition to Sears's "interest" argument, Sears also challenged the way the EEOC defined the relevant market, though its "interest" argument was clearly the core of its defense. For background on the use of statistical evidence in Title VII cases, see David C. Baldus & James W.L. Cole, *Statistical Proof of Discrimination* (New York: McGraw-Hill, Inc., 1980): 101–41.
14. For the arguments cited, see also Brief of Appellee and Cross-Appellant Sears, Roebuck and Co. at 20–24, *EEOC v. Sears*.
15. The testimony of Rosenberg and Kessler-Harris has been extensively discussed both in scholarly journals and the popular press. Scholarly journals: Thomas Haskell and Sanford Levinson, "Academic Freedom and Expert Witnessing: Historians and the *Sears* Case," *Texas Law Review* 66 (1988): 1629; Alice Kessler-Harris, "'Academic Freedom and Expert Witnes-

sing'—A Response to Haskell and Levinson," *Texas Law Review* 67 (1988): 429; Katherine Jellison, "History in the Courtroom: The Sears Case in Perspective," *The Public Historian* 9 (Fall 1987): 9; Ruth Milkman, "Women's History and the Sears Case," *Feminist Studies* 12 (Summer 1986): 375; Jacquelyn Dowd Hall, "Women's History Goes on Trial: E.E.O.C. v. Sears, Roebuck and Company, Preface by the Board of Associate Editors," and Sandi E. Cooper, "Introduction to the Documents," *Signs: Journal of Women in Culture and Society* 11 (1986): 751; Alice Kessler-Harris, "Equal Employment Opportunity Commission v. Sears, Roebuck and Company: A Personal Account," *Radical History Review* 35 (April 1986): 57. Popular press accounts include Karen Winkler, "Two Scholars' Conflict in Sears Sex-Bias Case Sets Off a War in Women's History," *The Chronicle of Higher Education,* February 5, 1986, p. 1, col. 2; Jon Weiner, "The Sears Case: Women's History on Trial," *The Nation,* September 7, 1985, 161, 176–180; Samuel G. Freedman, "Of History and Politics: Bitter Debate," *The New York Times,* June 6, 1986, p. B1, col. 1; John Leo, "Are Women Male Clones," *Time,* August 18, 1986, 63–64; Darcy O'Brien, "A Coming of Age," *Savvy,* October 1986, 73–75, 83; David Tell, "Women's History and EEOC v. Sears, Roebuck and Co.," *New Perspectives* 18 (Summer 1986): 21–34; Carol Sternhell, "Life in the Mainstream," *Ms. Magazine,* July 1986, 48–51, 86–91.

16. Joan C. Williams, "Deconstructing Gender," *Michigan Law Review* 87 (1989): 797; Carol Gilligan, *In a Different Voice: Psychological Theory and Women's Development* (Cambridge, Mass.: Harvard University Press, 1982). For reassessments of the women's culture literature by historians, see Scott, "Deconstructing Equality-versus-Difference;" Linda K. Kerber, "Separate Spheres, Female Worlds, Women's Place: The Rhetoric of Women's History," *Journal of American History* 75 (June 1983): 9.

17. Katherine Kish Sklar, *Catherine Beecher: A Study in American Domesticity* (New York: W.W. Norton & Co., 1976); Offer of Proof Concerning the Testimony of Dr. Rosalind Rosenberg, *EEOC v. Sears,* ¶¶10–19.

18. For discussions of human capital theory, see Cynthia B. Lloyd and Beth T. Niemi, *The Economics of Sex Differentials* (New York: Columbia University Press, 1979); *Sex, Discrimination and the Division of Labor,* ed. Cynthia B. Lloyd (N.Y.: Columbia Univ. Press, 1975): 90; Barbara R. Bergman, *The Economic Emergence of Women* (N.Y.: Basic Books, 1986): 25. For Rosenberg's reasoning, see Rosalind Rosenberg, "What Harms Women in the Workplace," *The New York Times,* February 27, 1986, p. A23, col. 1; Tell, op. cit., p. 24, 29. Rosenberg's major book is *Beyond Separate Spheres: Intellectual Roots of Modern Feminism* (New Haven: Yale Univ. Press, 1982). Representative works by Alice Kessler-Harris include Alice Kessler-Harris, *Out To Work: A History of Wage-Earning Women in the United States* (New York: Oxford University Press, 1982); *Women Have Always Worked* (Old Westbury, N.Y.: The Feminist Press, 1981).

19. An example of the women's culture literature in women's history: Suzanne Lebsock, *The Free Women of Petersburg: Status and Culture in a Southern Town* (New York: W.W. Norton, 1984) p. 143. The focus on women's diversity began before *Sears.* An influential early contribution was Nancy Hewitt's "Beyond the Search for Sisterhood: American Women's History in the 1980's," *Social History* 10 (October 1985): 299; a recent one is Kerber, "Separate Spheres." For examples of the theoretical literature, see Joan

Scott, "Deconstructing Equality-Versus-Difference;" Joan Williams, "Deconstructing Gender."

20. Rosenberg Testimony, *EEOC v. Sears,* paragraphs 1, 3.
21. Ibid., par. 18.
22. Cott, *Bonds of Womanhood,* p. 59–69.
23. Rosenberg testimony, par. 5.
24. Ibid.; L urel Thatcher Ulrich, *Good Wives: Image and Reality in the Lives of Women in Northern New England* (New York: Oxford Univ. Press, 1982). For a review of the literature on the controversy over whether the 18th century was a "Golden Age," see Marylynn Salmon, "The Legal Status of Women in Early America: A Reappraisal," *Law and History Review* (1983): 129.
25. Rosenberg testimony, par. 18; Ruth H. Bloch, "American Feminine Ideals in Transition: The Rise of the Moral Mother, 1785–1815," *Feminist Studies* 4 (June 1978): 101; Ann Daly, *Inventing Motherhood* (New York: Schocken Books, 1983).
26. Rosenberg testimony, par. 23.
27. Ibid., par. 17.
28. Barbara Welter, "The Cult of True Womanhood: 1820–1860," *American Quarterly* 18, no 2 (Summer 1966): 151; Rosenberg Testimony, par. 4–11. For examples of the literature on black and working class women, see Jacqueline Jones, *Labor of Love, Labor of Sorrow: Black Women, Work, and the Family from Slavery to the Present* (New York: Basic Books, 1985); Kessler-Harris, *Out To Work.*
29. Hewitt, "Beyond The Search For Sisterhood."
30. Written testimony of Alice Kessler-Harris, *EEOC v. Sears,* par. 2b. In her written testimony, Kessler-Harris limited her statement to the twentieth century. In her oral testimony, the limitation was far less clearly drawn. Trial Transcript, 16542–47. Kessler-Harris is well aware that she might have worded her statement better. Tell, op. cit., p. 30.
31. Kessler-Harris, *Out To Work;* Written Rebuttal Testimony of Rosalind Rosenberg, *EEOC v. Sears,* par. 4.
32. *EEOC v. Sears,* 428 F. Supp. at 1305; Trial Transcript, 16545–46.

*An earlier version of this study was prepared for the session
"Does He Who Pays the Piper Really Call the Tune?" at the
1983 Meeting of the National Council on Public History.*

6

THE PUBLIC HISTORIAN AND BUSINESS HISTORY: A QUESTION OF ETHICS

Carl Ryant

In recent years historians have changed their attitude toward business history, as a field for research but particularly in terms of new kinds of employment, partly in response to scholarly evaluation of the role of business in society and partly as the result of declining opportunities for academics who wish to teach. But this growing interest in business history, especially as evidenced by business's support for research, has spurred an interest in the ethical issues involved. Undoubtedly ethical problems exist for the historian at large, just as they do for any other professional. The problem is to identify the particular ethical problems of business history for the public historian.

Within public history (of which business history is just one part), this issue has often been raised, even if not so often satisfactorily answered. Two articles from *The Public Historian,* written from quite different perspectives, illustrate the profession's concern. In the Summer 1981 issue, which was devoted to the theme, "Business and History," Albro Martin, discussing the emerging position of the corporate historian, asked: "For whom is the corporate historian working?" Martin's context was administrative, and his answer was pragmatic: "Like all staff people, historians will have to find out for themselves, in the end, for whom they are working."[1] In the Winter 1982 issue, Terrence O'Donnell's "Pitfalls Along the Path of Public History" appeared. From a survey of back issues of *The Public Historian,* O'Donnell detected a common theme: "History is usable and must be sold." The problem, he argued, is that "in

The Public Historian, Vol. 8, No. 1 (Winter 1986) © 1986 by the Regents of the University of California the marketplace, the pressures for ethical compromise are greater than in the academy, though of course they exist there as well. Our principal ethical obligation is very simple: to tell the truth, insofar as we are able."[2]

Rather than raise the issue of ethics for the public historian doing business history entirely in the abstract (or discuss it primarily in terms of the works of others), this article will draw upon my own experiences, particularly through projects of the University of Louisville Oral History Center. These latter studies provide the context in which this problem is defined (although perhaps not entirely resolved) for me. My own training and experience are in an academic setting. For some time I have been interested in aspects of the history of mass merchandising. Thus, I have been both a consumer of the works of other scholars and a researcher interested in producing such material himself.[3] But more and more in recent years, as a result of my position as co-director of the University of Louisville Oral History Center, I have participated in oral history projects that concern business history, with business both the subject and the sponsor of study. In the conception and execution of these studies, particularly through the development of their funding, the ethical dimensions of business history for the public historian have become more apparent to me. Participation in sessions involving this problem at two meetings of the Oral History Association and one meeting of the National Council on Public History has convinced me of the importance of this problem, of the widespread interest in it, and of the difficulties inherent in resolving it.[4]

Various professional groups have attempted to deal with ethical problems of a related nature. The Oral History Association, after much debate, has produced several documents, the most recent of which is the so-called Wingspread Report—*Oral History Evaluation Guidelines.* The Society of American Archivists has produced its "Guidelines for Business Archives." The California Committee for the Promotion of History has developed "Standards of Professional Conduct." And the National Council on Public History, after serious debate, has developed its own statement on ethics. But such discussion of business history and ethics reveals that often historians with academic employment (in universities, libraries, or archives, for example) feel that their ethical problems are soluble while those of the nonacademic historian (working directly or indirectly for business) are insoluble. At the same time, many nonacademic historians argue that they do have special problems; some even suggest that a different set of guidelines must apply to their work than to that of the academic historian.[5]

The basic problem confronting the public historian doing business history is the more general question of the extent to which funding incorporates control. A related concern is whether the control exercised by an academic institution is preferable to that exercised by a business. Control may involve such matters as who is interviewed (and by whom) during an oral history project; what topics are or are not covered; who administers the use of the resulting tapes and transcripts (and subject to what restrictions); and in what form the results are published (films, articles, books, or exhibits, for example). If manuscript collections are involved, the same questions of access and use apply. And with any finished product—oral or written—questions of authorship, editing (censorship to some), and audience arise. Certainly there is a feeling common within academic circles that an in-house history is inferior to an academic history done from outside the company.

The University of Louisville Oral History Center has conducted three major business history projects and currently is engaged in a fourth. In the first study, university funds and a grant from the Kentucky Oral History Commission (a state agency which coordinates and helps finance oral history in Kentucky) were combined to conduct a study of the Louisville black community, with a special emphasis on business (large and small). In this project, there was no funding from the group being studied.[6]

The main difficulties, then, were those common to all such projects—identifying narrators and interviewers, doing necessary background research, making certain that proper transcripts and finding aids were prepared (for financial reasons not all interviews were transcribed fully although all were indexed), and seeing to it that proper release forms (understood by the narrators) were signed. The issue of restrictions was not often raised. In fact, occasionally the rights of the narrator demanded that we suggest some restrictions ourselves. But there was no pressure upon the university from any outside source with respect to how the project should be conducted. Responsibility for university and Oral History Commission funds involved only expending moneys as budgeted and conducting those interviews which were promised.

The two other completed projects (and the one now in process) were funded differently. While university moneys and grants from the Kentucky Oral History Commission were obtained, in these cases grants were also secured from the firms being studied. The university received funds from the Louisville and Nashville Railroad (L&N)—an important regional and national transportation firm—to study its history. The Louisville *Courier-Journal* and Louisville *Times* newspapers supplied money to document their past. And in the most recent project, Brown-Forman Distillers (a leader in the field) is providing support for a study of its industry. In the case of the railroad, the University of Louisville Archives was already the repository for some noncurrent records. The archives is working with the other two companies in order to obtain some materials and advise on record retention.[7]

In all of these projects, the University of Louisville is the ultimate holder of tapes, transcripts, and other documents. All such materials are released to the university on its standard release form, almost always without restrictions. The corporations involved neither seek nor are given copies of the interviews on a regular basis in order to monitor them, although some sample interview materials are provided to illustrate the progress of the projects. Of course, these companies may request copies of all unrestricted materials when they become available for public use—as could anyone—in accordance with the archives' policy of supplying copies of such materials at cost.

On the basis of experience with these projects, several problems (or potential problem areas)—which could create ethical tests for the public historian doing business history—arise. These areas are not necessarily unique to oral history, business history, or public history; but they represent common problems which demand solutions. For example, how are narrators for oral history interviews selected? A company may quite reasonably suggest employees (or former employees) whom they believe would make good informants. But to what extent does this nomination of individuals color the nature of the information obtained? Are certain other individuals, whose testimony might provide a different perspective, left uninterviewed—even if the error is inadvertent? (A similar problem arises in terms of what corporate records a firm makes available for background research and what materials remain unexamined.) Also, to what extent are current employees of a company reluctant to provide candid answers to questions, even when no pressure to give the "correct" response is applied by management? What of retirees concerned about pensions or former employees who need recommendations for new posts? There need not be a real threat of retribution in order for narrators to perceive that one exists. In such cases, the promise of protection through the use of restrictions on the release of materials may not obviate the problem.[8]

Other concerns include such matters as who selects the question areas. Are any topics closed to investigation? Who holds the tapes, transcripts, and other materials, and who administers their use? At the University of Louisville, the University Archives controls these matters. The release agreements are between each individual narrator and the university; the cooperating corporation has no legal control over the interviews—even though it has helped to pay for them. We have been fortunate in working with firms that have been willing to fund projects conducted in the manner just described.

These firms have certain special characteristics. The L&N Railroad had a long history of significant corporate identity, but this is no longer the case. Merger with other railroads has changed the corporate name, transferred administrative offices from Louisville, and caused some employees to face either movement to a new city or unemployment.[9] The newspapers have had a long history of family ownership which some people speculate may end with the passing of the current generation of publishers. The distilling industry represents an old and tradition-laden occupation that now is experiencing rapid technological change, substitution of corporate ownership for family ownership, and diversification into production areas totally unrelated to alcohol. Thus, in each case there is real concern that a treasured history may soon be lost if not properly documented. Also, these businesses probably do not fear that documenting past history will reveal any information damaging to their current image and profitability. This does not mean that there are no questionable events in their corporate pasts, but like most companies, these corporations find their immediate problems to be present and future decisions, not those of the past. In fact, the triumphs and mistakes of the past may provide guideposts to explain present positions and aid in future planning.

Apart from the possible difficulties of dealing with businesses, there are other, perhaps hidden, problems. For example, the biographer of a corporation (like the biographer of an individual) often forms either an intense like or an intense dislike for the subject. This must be recognized. Sympathy for a corporation (particularly when it is helping to fund a project) may cause an interviewer to leave certain questions unasked, in the belief—perhaps honest—that protecting the subject's image will do no real damage to the integrity of the research. This behavior need not be in response to any pressure from the business being studied. It can come from within the researcher. Ethical problems such as this face all practitioners, not just those who are deemed to have "sold out" for money.

It is appropriate at this point to distinguish among the various types of public historians doing business history: those employed by a corporation, those working independently as consultants to corporations, and those working through a university or other academic institution. This categorization does not mean that the ethical issues so far raised can be set aside in some cases and not in others. But it does recognize that different relationships and objectives place some restrictions upon the range of practical responses available to the various questions that can arise.

The reasons for corporate interest in history are varied, but among them are the desire for an in-house study to help explain past positions and determine future ones, the need for public relations tools, and the provision of projects for tax-deductible distribution of funds.[10] Understandably, a firm is concerned about the impact upon itself of such projects, particularly when it is financing them. What is objectionable, from the historian's point of view, is any deliberate attempt to falsify history. This is particularly disturbing if the professional status of the historian is being used to legitimate the process and remove any suspicion about the product's honesty.

Ultimately, the problem for the historian, whatever the subject being studied, is to be as honest as possible—honest more than objective, because honesty is the more easily attainable goal. Although objectivity is certainly worth striving for, there are many arguments as to whether one can achieve it. Furthermore, there is nothing wrong with the use of historical evidence (which by nature will be selective) to support a position, as long as one is honest about the material used and about the bias that is brought to the process. To assume that no ethical problems are involved, however—or to refuse to discuss them—will not promote honesty, scholarship, or the professionalization of public history. Nor will the market for public historians be protected or enlarged, certainly goals of considerable significance. Whatever the reasons that corporations advance as justifications for writing their histories, if no outsider will accept the work of the historians involved, then little permanent benefit will result. Loss of confidence in the product will ultimately imperil the public history industry, just as it has damaged other American industries.

The challenge to the public historian doing business history with business support, then, is to realize that potential problems exist and attempt to design projects in a manner which both recognizes and minimizes these difficulties. The guiding rule should be to maintain honesty by accepting as few restraints upon process and product as possible and freely admitting those restrictions that do exist and their potential impact upon the study.

For example, if a corporation agrees to full academic control of the project, then it can be funded by a grant from the corporation. If the corporation seeks academic expertise but has corporate needs which demand certain scholarly acceptable restrictions (such as time seals, limited areas of research, or limited use for publication), then a contract for consultancy is appropriate. For those firms whose goals are essentially in-house, but which wish to utilize a trained historian, the best approach is direct employment by the company. (This could be on a short- or long-term basis.) This model allows for flexibility in the establishment and attainment of goals, but it does not surrender the fundamental concept of academic honesty.

Such an approach applies both to those working from an academic, institutional base and those working independently (or as direct employees of a business). Clearly, however, it is easier for the academic historian to decline to accept a grant, contract, or temporary position in business than it is for the independent historian or corporate employee to refuse an assignment. Thus, it is the role of the public historian doing business history to educate the business community as to the professional and ethical standards related to collecting and publishing history. At a minimum, firms must know what these standards are and to what extent their projects conform to them. Companies must recognize when they make requests or decisions that run counter to such standards, even though their perception of corporate needs may cause them to conclude that such standards must be violated. In this educational process the National Council on Public History should play a vital role. When, as a professional organization for those doing business history in cooperation with business (or in its employ), the National Council on Public History suggests standards of conduct or provides forums for the discussion of such issues, it provides historians with evidence to use in arguing for the honest conception, execution, and dissemination of corporate-sponsored history. This is the best way to avoid undue interference with research, by establishing rules which will provide useful and accepted guidelines for others.

The ultimate tool of the independent historian who doubts the academic integrity of a project is to refuse employment in it. While the institutionally based historian has similar recourse, it is an easier financial decision for those with an additional source of support for themselves and their research. To take such action is an extreme measure, but one which would not have to be resorted to often. Acceptable arrangements with business are possible (as this article has indicated)—arrangements which accept legitimate need for control but openly identify such control, recognize its impact upon scholarship, and seek to minimize its use. If the employment of public historians in business history cannot be maintained in a manner which permits such an honest statement of the viewpoints and goals involved; if restraints must exist at the expense of academic honesty; then there is no profession of academic, business-oriented, public history. But this is not the case. The problem is not whether it is possible for the public historian to produce good business history, only how best to achieve that end.

REFERENCES

1. Albro Martin, "The Office of the Corporate Historian: Organization and Functions," *The Public Historian* 3, no. 3 (Summer 1981), 16.
2. Terrence O'Donnell. "Pitfalls Along the Path of Public History," *The Public Historian* 4, no. 1 (Winter 1982), 66, 70.
3. See, for example, Carl G. Ryant, "The South and the Movement Against Chain Stores," *Journal of Southern History* 39 (May 1973), 207–22; idem. "Kentucky and the Movement to Regulate Chain Stores, 1925–1945," *Filson Club History Quarterly* 57 (July 1983), 270–85, idem. "New Merchandising in the New Era: Change in the Kentucky Retail Trade During the 1920s," *Journal of Kentucky Studies* 1 (July 1984), 202–10.
4. Carl Ryant, commentator, "Oral History and Business History: From Inside and Outside the Industry," 1981 Meeting of the Oral History Association; idem, panelist, "Special Problems of Business History: A Roundtable," 1982 Meeting of the Oral History Association.
5. Oral History Association, *Oral History Evaluation Guidelines* (1980); Linda Edgerly, "Business Archives Guidelines," *American Archivist* 45 (Summer 1982), 267–72; California Committee for the Promotion of History, "Standards of Professional Conduct," adopted October 28, 1984; National Council on Public History, "Ethical Guidelines," adopted April 1985 (see *NCPH Newsletter* 5 [Spring–Summer 1985], 3).
6. A slide-tape presentation, "Just Around the Corner," resulted from the black history project, which has also been reported on in Carl Ryant, "Roundtable Session on Oral History," 1979 Missouri Valley History Conference; idem, "Reconstruction of a Black Business District," 1979 International European Conference on Oral History; idem, "Kentucky's Minorities and Oral History," 1980 Kentucky Conference on Oral History; idem, "Louisville's Black Community: Oral History," 1982 Meeting of the Central States Anthropological Society; idem, "Louisville's Black Community: A Family Perspective," 1982 Meeting of the American Culture Association; idem, "Class, Continuity, and Community: Oral History and Collective Identity," 1984 Meeting of the American Culture Association. The black community project is also discussed, along with the railroad project and the newspaper project, in Carl Ryant, "Real Versus Perceived Power in an American City: Louisville, Kentucky, 1920–1970 (Three Case Studies)," in Mercè Vilanova and Jordi Planes, eds., *V Col-loqui Internacional d'Història Oral: "El Poder a la Societat,"* (Barcelona: Universitat de Barcelona, 1985),

405–11. See also Carl Ryant, "Louisville's Black Population Advancement Begins from Within," Louisville *Defender,* February 19, 1981; idem, "Louisville's Black Population Spoke Loudly (And Well)," Louisville *Defender,* February 18, 1982; idem, "Socioeconomic Mobility in the Louisville, Kentucky, Black Community," in Nelleke Bakker and Jaap Talsma, eds., *Papers Presented to the International Oral History Conference* (Amsterdam: University of Amsterdam, 1980), I, 49–64.

7. For the L&N project, see Carl Ryant, "'Where the Railroad Was, the River Is': Oral History from L&N Workers," *Register of the Kentucky Historical Society* 82 (Winter 1984), 60–71. The University of Louisville Archives has 155 linear feet of the railroad's records as well as 39 reels of microfilm. In the railroad project, 45 persons (9 women and 36 men) were interviewed. The youngest was 40; the oldest 86. The median age was 67; the mean 67.9. Seventeen held blue-collar jobs; the rest white-collar. Six blacks were interviewed—2 women and 4 men. All of those interviewed had long work records with the L&N—often 30 to 50 years. The median length of service was 36 years; the mean 36.08. In the newspaper project, interviews were conducted with 31 employees, 27 men and 4 women. The age range was from 38 to 79 years, with a median of 66 and a mean of 63.9. Length of service was from 6 to 55 years, with a median of 35 and a mean of 32.74. In the case of the distilling project, more than 60 interviews have been conducted.

8. Preliminary comparison of interviews from the L&N project—where there were a good number of interviews with retired workers—with those from the distilling project (where most interviews, particularly on the line, have been with active employees) suggests that there may be somewhat less candor in the latter case.

9. *Louisville Courier-Journal,* October 15, 1982.

10. See Enid Hart Douglass, "Corporate History—Why?" *The Public Historian* 3, no. 3 (Summer 1981), 75–80.

7
ETHICS AND THE PUBLICATION OF COMMISSIONED HISTORY

Donald Page

Because publication is usually an integral part of the work of the public historian, some ethical issues associated with it should not be overlooked. Unlike the academic or free-lance historians, who contend primarily with peer review and the demands of publishers' contracts, public historians have the added and frequently more troublesome dimension of their clients[1] or employer's insistence on using history for their own ends. While academic historians have the luxury of working in the freedom afforded by a long tradition of open inquiry and public presentation in the pursuit of truth, that freedom may not exist to the same extent in the corporate world of the public historian outside of academia.

In the general debate about the ethical issues faced by historians there has been much attention directed to resisting the pressures of employers who try to deflect the historian's judgments by seeking to suppress evidence or by tailoring the conclusions to their own preconceived point of view. That concern must also extend to the employers' use of the historians' end products otherwise, historians may find themselves responsible for a product that may not be entirely of their own making. The "Principles and Standards for Federal Historical Programs," issued by the Society for History in the Federal Government partially addresses this issue in so far as historians "will be free to determine the scope, organization, format, and contents of the study" and "the agency shall have the right to control dissemination and use of the study."[2] What also needs to be addressed is the right of the agency or employer to change the manuscript before publication. Can, for example, the employer disallow the use of certain sources, expunge parts of the text, deny authorship, or refuse to publish it with or without changes? Historians are not the only ones to require a code of professional ethics. Employers must also be held accountable to the historians in publishing the results of historical inquiry.

While the public historian may have a great deal to say about what goes into making the corporate image that will eventually be presented to the public, it is the corporation or institution which will want to deter-

mine the final content and format before publication. Few, if any, organizations could be expected to knowingly allow the publication of a work
which would damage their public credibility, aid their competitors, or
harm or destroy consumer confidence. While the public historian's
interest in publication may be based on professional development or
contribution to a body of scholarship or public debate, the client or employing organization thinks primarily about its impact upon future business operations. Information or views considered to be inimical to that
desired future may be suppressed or severely edited. Because the historians are more concerned about the integrity of the history and the preservation of the truth, they may have different perceptions of what could be
injurious to the operations and image of the organization that would justify withholding publication. With due regard to potential libel or slander, the historian would be less concerned than the employer about
preventing a potential embarrassment to incumbent or former officials.
Public historians must live and produce in this environment, so it is important that some mutually agreeable guidelines be established at the
outset of their work, lest an author labor in vain on a history never to be
published. Such an arrangement may also go a long way in avoiding the
ethical problems associated with client or employer censorship.[3]

Long before the writing stage begins, it is important to establish the
ground rules on what materials can be seen and used. Unless this understanding is clearly delineated from the beginning, there may be disagreements later about the right to quote or cite certain documents or
information. Historians need to know precisely what records will not be
available for research so that they may make an initial assessment of the
viability of the project.

In the public sector, restrictions may be defined by laws pertaining to
secrecy or access, such as an official secrets act or a freedom of information act. Businesses seldom have these legal constraints unless the nature
of their work is defined by the law, as in defense contracts. Most often,
their restrictions are voluntary, based on the requirement to remain
competitive and to protect the privacy of their employees. For historians
working within an establishment, the line may be somewhat blurred because they possess permission or security clearance that allows access to
all or most documentation. However, privileged access does not negate
the importance of defining the limits for studies that eventually are to be
published in order to avoid problems later in determining what has been
obtained from classified sources.

The longer the historian works in a cloistered security conscious environment or within a private institution, the more difficult it may be to
distinguish between classified and public sources. Part of the public
historians' job is to be thoroughly familiar with operations of the institution. Consequently, they may be privy to conversations and interpersonal notes, which never go to file, containing information the
employer assumes is confidential. Since this protected information
often answers the questions of causation and becomes the bridge for
making sense of a fragmentary but more formal documented record of

decision making, its use must be carefully regulated. Often, it will be necessary in order to not perjure the historical truth, to work out in advance a mutually acceptable way of acknowledging sources.

Historians will also wish to describe in the preface to their work the limitations of their research to protect themselves from the impact of subsequent revelations when previously restricted information is released to others. This is a particularly important procedure when a published version emanates from a more comprehensive classified study.

Few contemporary studies can be published without some limitations. In the past, this has led many historians to argue that presentist history should not be written at all. In the last few decades, the force of this argument has waned as historians have increasingly sought to participate in contemporary issues and have become more conscious of the declining importance of paper records due to modern means of communication and decision making. This, of course, is one of the great values of oral history. The institutional historian must supplement and verify the printed or machine readable record in order to present a more complete and accurate account.[4] It is often only through oral history that the historian can expect to discover the substance and the significance of interpersonal relationships, telephone conversations, and the dynamics of collective decision making within a bureaucracy. In some cases, especially after the introduction of freedom of information legislation, officials have been encouraged, or for their own self protection have decided, to work with a minimum of documentation on controversial matters.

There is also the problem of selective preservation. Those who are most conscious of their place in history, can be very skillful in preserving only the record that will support their view. This selectivity is a particularly difficult problem for historians if their subjects have used and abused their files in writing autobiographies or other essays. Evidence that does not meet their recollections or desires may be destroyed or added to in such a way as to fill in the missing pieces in the documentary record to their benefit.[5] For public historians involved in policy studies it is often a question of balancing access with assessment.

While the prefatory statement on access and usage may not be written until the end, its parameters must be spelled out at the outset of the work. Once the manuscript has been submitted, public historians are always at the mercy of the owners of the records who can legitimately deny publication of personal or classified information or raise troublesome ethical questions over its use. For example, I was once asked to review an unpublished autobiography as preparation for a series of oral history interviews with the author. Recognizing the importance of the information in the autobiography, I later sought and was given permission to use the memoir for enhancing a history that I was writing. When my work was subsequently completed it contained some revelations from interviews which made the author uncomfortable and, in a retaliatory mood, he insisted that all references to his autobiography be removed from my history. This was easy enough to execute but it resulted in a distorted picture of the individual's motive, thereby destroying the objective balance that I was seeking. Had conditions of access been agreed to in writing in the first place, much subsequent grief could have been avoided.

Even more difficult was the case of a colleague who had been given access to a collection of unsorted private papers of the editor and owner of a prominent newspaper before they were deposited in a public archive. While he was researching a biography of the editor, he discovered cheque book stubs that made it quite evident that the editor had some significant joint financial investments with the leader of the political party which his newspaper vehemently opposed. The historian had been granted access to the paper's by the editor's widow. She knew the purpose of the research project, and placed no restrictions on his use of the information. As a courtesy to the widow the historian drew her attention to the existence of the stubs. As it happened, her new husband, who was connected to the family of the leader of the opposition, quickly removed this information from the collection before it was transferred to the public archives. The historian was then confronted with the question, whether he should use such material in the biography. To do so would almost certainly involve him in giving testimony on the missing cheque stubs in a subsequent court battle over the assets of the late editor's estate, in particular over who owned the joint assets of the editor and the leader of the opposition. The use of such material is often a judgment call of the historian but without prior written agreement, unforeseen problems may develop.

In some cases historians may find that they are asked to remove documented citations of quotations from what are normally regarded as public sources, when they do not fit the right corporate image.[6] As Stanley Hordes has pointed out, the short-term rewards of altering a manuscript to meet the unhistorical demands of the employer can send the historian down the slippery road to professional disrepute.[7] If the price of publication is the removal of certain portions of the text, then historians must decide if this is sufficient reason to warrant it not being published with their blessings. In most cases, the solution may be found in the wording of the preface to explain the limitations, i.e., the degree to which the text has been censored. Such protection is the best hope of preserving the historian's reputation for presenting the unvarnished, if somewhat limited truth, without missing the professional credit acquired through publication of commissioned history.

While it is customary in publishing contracts for the author to have the final say on what will be published, public historians in the employment of large institutions normally find that publication contracts are either non-existent because of in-house publishing capabilities or are drawn up between the publisher and the organization to bypass the author. The nature of internal operations often makes it difficult for authors to retain rights over the manuscript that goes to printing. In their own interests, they must insist in writing on holding the organization responsible for protecting their rights as authors beyond the normal copyright provisions. They must be able to ensure that their manuscript is not altered before publication except by their explicit permission.

If the employer insists on publishing a text which is unsatisfactory to the historian, then the only resort is to insist on withholding from publication the name of the author. This may not, however, always be an agreeable solution to the organization which wants the credibility derived from a professional historian's reputation. It is therefore very important that historians have the legal right in a contract or in their terms of employment to withhold their names from any publication as a means of protecting their professional standing.[8]

The historian may also experience the opposite result, though this is less common today than it used to be. The notion that government and, to a lesser extent, business historians should remain anonymous because they are being paid and, therefore, the credit belongs to either the organization as a whole or its most senior official or owner, has largely been disregarded. It has normally been found more convenient for the organization to have the protection of claiming that the views are those of the author and may or may not coincide with those of the organization.[9]

Historians' gossip is filled with stories of colleagues who have completed their work but their client or employer has refused to have it published, even though that was the original intention. The reasons are as numerous as the stories and may involve issues such as an inability or unwillingness to meet the inflationary costs of publication or a change in priorities away from publicizing the corporate image into more direct means of marketing the institutional image. In one case the financial officer who had not been involved in the project had neglected to make the necessary budgetary allocation in the annual estimates. When it came time to make an allocation the following year, a new manager, who regarded the project as a white elephant, had it consigned, forever, to the archives. These reasons were quite unrelated to the author and were much less nefarious than those the aggrieved author imagined.[10] Having been on both the historian's side and the employer's side in these disputes, I have found that the problem is not always with the employer. Often the finished product does not meet the legitimately high standards of scholarship demanded for publication by the organization which, after all, has its own reputation and investment to protect. On the other hand, the author has every right to feel aggrieved that his labors are not being recognized in the only way that he can receive professional recognition for them.

In spite of the arduous efforts of institutional historians, it is true that they have been paid for producing the manuscript, and the piper has the right to determine the reward. Disputes are not easily resolved, though professional history associations could assist by establishing a mechanism for mediation with an impartial assessment of the manuscript and a review of the concerns of the organization. In the absence of such a system, it would seem that, at the very least, the historian has the right to know the reasons why publication has been rejected and should have the opportunity to rectify any inadequacies in order to permit publication.

Contract clauses that allow adjustments should be no different from those of the tradesmen who guarantee the quality of their work. It also opens up the possibility that the client may withhold payments until revisions have been completed by the historian. Delays and adjustments would be more acceptable to the author if adjudicated by a professionally constituted tribunal. Contracts involve not only a code of ethical standards but a guarantee of performance which can be upheld in the courts. No organization can be expected to guarantee the right of publication to historians without seeing their final product. For historians to demand that right would only serve to debase the quality of their work. Let their peers along with representatives of the contractor or employer make that judgment based on professional standards. Only in this way can we ensure that substandard history will not be pushed through merely to satisfy the historian's pride. At the same time, good history will receive its just reward with publication.

Historians must try to obtain recognition prior to the completion of the manuscript, that pending a disagreement with the employer over publication, the historians have the right to seek another publisher. Some difficult questions could arise about the use of sources, what if any acknowledgment should be given to the original sponsor of the project, who should receive royalties from publication (given the financing of the research provided by the organization), and what would happen in any subsequent effort by the organization to produce its own version. It is clear that historians have frequently been naive in working out these details in advance.

Given the number of reportedly good manuscripts that are gathering dust in private archives, perhaps it is time to be more insistent on working out an insurance clause for commissioned studies. The organization, for its part, usually relies on the established professional competence of the historian and peer evaluations to ensure, as far as possible in advance, that the end product would meet their standards while at the same time would be a sound, objective history. Employers have the right to these expectations from professionals who pride themselves in the quality of their work. At the same time, this very pride in the quality of their work should cause public historians to hold their employers accountable to a mutually agreed code of ethics regarding the publication or non-publication of their work.

REFERENCES

1. The views expressed in this article are those of the author and do not necessarily represent those of the Department of External Affairs.
2. The Society for History in the Federal Government, "Principles and Standards for Federal Historical Programs," *The Public Historian*, 8 (Winter 1986) 61–62.
3. Wayne D. Rasmussen, "Some Notes on Research and the Public Historian," *The Public Historian*, 1 (Spring 1979) 68–71, and Vincent Gambi, "Going Public," *Canadian Business*, (March 1983), 74–79.

4. D. M. Page. "Whose Handmaiden?: The Archivist and the Institutional Historian," *Archivaria* 17 (Winter 1983–1984) 162–72.
5. Secretary of State for External Affairs, Paul Martin, is remembered for doing business with other foreign ministers over the telephone. When several of his closest advisers were asked to verify the accuracy of some of the stories in his autobiography, they were unable to do so because they had never been privy to these telephone conversations. Mr. Martin's account could not be supported or refuted by the remaining records in his department. It remains to be seen whether his interlocateurs have left their own records of these conversations. In the meantime, we must be content with the author's version to enhance our understanding of important diplomatic initiatives of the 1960s. Paul Martin, *A Very Public Life,* volume II *So Many Worlds,* Toronto: Deneau, 1985.
6. D. M. Page, "History and Foreign Policy: The Role and Constraints of a Public Historian in the Public Service." *The Public Historian,* 6 (Spring 1984) 21–36.
7. Stanley M. Hordes, "Does He Who Pays the Piper Call the Tune? Historians, Ethics, and the Community." *The Public Historian,* 8 (Winter 1986) 53–56.
8. Historical Researchers in the employment of the Government of Canada have in their collective agreement the following article 31 on authorship. "When an employee acts as a sole or joint author or editor of an historical publication his authorship or editorship shall normally be shown on the title page of such publication. Where the employer wishes to make changes in material submitted for publication with which the author does not agree, the author may request that he not be credited publicly." Treasury Board Canada, *Group: Historical Research (all employees),* Agreement between the Treasury Board of Canada and the Professional Institute of the Public Service of Canada, (1981), 54.
9. The Canadian Department of External of Affairs, for example, held this position on anonymity for its historians for many years. The first volume of *Documents on Canada's External Relations* appeared in 1967 without listing the editors and none of the articles appearing in its journal, *External Affairs,* were signed. Volumes of Documents published after 1969 contain the names of editors and authors are mentioned in *International Perspectives* which replaced *External Affairs* the following year.
10. Ann Silversides, "Corporate Histories Can Be Costly Vanity," *The Globe and Mail, Report on Business,* January 22, 1983.

PART II: PUBLIC HISTORY CODES OF ETHICS

1

DOES HE WHO PAYS THE PIPER CALL THE TUNE? HISTORIANS, ETHICS, AND THE COMMUNITY

Stanley M. Hordes

Several years ago, at my first public history conference, two successful public historians offered testimony as to how they had "made it" in the real world. The first, a historian for a large private corporation, began by offering an account of the wonderful contributions his company had made to mankind over the century or so that it had been in existence. He then proceeded to describe his role in collecting and interpreting materials relevant to the company's development. The second speaker, also a corporate historian, discussed his role as a company speech writer. His primary function was to extract from corporate records historical material for executives to use in their public speeches.

Although I had been employed as a historian in the public sector for several years, and was a strong advocate of historians' participation in the community, I was troubled by the advocacy approach to history maintained by the two speakers. While none of us can be totally objective and free from cultural biases, it appeared to me and to several colleagues in the audience that both of the speakers had undermined their credibility as historians.

More than a few years and several dozen conferences later, my concerns over the potential for conflict of interest for historians, both in the public and private sectors, has not diminished. To the contrary, many of my colleagues in museums, historic preservation agencies, private companies, and contracting firms regularly face critical ethical conflicts. Some agonize over these decisions, while others dismiss them as irrelevant and go about their business. Curiously, the two principal dangers faced by public historians reflect the experiences articulated by the two speakers cited above. The first danger is the risk that we as historians become public relations agents for our companies or agencies. Perceiving

The Public Historian, Vol. 8, No. 1 (Winter 1986)

that our standing in the eyes of our superiors would improve if we shaped the past to fit a preconceived pattern, we proceed to search into the documents to unearth facts that relate not only how wonderful our company *is,* but how great it *has been* through history.

Take, for example, the hypothetical case of an in-house historian for a chemical company that had manufactured a highly toxic defoliant used against civilian populations in a recent war.[1] In the course of writing the history of the company, how will the historian treat this chapter of its history? If he or she determines that the developers of the substance indeed knew in advance the detrimental effects on humans, and that civilians would likely suffer the ill effects of its application, then an objective methodological training would dictate that this be spelled out. However, since the company prides itself on its long record of bringing wonderful consumer products to a growing world, the company's board of directors wishes to present to the public a positive view of its present and its past. It is all too likely that the historian in question would be tempted to play down the role of the company in the development of the defoliant, and instead would emphasize its role as good citizen.

The second principal danger is more subtle, and thus poses a far more serious threat to the historian's credibility. In an effort to please our client or our employers, we consciously or unconsciously anticipate the kind of historical information that they want, and mold the facts to fit their perceived needs. The historian assessing the significance of a structure potentially eligible for the National Register of Historic Places, for example, if often motivated as much by the financial consideration of his or her client as by the criteria for significance of the importance of the resource. A colleague undertaking an architectural survey in a large eastern state recently admitted to me that he had omitted a potentially significant structure from the list of eligible structures. He did this in consideration of his perception that his client did not want to expend the funds necessary to maintain the structure. He thus "bent" the criteria of significance to suit the exigencies of the party paying for his services.

Such problems are not confined to the private sector. A preservation planner with a Ph.D. in history working for a county in a southeastern state was recently called upon to contribute an article on historic preservation in her area. After carefully researching the subject, she arrived at the conclusion that the county planners had allowed the destruction of several significant archaeological sites in the construction of a new housing development. The chair of the County Commission, who was also the planner's boss, however, fancied himself quite a historic preservationist, and wished to present himself as a protector of old ruins. So the planner faced a most difficult decision. Should she present her analysis as she understood it to be, or should she play it safe and sugar-coat the recent past to placate the counter commissioner? As it turned out, she followed the latter course, placed her boss's actions in a favorable light, and secured her position for years to come.

Examples of both of the problems cited above abound in the profession today,[2] and the community of public historians is sharply divided about how to respond to the problem of ethics and the potential for conflict of interest. One group of historians feels strongly that their sole function is to serve their clients' short-term interests, and that merely by their presence in the public arena their role as advocates is natural, open, honest, and even desirable. On the opposite side of the spectrum are the historians who, despite pressures to the contrary, strive for objective, thorough analysis, regardless of the implications for their clients or employers. They maintain that recipients of historical information can only make informed judgments and sound policy decisions on the basis of unbiased, professional research and presentation.

What then should comprise the parameters of the advocacy role played by historians in the community? First and foremost, historians should serve as advocates for history, and should work to protect historical resources, be they documentary, architectural, or archaeological. Concurrently, we are obliged to promote a greater awareness of and appreciation for history in our schools and communities. Beyond this "motherhood and apple pie" role, historians should exercise discretion. In the course of their work, historians should represent their research to the public in a responsible manner and should serve as advocates of economic or political interests only when such a position is consistent with objective, historical truth.

The development of new fields for historians in the public and private sectors has stimulated exciting opportunities for historians, but presents serious challenges as well. The responsibility for meeting these challenges must be shared both by the individual historian and by the profession collectively. The National Council on Public History's approval of a Code of Ethics is one step in the right direction. Once this code has gained acceptance among the profession, individual historians will be able to use it as a yardstick, both in guiding their own conduct, and also in justifying their approach to their work to their employers and clients. Armed with the support of the professional community, historians may set about their work with an awareness of the potential for ethical conflicts, and take them into consideration in the formulation of their research designs. This will put them in position to act upon, rather than react to, a potentially dangerous situation.

As the historical profession, we need to ensure that our credibility is maintained. The community—employers and clients as well as the general public—has entrusted us with responsibility for interpreting the past. We must not abuse this trust by straying from our mission to undertake this interpretation in the most objective, unbiased, professional manner possible.

REFERENCES

1. All examples cited in this article are either hypothetical or represent a composite of several actual experiences. Any similarity between any one example and an actual person or circumstance is purely coincidental.
2. See, for example, Thomas King, Patricia Hickman, and Gary Berg, *Anthropology in Historic Preservation* (New York: Academic Press, 1977).

Ethical Guidelines for the Historian
National Council on Public History

I. Historians' Relationship to Sources
   A. Historians work for the preservation, care, and accessibility of the historic record. The unity and integrity of historical record collections are the basis for interpreting the past.
   B. Historians owe to their sources accurate reportage of all information relevant to the subject at hand.
   C. Historians favor free and open access to all archival collections.

II. Historians' Relationship to Clients (Employers)
   A. Historians owe their employers the historical truth insofar as it can be determined from the available sources.
   B. Historians at all times respect the confidentiality of clients, employers, and students. Information gained through a professional relationship must be held inviolate, except when required by law, court, or administrative order.
   C. Historians seek to perform professional quality work in accordance with their employment agreements or research contracts.

III. Historians' Relationship with Colleagues
   A. Historians share knowledge and experience with other historians through professional activities and assist the professional growth of others with less training or experience.
   B. Historians handle all matters of personnel, including hiring, promoting, pay adjustments and discipline, on the basis of merit without regard to race, color, religion, sex, national origin, political affiliation, physical handicap, age, or marital status.
   C. When applying for employment or awards, historians submit applications and letters of recommendation which are accurate as to all pertinent details of education, experience, and accomplishment.
   D. Historians give appropriate credit for work done by others.

IV. Historians' Relationship with the Community
   A. Historians serve as advocates to protect the community's historical resources.
   B. Historians work to promote a greater awareness of and appreciation for history in schools, business, voluntary organizations, and the community at large.
   C. Historians represent historical research to the public in a responsible manner and should serve as advocates of economic or political interests only when such a position is consistent with objective historical truth.

V. Historians' Responsibility to the Canons of History

    A. Historians are dedicated to truth. Flagrant manifestations of prejudice, distortions of data, or the use of deliberately misleading interpretations are anathema.

    B. Historians represent the past in all of its complexity.

The views expressed in this article are those of the author and do not reflect those of the U. S. Army Corps of Engineers, the Department of the Army, or the Department of Defense.

2

FEDERAL HISTORIANS: ETHICS AND RESPONSIBILITY IN THE BUREAUCRACY

Martin Reuss

A free exchange of information is vital to the functioning of a democratic society. Both as citizens and historians, federal historians have a vested interest in preserving and contributing to that exchange. To some extent, consequently, they are institutional mavericks in any bureaucratic setting. Their desire is to gather, analyze, and communicate sufficient information to portray an accurate picture of events. However, the managers of government agencies may wish to limit the exchange of information for a variety of often justifiable reasons. There is then an inherent tension in the relationship between historians and senior officials. In light of this, it is no small wonder how many genuinely first-class "official" histories have been written. Indeed, the occasional story of historians denied access to information for unconvincing reasons must be put in perspective: federal historians enjoy access to an overwhelming amount of information in archives and official files.

Still, like public historians elsewhere, federal historians experience subtle pressures to ignore or de-emphasize topics that managers believe may reflect adversely on them or their agency. Government managers may value historical expertise but will also be wary of information being released that could prove embarrassing to themselves or the bureaucracy. Their appreciation of federal historians usually depends on the quality and amount of information historians give to *the agency,* not to the general public or the scholarly community. Max Weber said it best:

The Public Historian, Vol. 8, No. 1 (Winter 1986)
© 1986 by the Regents of the University of California

"Every bureaucracy seeks to increase the superiority of the professionally informed by keeping their knowledge and intentions secret."[1]

Faced with situations that may place their commitment to their profession in conflict with their loyalty to their agency, government historians must be flexible, and must have a sense of humor and plenty of
common sense. But all the flexibility in the world will not work if managers simply do not understand what historians can and cannot do. Historians must educate senior managers (and, yes, some historians) about
the nature of their craft. Beyond this aim lies the most basic goal of all:
to have federal historians treated as professionals and not as clerks. For
these reasons and more, a statement defining professional responsibilities is needed in the federal government. The statement became reality
at the end of 1984.

I

At first it was called an ethics statement. The idea was not new. For
several years, proponents (including this writer) had argued that such a
statement would educate federal officials about what should and should
not be expected of federal historians. This did not mean that the statement was to list job requirements. It was to be a code, not a certification.
Ideally, it would offer helpful guidance to all who cared about federal
history by articulating the heretofore unwritten assumptions of the professional historian in government service. Above all, enthusiasts argued
that the statement would help convince senior officials that historians
did, indeed, belong to a true profession grounded in common values and
goals.

The Society for History in the Federal Government, created in 1980,
provided the organizational strength needed to give an ethics statement
both credibility and necessary publicity. In the spring of 1983, Sam
Walker of the Nuclear Regulatory Commission, chairman of the society's
Federal Historical Programs Committee, agreed that a subcommittee on
ethics should be created within his committee. As the subcommittee's
chairman, I invited people who represented many different sectors of the
federal historical community to join the subcommittee.

In our first meeting, each member of the committee took the responsibility of drafting a statement that particularly related to his or her expertise. Mary Loughlin, a free-lance editor, accepted the assignment of
drafting a statement dealing with relations between federal historical offices and contractors. Donald Ritchie of the Senate Historical Office
drafted a section dealing with oral history. Heather Huyck of the National Park Service wrote a draft dealing with historical interpretation,
and Donald Jackson of the Historic American Buildings Survey/
Historic American Engineering Record (HABS/HAER) authored a section dealing with cultural resources. Paul Theerman of the Joseph Henry
Papers, Smithsonian Institution, submitted a statement dealing with editing. I took the responsibility of drafting sections dealing with research

and relations with senior managers. Everyone joined in what became very much a cooperative committee effort.[2]

Meetings were held about once a month thereafter. As discussions progressed, it became obvious that what we were drafting was not an ethics statement but a statement of responsibilities. To take two examples at random, principles that documentary editors should preserve a full and faithful transcription of their texts or that oral history interviewers should make each interview as complete as possible hardly seemed ethical matters, but they did suggest what was expected of a professional documentary editor or historian. Moreover, many of these principles responded to what the subcommittee members thought were genuine issues that required resolution. In going over each contribution to the ethics statement, the committee began to eliminate all but the most important of these responsibilities and to identify where these responsibilities overlapped and could be consolidated.

By December 1983, approximately nine months after work had begun, the subcommittee was ready to send a draft statement to the society's Executive Council for its consideration. The final typewritten 2 1/2-page draft statement had been reduced to five parts: general principles (preface), research, writing, contract history, and oral history. Also, the name of the document had been changed from "Ethics Statement" to "Principles and Standards." The change was carefully considered. As I explained in a December 6, 1983, letter to Wayne Rasmussen, the society's president, the new title helped focus attention on "the more basic question of the professional responsibilities of federal historians." For instance, one of the points made under "general principles" was that historians can act as advisers to policymakers. This was hardly an ethical matter, but it addressed one of the key justifications for there being historians within the federal government at all.

The draft "Principles and Standards" was intended to be applicable to all those engaged in federal historical work, not just to GS-170 career historians. The subcommittee hoped that it would offer guidance and support, for example, to park rangers and historical interpreters who do much public history but are generally not made to feel part of the federal historical community. Indeed, it seemed especially important that those without the benefit of substantial graduate training in history be made aware of the statement. Subcommittee members asked for the widest possible circulation of the statement and its publication in the society's newsletter, *The Federalist*. We also recommended that it be discussed at the next annual meeting, to be held in April 1984.

The Executive Council met in the middle of February to consider the statement. Various council members questioned both the wording and the necessity for the document. One member asked whether disciplinary measures were envisioned for not adhering to the principles. I replied in the negative and noted that the statement was meant for both historians and historical managers. Its strength would come when it was generally accepted first, by the society, and then by the federal historical community as a whole. Council members agreed to submit their thoughts in writing to Rasmussen.

In the spring, Rasmussen sent me the comments of the Executive Council. Only two members seemed to support the idea generally. One member could not "fully appreciate the need for this document. The conduct proscribed should come naturally to any professional historian, whether or not he/she is working in the federal sector." Another expressed concern that the statement "will fall into the hands of our academic brethren, confirming their darkest suspicions about our branch of the craft." Still another council member, who generally supported some sort of statement, called the draft "basically flawed" and continued, "It is not up to us to make a special point of reminding federal historians that plagiarism is immoral, that use of primary sources is usually better than reliance on secondary sources, or that records should be returned to file drawers." Others questioned specific wording. In short, according to President Rasmussen, "The members of the Executive Council . . . are far from agreement on the need for such a statement and upon the wording your subcommittee has proposed."[3] The council agreed that the draft statement should be given wide circulation but thought that any final version should await a decision then pending before the National Council on Public History to adopt an ethics statement of its own.

Obviously, a substantial difference existed between what even the most supportive council members wanted and the desires of the subcommittee. The major point of contention seemed to be whether the statement should address only those responsibilities unique to the federal government or should address responsibilities that all historians share. Because subcommittee members thought the statement as much an educational document for nonhistorian managers as a guide for federal historians, they had been inclined to the broader view. I was particularly concerned by (1) what seemed an inordinate sensitivity to what academicians might think and (2) ignorance of the problems professionally (and often geographically) isolated field historians face as they attempt to educate their supervisors about the proper role of the historian.

The subcommittee generally agreed that the society's adoption of a "Principles and Standards" statement should not depend on what the NCPH did since the society's statement dealt exclusively with federal history. At the annual meeting, held in April, the subcommittee's version was distributed, and I encouraged members to write or call with their reaction. Although I received very few comments in response, most of those were positive.

In June, the subcommittee decided to invite three Executive Council members to help redraft the "Principles and Standards." Richard Baker, David Allison, and Richard Hewlett agreed to come to our July meeting and discuss their concerns and suggestions. At that meeting, Hewlett presented a draft he had authored. Everyone thought that Hewlett's draft satisfactorily responded to many of the Executive Council's suggestions, but some were concerned that several important points of the subcommittee's draft had been dropped. In subsequent correspondence, these points were added, and the draft was substantially revised. At the end of October, this revised draft was sent to the Executive Council for reconsideration. The council unanimously adopted it on December 18, 1984. It became the first "Principles and Standards" statement adopted by a national historical organization.

While "Principles and Standards for Federal Historical Programs" will probably not satisfy anyone entirely, it does have the virtue of explaining the special responsibilities of federal historians and, perhaps more important, of *relating* those responsibilities to the work of others in the federal establishment, including policymakers, records managers, archivists, contractors, and supervisors. In so doing, the document stresses the *reciprocal* responsibilities and obligations of historians and agency officials. For the first time a statement exists that clearly says that federal historians should be treated as professionals and should not be expected to bias their interpretations in favor of "current policy considerations." Conversely, as federal employees, they accept limitations on their work resulting from the use of classified or Freedom of Information Act-exempt material. The statement covers oral history and cultural resources as well as writing and archival research, suggesting the many areas in which historians are active. In emphasizing that historians should be treated as advisers to policymakers, the statement implies the analytical abilities of historians, abilities that some senior officials have overlooked.

"Principles and Guidelines" comes closest to identifying ethical positions as distinct from responsibilities in the middle of section C, where historians are enjoined to "use the highest standards of their profession." These standards include "balanced and fair interpretation of all the evidence available, careful analysis of the evidence, honest and forthright conclusions based on the evidence, clear and concise writing, accurate and clearly attributed quotations, and proper citation of all sources." While these points may seem obvious to most historians, they are not to all government bureaucrats. If even a few federal managers who read the statement are persuaded that historians must be allowed to abide by their professional standards, the statement will have served a useful purpose.

II

In accepting the "Principles and Standards" statement, the Society for History in the Federal Government has taken a noteworthy step toward improving the professional status of federal historians. The document is hardly perfect, however, and in retrospect, it appears to contain some unfortunate omissions. For one thing, the statement does not mention the obligation of the government historian to recognize and explain the limitations of his craft. Knowledge of history does not guarantee wisdom, and there are many areas of human knowledge that may be better explored using some other methodological approach. Historians must distinguish between questions that can and cannot be answered through

historical research. While they have borrowed some social science methodologies in recent years, there are certain areas where professionally
trained social scientists may be able to develop more insights than historians. If we expect social scientists to recognize the particular skills of
historians, we owe them the same in return.

Federal historians also need to be candid about those issues where one
simply *cannot* learn from history. Arguing by analogy is a favorite device
of senior officials, and they often ask historians to use historical analogy
to illuminate a current problem.[4] Sometimes, the analogy does not exist;
or, if it does, the differences are more profound than the similarities.
Historians are obliged to tell officials when analogies are appropriate or
not—and preferably not after much time and money has been spent on a
study which, from the officials' viewpoint, is unrewarding. Policymakers
should value a historian as much for singling out an inappropriate analogy as an appropriate one.

Another insight that is missing from the "Principles and Standards"
statement is that "the historian's work is above all a work of criticism,"
in the words of the French historian Charles-Victor Langlois.[5] This is an
important point that should be shared with federal supervisors. In
stressing the historian's critical approach, Langlois was primarily concerned with questions of objectivity. He warned against historians who
did not "guard against instinct," who did not exercise sufficient
dispassion to be able to divorce themselves, with all their prepossas-
sions, from the sources they were studying.[6] The biases of the present
cannot be mixed with the battles of the past. In a government bureaucracy, this is not always an easy principle to follow. Immersed in day-to-
day routine, it is easy for a historian to be "captured" by his agency.
What both the historian and his supervisor must realize is that, once this
happens, the historian can no longer be faithful to his craft. If he does
not scrupulously evaluate the evidence, his interpretation may be inac-
curate. Far worse, the agency may be led into a fundamental misunder-
standing of its character and development.

Government historians should not oversell history, nor should historical offices be "make work" offices, but there is no reason why federal
historians should not make maximum use of their analytical abilities to
increase the agency's self-knowledge. Policymakers sometimes overlook
the fact that a fair characterization of an agency is possible only after examining its long-term development. When the data seems conclusive,
after studying several sequences of decisions or actions, the historian
may be able to offer some helpful generalizations about agency performance. If the generalizations seem relevant to current concerns (which
means keeping abreast of ongoing agency activities), they should be
brought to the attention of the policymakers. If, partly in consequence,
senior officials grant historians greater respect and status, historians
may find their own set of somewhat unbureaucratic values less frequently challenged. That means less tension for the historian and better
history for the agency.

III

Much of what has been discussed above, and much that is in the "Principles and Standards" statement, has to do with honesty and truth. Federal historians should not claim more for historical research than can reasonably be produced, and they should certainly be careful to supply the agency and the public with accurate information, always avoiding the obfuscation so characteristic of bureaucratic documents. Obviously too, they must be willing to subject their interpretations to professional review in order to allow the development of alternate interpretations and further research, i.e., to come closer to the truth. Keeping their work almost literally behind closed doors, as occurs in too many cases and for no good reason, not only prevents that search for greater understanding that historical research is all about, but it also precludes the possibility of holding the historian accountable for his work. Only through constructive dialogue and mutual criticism with other public and academic historians will government historians enhance their own credibility, while providing their agencies with the full benefits of historical inquiry.

As public servants, federal historians are obligated to serve the agency that, in the end, must answer to the public. In doing so, they perform a wide range of tasks—writing histories, reports, and speeches; helping to manage files; editing material; and providing information to Congress, other federal agencies, and the public, to name just a few. Given this range of responsibilities, it is essential that historians remember that their primary duty is to impart to government officials a sense of historical place and proportion that will lead to better programs and policies. To do so successfully requires that historians be flexible (without prostituting their skills) and that senior managers understand the historical profession. The "Principles and Standards" will help insure that both qualities endure in the federal bureaucracy.

REFERENCES

1. H. H. Gerth and C. Wright Mills, eds. and translators. *From Max Weber: Essays in Sociology* (New York: Oxford Univeristy Press, 1958), 233.
2. Sam Walker, representing the Federal Historical Programs Committee, contributed substantially to this effort. Merlin Berry, from the Office of Personnel Management, also provided helpful information at the initiation of the subcommittee's deliberations.
3. Rasmussen to Reuss, March 23, 1984. This and all other communications cited in this essay are in the archives of the society either in original or photocopy form.
4. I go into greater detail on how federal managers use history in "Public History in the Federal Government," in Barbara J. Howe and Emory L. Kemp, eds., *Public History: An Introduction* (Melbourne, Florida: Krieger Publishing Company, 1986), 293–309.
5. Quoted in Fernand Braudel, *On History,* translated by Sarah Matthews (Chicago: University of Chicago Press, 1980), 8.
6. *Ibid.*

Principles and Standards for Federal Historical Programs
Society for History in the Federal Government

The Society for History in the Federal Government urges all persons serving as historians in the federal government and all government officials administering historical programs to use this statement as a guide in their historical activities.

General Principles
1. Federal historians with professional training and experience have a right to expect that they will be treated as professionals in their work.
2. Federal historians have a responsibility to serve their scholarly profession and the public as well as the federal agencies for which they work. They should not be expected to bias their historical interpretations to accommodate current policy considerations.
3. Historians also have a responsibility as federal employees to accept limitations on their right to publish material or to make public statements when such information has not been reviewed for classified content or for data exempt from disclosure under the Freedom of Information Act.

These principles have specific application as follows:

A. In Collecting Historical Records
1. A primary function of federal historians is to collect historical evidence relating to the history of their agencies. Historical evidence includes documentary materials, oral history, artifacts, and historical sites.
2. Federal historians should assist personnel in the National Archives and Records Service to identify records of historical significance for eventual deposit in the National Archives. Until the National Archives can accept such materials, agency historians, archivists, and records managers should have the authority and resources to maintain control of these records as agency archives.
3. Federal historians should cooperate with their agency's records management personnel in drafting retention schedules that will assure permanent preservation of historical records.
4. Federal historians who retain records of archival quality in agency files have an obligation to make such records available to the public in accordance with the access standards of the National Archives.

B. In Conducting Historical Research
1. Federal historians should have access to all pertinent records relating to their research for official purposes, and they should make every effort within time limits and other constraints to consult all available

records. Primary sources should be used whenever possible. When, for legitimate reasons of security or policy, access to pertinent records is limited, the historians' supervisor should accordingly limit the declared scope of the study. Federal historians should then be free to evaluate for historical purposes all available evidence related to the study. This right does not extend to public release of such conclusions.

2. Federal historians should be encouraged to bring to the attention of their superiors any historical facts or conclusions which they believe may be pertinent to policies being formulated in the agency. The disposition of this information, however, remains within the discretion of the agency.

3. Federal records in the public domain or clearly eligible for public access should be available on an equal basis to all persons seeking access for reasonable purposes. Federal historians should enjoy no special privileges in access to such records. Federal historians should neither be required not permitted to withhold such records or information about their existence from the public; the historians should use accepted procedures for announcing the availability of such records to the scholarly community.

C. In Writing Historical Studies

Federal historians will be held accountable for the quality of their work by their professional colleagues as well as by agency officials. Accordingly, completed studies should bear the names of the authors.

When federal historians have been assigned the task of writing *official histories to be published for public use,* they have the right to expect that:

1. They will have access to all records, including classified and privileged documents, pertinent to their assignment.

2. They will be free to draw their own conclusions and interpretations reasonably supported by the evidence.

3. They will be free to determine the scope, organization, format, and contents of the study.

4. Their work will be reviewed by the agency for classified information and by the agency historians and technical experts to assure historical accuracy. When appropriate, independent historians should be invited to judge the quality of the work. The agency historian may also wish to invite managers of current programs to review the work.

Agency officials and administrators of historical programs should define the scope and time period to be covered by published histories so that the freedom of action defined above will not be impaired.

The historians, for their part, will be expected to perform their research and writing in accordance with the highest standards of their profession. The standards include: balanced and fair interpretation of all the evidence available, careful analysis of the evidence, honest and forthright conclusions based on the evidence, clear and concise writing, accurate and clearly attributed quotations, and proper citation of all sources.

When federal historians have been assigned to prepare *internal policy studies or reports:*

1. They have a right to clarify with their superiors whether the assignment is to be treated as historical work or as a staff study which merely uses historical material for a nonhistorical purpose (e.g., a speech, press release, congressional testimony, or policy paper).
2. If the assignment is to prepare a historical study, the discretion allowed for published historical work should apply, except that the agency shall have the right to control the dissemination and use of the study.
3. If the assignment is for a purpose other than preparing a historical study, the historian is subject to the same directions and restrictions that may appropriately be established by the agency for any other employee.

D. In Using Oral Evidence

1. The collection of oral evidence from persons who participated in events of interest to the historian is the oldest form of historical research, and it is a source that should not be neglected.
2. Federal historians should be provided reasonable opportunities to conduct oral history interviews with departing or retired senior exec-. utives and program managers of the agency, either to enhance the historical records of the agency or to fill in gaps in research for official histories.
3. Interviews should be recorded on tape but only after the person to be interviewed has been informed of the mutual rights and responsibilities involved in oral history, such as editing, confidentiality, disposition, and dissemination of all forms of the record.
4. Such agreements with the interviewee should be documented.
5. To the extent practicable, oral interviews should encompass the potential interest of other researchers and not just the immediate needs of the interviewer.

E. In Advising Policy Makers

1. Agency officials should recognize that staff historians, as the most reliable and available source of institutional memory, can be valuable advisers on policy issues.
2. The senior staff historian should have access to current policy records in order to identify issues on which historical research may be illuminating.
3. Agency officials should recognize that the staff historian has a responsibility to call attention to opportunities for historical research on current policy issues.
4. Staff historians should be encouraged to write accurate and candid histories of policy issues for their superiors independent of staff or program review.
5. Staff historians should recognize that their professional responsibili-

ties extend only to preparing historical studies and not to advocating courses of action.

F. In Preserving Nonverbal Historical Materials

1. Federal historians have a responsibility to preserve all types of historical evidence, not just documentary records. Nonverbal sources include archaeological and other historic sites, historic structures, artifacts, works of art, and photographic records. This responsibility extends not only to materials related to the history of the agency but also to those significant in local, state, and national history.
2. In historic preservation, federal historians should apply ethical and professional standards equal to those expected in documentary research and writing. Federal historians should act only within their area of competence and call upon specialists for advice when needed.
3. Agency historians should review all proposals for disposing of federal land, buildings, and equipment of possible historical value. Historical significance should be a factor in determining the course of action.
4. Federal historians should recommend practical ways of preserving artifacts and other nonverbal materials either in museums or in storage.
5. Federal historians should maintain inventories of historic sites, buildings, and artifacts in their agency's custody and, when appropriate, prepare interpretive materials explaining their significance.

G. In Negotiating and Administering Contracts

1. Federal historians should follow procurement and contracting procedures established by federal law and regulation.
2. Statements of work should set forth clearly the scope and requirements of the contract, the specifications of the work product, and well defined benchmarks for completing each phase of the work.
3. Selection criteria for contractors should not be defined so rigidly as to exclude all but a few candidates.
4. Contract opportunities should be advertised as widely as feasible.
5. Federal historians administering contracts should monitor the work of the contractor to provide adequate guidance to the contractor and to assure timely completion of a high-quality product.

3

STANDARDS OF PROFESSIONAL CONDUCT IN CALIFORNIA

James C. Williams

The debate continues as to whether historians are correct in adopting a formal code of ethics or set of standards for professional conduct. The need for such a statement for public historians, however, clearly has grown during the past decade. First, as more and more qualified historians turn to public history, professional standards guiding academic historians seem inadequate. Second, there is the increasing need for operative standards in cultural resources and planning analysis work, where the demand for historical expertise is now too often met by persons poorly qualified as historians.

The professional standards guiding academic historians, which are codified in the American Association of University Professors' (AAUP) "Statement on Professional Ethics" (1966), assumes that the historian's work will be influenced only by scholarly interests. Professor Ronald Tobey of the University of California at Riverside observed at the 1984 meeting of the National Council on Public History: "The standard of disinterested scholarship is maintained according to the AAUP Statement of Professional Ethics, by a community of free scholars, of which the professor is a member, whose evaluation and criticism test the veracity of scholarship." Unfortunately, historians working for corporations and government and those consulting privately often find that they are influenced by nonscholarly interests—the political climate within the public or private agency, the availability and use of confidential data, and the potential advocacy role which often accompanies such work. These may influence negatively the historian's freedom of research, analysis, and presentation of material, thus raising questions about the overall integrity of historical work completed for a fee.

The second need for standards of professional conduct in public history stems from the expanding fields of historic preservation and cultural resource management. Federal law now fully recognizes the importance of historical resources, as particularly evidenced by the pro-

The Public Historian, Vol. 8, No. 1 (Winter 1986)

visions of the National Historic Preservation Act (NHPA). The NHPA mandates identification, protection, and analysis of impacts on historical resources located on federal lands and on lands over which federal agencies have permit, licensing, or financial authority. History has become a necessary consideration in resource management and in urban and rural planning.

Similarly, there has been growing interest in other areas dealing with history. A revival of community history has prompted a dramatic increase in the number of local historical societies during the past two decades, and many more museums are focusing on history. In the private sector many corporations are developing historical archives, records management programs, and museums. In addition, history is gaining increased currency in the private sector as a valuable tool for policy planning. Society generally is finding greater value in historical insight and the skills possessed by historians.

Yet, because most historians carry on their work in the academy, few have paid attention to the growing need for historical work in the world of cultural resource management, historic preservation, policy planning, museums, and historical societies. Encouraged, perhaps, by the notion that anyone can do history, employers often give positions in these fields to individuals with little or no historical training. Inevitably, cases of poor historical practice surfaced in the public and private sectors.

Neither academic nor public historians have found it easy to agree on a response to these issues, for the tradition of standards borne of honor and scholarly truth holds strong in the profession. But public history is breaking ground where such tradition, regrettably, seems almost quaint. In California, where the first public history graduate program was launched and where inadequate historical practice surfaced early in cultural resources work, the California Committee for the Promotion of History (CCPH) adopted a formal statement of professional standards of conduct for public historians in October 1984.[1]

The CCPH Standards of Professional Conduct for public historians are particularly significant because the CCPH also offers a meaningful vehicle for addressing the problems which initially raised the need for standards or ethics. This vehicle, the CCPH Register of Professional Historians, is a listing of those historians who agree to sign and abide by the standards, supply an appropriate resume, and meet minimum standards of proven training, education, and/or experience in various areas of public historical practice (e.g., cultural resource management, litigation support services, historic preservation). The CCPH is providing copies of the register to as many potential California clients of public historians as CCPH can identify. Thus, the register provides a means for clients to identify qualified historians, and with the CCPH Standards of Professional Conduct, should go far toward eliminating potential conflicts, assisting in guaranteeing high quality historical work for employers, and enhancing the integrity of public historians.

CCPH does not pretend that its adoption of professional standards of conduct will be a panacea for all issues facing public historians, but it does believe that the use of the register and the implementation of the standards will have meaningful, operative value beyond a more generalized statement of ethics. There is some risk, of course. Some members have expressed concern that the standards and register may someday embroil the CCPH in costly litigation which may hurt the organization, even though the CCPH stops short of certifying historians listed on its register. Nevertheless, CCPH members believe that the standards, accompanied by the register, will assist both public historians and their clients in carrying out their professional responsibilities.

REFERENCES

1. The CCPH Standards of Professional Conduct are reprinted in the Appendix to this roundtable.

Standards of Professional Conduct
California Committee for the Promotion of History

(The Standards of Professional Conduct were adopted at the annual meeting of the California Committee for the Promotion of History, October 28, 1984, and amended on October 27, 1985.)

History is a profession, and the privilege of professional practice requires professional responsibility, professional competence, and an adherence to professional principles on the part of each practitioner.

I. The Historian's Responsibility to the Public
  1.1 The historian shall:
- (a) Recognize a commitment to represent history and its research results to the public in a responsible manner;
- (b) Actively support conservation of historical resources;
- (c) Avoid and discourage exaggerated, misleading, or unwarranted statements about historical matters that might induce others to engage in unethical or illegal activity.

  1.2 The historian shall not:
- (a) Engage in any illegal or unethical conduct involving historical matters or knowingly permit the use of his/her name in support of an illegal or unethical activity involving historical matters;
- (b) Give a professional opinion, make a public report or give legal testimony involving historical matters without being as thoroughly informed as might reasonably be expected;
- (c) Engage in conduct involving dishonesty, fraud, deceit, or misrepresentation about historical matters;
- (d) Undertake any research that affects historical resources for which he/she is not qualified.

II. The Historian's Responsibility to his/her Colleagues
  2.1 The historian shall:
- (a) Give appropriate credit for work done by others;
- (b) Stay informed and knowledgeable about developments in his/her field or fields of specialization;
- (c) Accurately prepare and properly disseminate a description of research done and its results;
- (d) Communicate and cooperate with colleagues having common professional interests;
- (e) Give due respect to colleagues' interest in, and rights to, information where there is a mutual active or potentially active research concern;
- (f) Know and comply with all laws applicable to his/her historical research, as well as with any relevant proce-

dures promulgated by duly constituted professional organizations;

(g) Report violations of these standards to proper authorities.

2.2 The historian shall not:

(a) Falsely or maliciously attempt to injure the reputation of another historian;

(b) Commit plagiarism in oral or written communication;

(c) Undertake research that affects historical resources unless prompt, appropriate analysis and reporting can be expected while respecting client confidentiality.

(d) Refuse a reasonable request from a qualified colleague for research data while respecting client confidentiality.

(e) Submit a false or misleading application for accreditation by or membership in any professional historical organization;

(f) Remove archival material, artifacts, or other historic and cultural resources from their legal repositories without prior authorization.

2.3 Historians working in specialized subfields and appropriate professional contexts, including—but not limited to—oral history, museology, conservation and curatorial care, historic preservation, historic archaeology, archival and records management, shall:

(a) Perform their duties with respect and care for the material resources being studies and/or preserved;

(b) Exhibit respect, care, and proper concern for the people, including informants, with whom they work;

(c) Subscribe and adhere to such additional codes or standards as have been adopted by the appropriate professional organization or association, understanding that subscription to the CCPH standards shall not preclude or substitute for similar codes or standards established by appropriate professional organizations.

III. The Historian's Responsibility to Employers and Clients

3.1 The historian shall:

(a) Respect the interests of his/her employer or client, so far as is consistent with public welfare and these standards;

(b) Refuse to comply with any request or demand of an employer or client which conflicts with these standards;

(c) Recommend to employers or clients the employment of other historians or other expert consultants upon encountering historical problems beyond his/her own competence;

(d) Exercise reasonable care to prevent his/her employees, colleagues, associates, and others whose services are utilized by him/her from revealing or using confidential information. Confidential information means information of a nonhistorical nature gained in the course of employment which the employer or client has requested be held inviolate, or the disclosure of which would be embarrassing or would be likely to be detrimental to the employer or client. Information ceases to be confidential when the employer or client so indicates or when such information becomes publicly known.

3.2   The historian shall not:
  (a) Reveal confidential information, unless required by law;
  (b) Use confidential information to the disadvantage of the client or employer;
  (c) Use confidential information for the advantage of himself/ herself or a third person, unless the client consents after full disclosure;
  (d) Accept compensation for recommending the employment of another historian or other person, unless such compensation is fully disclosed to the potential employer or client;
  (e) Recommend or participate in any research which does not comply with these standards.

IV. The Historian's Research Responsibilities

4.1   The historian has a responsibility to prepare adequately for any research. Before entering into any undertaking, the historian must:
  (a) Assess the adequacy of his/her qualifications and when necessary acquire additional expertise, bring associates with the needed qualifications into the undertaking, and/or modify the scope of the undertaking while respecting the client's needs;
  (b) Inform himself/herself of relevant previous research;
  (c) Develop a plan of research which specifies the objectives of the project, takes into account previous relevant research, and employs suitable methodology;
  (d) Ensure the availability of adequate staff and support facilities;
  (e) Comply with all legal requirements; including without limitation, obtaining where appropriate all necessary governmental permits and necessary permission from landowners or other persons;
  (f) Determine whether the project is likely to interfere with the program or projects of other scholars and if there is such a likelihood, initiate negotiations to minimize such interference.

4.2   In conducting research the historian must follow his/her plan or program of research, except to the extent that unforeseen circumstances warrant its modification.

4.3   The historian shall meet where pertinent the following minimal research standards:
  (a) All sites, structures, buildings, and environmental and cul-

tural features must be fully and accurately recorded by appropriate means, including their location;

(b) All sources must be fully and accurately recorded including their location;

(c) The methods employed in data collection must be fully and accurately described;

(d) All records shall be intelligible to other historians. Terms lacking commonly held referents, when used, shall be clearly defined;

(e) Research records resulting from a project must be deposited at an institution with permanent curatorial facilities and open to qualified professional historians, while respecting client confidentiality.

4.4 The historian will meet the following minimal standards in accepting responsibility for appropriate dissemination of the results of his/her research to the appropriate constituencies with reasonable dispatch:

(a) Results viewed as significant contributions to substantive knowledge of the past or to advancements in theory, method, or technique should be disseminated to colleagues and other interested persons by appropriate means, such as publications, reports at professional meetings, or letters to colleagues;

(b) Requests from qualified colleagues for information on research results should be honored, if consistent with the researcher's prior right to publication and with his/her other professional responsibilities;

(c) Failure to complete a full scholarly report without prolonged delay after completion of research shall be construed as a waiver of a historian's right of primacy with respect to analysis and publication of the data. In the event of such failure, the research data should be made fully accessible for analysis and publication by other historians;

(d) Historians should seek to remove from agreements any terms that prohibit them from including their own interpretations or from having a continuing right to use the material after the undertaking has been completed;

(e) Historians have an obligation to accede to reasonable requests from the news media.

4.5 Historical research requires institutional facilities and support services for its successful conduct and for proper permanent maintenance of the resulting records. It is the responsibility of the historian to ensure that facilities and services are adequate to the scope of the project.

PART III: HISTORY AND RELATED FIELDS, CODES OF ETHICS

1

STATEMENT ON STANDARDS OF PROFESSIONAL CONDUCT

American Historical Association

The historical profession is diverse, composed of people who work in a variety of institutional settings and also as independent professionals. But all historians should be guided by the same principles of conduct.

1. SCHOLARSHIP

Scholarship, the uncovering and exchange of new information and the shaping of interpretations, is basic to the activities of the historical profession. The profession communicates with students in textbooks and classrooms; to other scholars and the general public in books, articles, exhibits, films, and historic sites and structures; and to decision-makers in memoranda and testimony.

Scholars must be not only competent in research and analysis but also cognizant of issues of professional conduct. **Integrity** is one of these issues. It requires an awareness of one's own bias and a readiness to follow sound method and analysis wherever they may lead. It demands disclosure of all significant qualifications of one's arguments. Historians should carefully document their findings and thereafter be prepared to make available to others their sources, evidence, and data, including the documentation they develop through interviews. Historians must not misrepresent evidence or the sources of evidence, must be free of the offense of plagiarism, and must not be indifferent to error or efforts to ignore or conceal it. They should acknowledge the receipt of any financial support, sponsorship, or unique privileges (including privileged access to research material) related to their research, and they should strive to bring the requests and demands of their employers and clients into harmony with the principles of the historical profession. They should also acknowledge assistance received from colleagues, students, and others.

Since historians must have **access to sources** archival and other in order to produce reliable history, they have a professional obligation to preserve sources and advocate free, open, equal, and nondiscriminatory access to them, and to avoid actions which might prejudice future access. Historians recognize the appropriateness of some national security and corporate and personal privacy claims but must challenge unnecessary restrictions. They must protect research collections and other historic resources and make those under their control available to other scholars as soon as possible.

Certain kinds of research and conditions attached to employment or to use of records impose obligations to maintain confidentiality, and oral historians often must make promises to interviewees as conditions for interviews. Scholars should honor any pledges made. At the same time, historians should seek definitions of conditions of confidentiality before work begins, press for redefinitions when experience demonstrates the unsatisfactory character of established regulations, and advise their readers of the conditions and rules that govern their work. They also have the obligation to decline to make their services available when policies are unnecessarily restrictive.

As **intellectual diversity** enhances the historical imagination and contributes to the development and vitality of the study of the past, historians should welcome rather than deplore it. When applied with integrity, the political, social, and religious beliefs of historians may inform their historical practice. When historians make interpretations and judgments, they should be careful not to present them in a way that forecloses discussion of alternative interpretations. Historians should be free from institutional and professional penalties for their beliefs and activities, provided they do not misrepresent themselves as speaking for their institutions or their professional organizations.

The bond that grows out of lives committed to the study of history should be evident in the **standards of civility** that govern the conduct of historians in their relations with one another. The preeminent value of all intellectual communities is reasoned discourse the continuous colloquy among historians of diverse points of view. A commitment to such discourse makes possible the fruitful exchange of views, opinions, and knowledge.

2. TEACHING

Communication skills are essential to historians' efforts to disseminate their scholarship beyond the profession. Those skills are not limited to writing books and articles but also involve teaching, which takes place in many locales, museums and historic sites as well as classrooms and involves the use of visual materials and artifacts as well as words.

Quality in teaching involves **integrity** as well as competence. Integrity requires the presentation of differing interpretations with intellectual honesty; it also requires fairness and promptness in judging students' work on merit alone and a readiness to discuss their views with an open mind.

When so applied, the **political, social, and religious beliefs** of historians may inform their teaching. The right of the teacher to hold such convictions and to express them in teaching, however, does not justify the persistent intrusion of material unrelated to the subject of the course or the intentional use of falsification, misrepresentation, or concealment.

Freedom of expression is essential to the task of communicating historical thought and learning. To this end, historians should have substantial latitude in realizing their objectives, although they are obligated to see that their courses or other presentations reasonably correspond in coverage and emphasis to published descriptions.

3. PUBLIC SERVICE

Historical knowledge provides a vital perspective in the analysis of contemporary social problems and political issues and at times may impose obligations on historians to enter policy arenas where difficulties abound. Oftentimes the work of historians may be used by others in ways that historians find objectionable. Some may seek to make partisans out of professionals or to discredit them by charging that they are not qualified to speak on an issue or are biased.

Historians entering public arenas as political advisers, expert witnesses, consultants, legislative witnesses, journalists, commentators, or staff may face a **choice of priorities** between professionalism and partisanship. They may want to prepare themselves by seeking advice from other experienced professionals. As historians, they must be sensitive to the complexities of history, the diversity among historians, and the limits as well as the strengths of their own points of view and experiences and of the discipline itself and its specialities. In such situations, historians must use sources, including the work of other scholars, with great care and should be prepared to explain the methods and assumptions in their research and the relations between evidence and interpretation and should be ready also to discuss alternative interpretations of the subjects being addressed.

4. EMPLOYMENT

Although some historians are self-employed, working as writers or contractors, most are employed by academic institutions, corporations, government agencies, law firms, archives, historical societies, museums, historic parks, historic preservation programs, and the media.

As professionals, historians should participate in the making of decisions governing the institutions in which they work and must **share responsibility** for the ways in which their professional principals are applied. They should endeavor to establish in administrations and governing boards a full understanding of the values relevant to hiring and promotion decisions. Academic institutions, for instance, should be advised to adhere closely to the 1966 "Statement on Government of Colleges and Universities," jointly formulated by the American Association of University Professors (AAUP), the American Council on Education, and the Association of Governing Boards of Universities and Colleges.

Employment principles include **fair practice in recruitment** to ensure that all professionally qualified persons may obtain appropriate opportunities. To accomplish this goal, historical institutions should accurately list all positions for which they are recruiting in appropriate sources, such as the AHA Employment Information section of the newsletter *Perspectives,* and note any contingencies that may affect the availability of the positions. Descriptions and selection criteria should not be altered without reopening the search.

In addition departments should acknowledge all applications, promptly notify those who are no longer under consideration, and invite finalists to visit the institution. Interviews should be marked by respect for individual dignity, and interviewers should avoid questions that may be in conflict with the letter and spirit of federal antidiscriminatory law.

Every candidate for appointment, reappointment, promotion, tenure, apprenticeship, graduate student assistantship, award and fellowship should be evaluated exclusively on **professional criteria.** Those employing historians should not discriminate against them on the basis of sex, race, color, national origin, sexual preference, religion, ideology, political affiliation, age, physical handicap, or marital status, except in those cases in which federal law allows specific preference in hiring.

Sexual harassment is a discriminatory practice which is unethical, unprofessional, and threatening to intellectual freedom. It includes all behavior that prevents or impairs an individual's full enjoyment of educational or workplace rights, benefits, environment, or opportunities, such as generalized sexist remarks or behavior; requests for sexual favors; sexual advances; sexual assaults; and the use of professional authority to emphasize inappropriately the sexuality or sexual identity of a student or colleague.

Decisions on personnel matters should be reached in accord with **established procedures** known to all members of the institution and leading to evaluations that are truthful, comprehensive, and consistent with the standards of academic freedom and fair professional practice. Appointees should be informed of the relative weight to be attached to scholarship, teaching, and other service. Procedures should provide for professional review, appropriate notification, and appeal for reconsideration. The candidate should have ample opportunity to provide a record of activities and achievements and evidence of professional merit. The institution should notify the candidate promptly of its decision and the explanation of it, and the candidate should have an opportunity to appeal.

The **dismissal or suspension** of a historian with tenure or on special or probationary appointment must follow procedures of due process equal to those set forth in the AAUP 1940 "Statement of Principles on Academic Freedom and Tenure."

Historians who work part-time should be compensated in proportion to the share of a full-time workload they carry, including a proportionate share of fringe benefits available to their full-time colleagues, and have access to institutional facilities and support systems. Those likely to remain part-time for extended periods should be offered multi-year contracts with the attendant obligation of participation in governance and administrative tasks and access to institutional appeal and grievance channels; they should also be represented on the appropriate advisory and governing bodies, such as faculty senates.

5. IMPLEMENTATION

Historians have a professional obligation to encourage the establishment of and to support guidelines and procedures concerning professionals in their employing institutions. Historians also have the responsibility to take appropriate action when confronted with violations of the profession's standards of conduct.

Initially, historians should utilize their employing institutions' grievance machinery. When this is not possible, feasible, or appropriate, alleged violations may be referred to the Professional Division of the AHA for consideration and possible resolution. The division is not an investigatory body, although it may solicit and receive documents on cases.

The division may refer cases to other organizations for formal arbitration or resolution; it may make statements on cases, or advise parties to the controversies to do so; and it may provide opportunities for persons to bring their views before the profession.

ADDENDUM ON POLICIES AND PROCEDURES

The Professional Division, elected by the AHA membership, shall have primary responsibility for the interpretation of the AHA Statement on Standards of Professional Conduct and any addenda, for the investigation of complaints brought under it, and for recommendations to Council pertinent to such complaints. Review of a case by the Professional Division cannot and should not, however, be viewed as a substitute for legal action.

All complaints of violation(s) of the AHA Statement on Standards of Professional Conduct should be directed in writing to the Executive Director of the Association, who shall acknowledge receipt of the complaint, send a copy of the statement and these procedures, and, where necessary, advise the complainant that a formal complaint must include specification of the time, place, persons, and events constituting the alleged violation and cite the section(s) of the statement alleged to be violated. The Executive Director shall communicate the entire complaint to the other party or parties, together with a copy of the statement and these procedures (by registered mail with return receipt requested) and request a response within ninety days.

After acknowledgement of the complaint and the receipt of a response from the accused or after the lapse of ninety days without response, the

Executive Director shall send copies of the complaint, responses, and supporting documents to all members of the Professional Division and to the complainant and the other party or parties involved. The Division shall treat cases with confidentiality, and all parties involved are expected to treat it with complete discretion. After consideration, the Division shall decide by majority vote whether:

1) the case should not be pursued further,
2) further information is needed,
3) the case should be referred to other organizations for formal arbitration or resolution,
4) mediation should be attempted,
5) an advisory should be issued, or
6) other action should be recommended to the Council.

If the Division decides:

1) there should be no further pursuit of the case, the Vice-President shall communicate the decision and the reasons therefor to the Executive Director, who shall notify all parties. The Division will not normally pursue a case if the dispute has been submitted to litigation in the courts.

2) that further investigation of the case is necessary, it may direct inquiries through the Executive Director to either the complainant or the other party, with copies of the request and responses thereto in every instance to the other party. All parties involved are under an obligation to respond to such requests.

3) to refer the case to another organization, the Vice-President shall communicate the decision to the Executive Director, who shall notify all parties and with the consent of the complainant, forward to the appropriate organization copies of the complaint, responses, and supporting documents together with a request for arbitration or resolution.

4) to attempt mediation, it shall appoint a mediator from among members of the Association, acceptable to both parties. The mediator shall in due course notify the Division that the matter has been resolved by written agreement of the parties, or if no such resolution has been achieved, the mediator may *a)* recommend that the matter be dropped, or *b)* recommend further action.

5) that an individual case is indicative of a larger problem, it may **issue an advisory opinion or guideline,** which shall be published in *Perspectives* and become an addendum to the Statement. An advisory opinion must not reveal names or details of specific cases. Individual cases shall not be publicized.

6) other action is needed, it may direct the Vice-President to seek approval for that action from the Council. The Executive Director shall notify all parties of the Division's recommendation, and the subject of the complaint shall have thirty days to comment in writing before the recommendation is forwarded to the Council. The Council, after examination of the Division's recommendation and comments thereto, shall make a final determination of the case on behalf of the Association, and either dismiss the case or take the recommended action. The Executive Director shall notify all parties of the Council's action.

Inasmuch as the Division is a part of the constitutional structure of the Association, appeals from or criticism of its action should go before the Council.

Editor's Note: The AHA Council adopted the preceding Statement on Standards of Professional Conduct in May 1987. The Addendum on Policies and Procedures for handling complaints of violations of the Statement was adopted by Council at its December 1987 meeting.

2
GOALS AND GUIDELINES OF THE ORAL HISTORY ASSOCIATION[1]

The Oral History Association recognizes oral history as a method of gathering and preserving historical information in spoken form and encourages those who produce and use oral history to recognize certain principles, rights and obligations for the creation of course material that is authentic, useful and reliable.

Guidelines for the Interviewee
The interviewee should be informed of the purposes and procedures of oral history in general and of the particular project to which contribution is being made.

In recognition of the importance of oral history to an understanding of the past and in recognition of the costs and effort involved, the interviewee should strive to impart candid information of lasting value.

The interviewee should be aware of the mutual rights involved in oral history, such as editing and seal privileges, literary rights, prior use, fiduciary relationships, royalties, and determination of the disposition of all forms of the record and extent of dissemination and use.

Preferences of the person interviewed and any prior agreements should govern the conduct of the oral history process, and these preferences and agreements should be carefully documented for the record.

Guidelines for the Interviewer
Interviewers should guard against possible social injury to or exploitation of interviewees and should conduct interviews with respect for human dignity.

Each interviewee should be selected on the basis of demonstrable potential for imparting information of lasting value.

The interviewer should strive to prompt informative dialogue through challenging and perceptive inquiry, should be grounded in the background and experiences of the person being interviewed, and, if possible, should review the sources relating to the interviewee before conducting the interview.

Interviewers should extend the inquiry beyond their immediate needs to make each interview as complete as possible for the benefit of others, and should, wherever possible, place the material in a depository where it will be available for general research.

The interviewer should inform the interviewee of the planned conduct of the oral history process and develop mutual expectations of rights connected thereto, including editing, mutual seal privileges, literary rights, prior use, fiduciary relationships, royalties, rights to determine disposition of all forms of the record, and the extent of dissemination and use.

Interviews should be conducted in a spirit of objectivity, candor and integrity, and in keeping with common understandings, purposes and stipulations mutually arrived at by all parties.

The interviewer shall not violate and will protect the seal on any information considered confidential by the interviewee, whether imparted on or off the record.

Guidelines for Sponsoring Institutions

Subject to conditions prescribed by interviewees, it is an obligation of sponsoring institutions (or individual collectors) to prepare and preserve easily useable records; to keep careful records of the creation and processing of each interview; to identify, index and catalog interviews; and, when open to research, to make their existence known.

Interviewers should be selected on the basis of professional competence and interviewing skill; interviewers should be carefully matched to interviewees.

Institutions should keep both interviewees and interviewers aware of the importance of the above guidelines for the successful production and use of oral history sources.

ORAL HISTORY EVALUATION GUIDELINES[2] (Revised, 1989)

Does a researcher who conducts interviews for a specific writing project have a responsibility to deposit those interviews in an archive after the book or article is published? Should interviewers announce that they intend to deposit their interviews in an archive without first notifying that archive? What are oral history archives' responsibilities toward their interviewers? What are interviewers' responsibilities toward their interviewees when their interviews are used in public programming? Is the use of anonymity ever acceptable in oral history? Can videotaping become intrusive and change the nature of an oral history? What guidelines should teachers set for students who conduct interviews?

These were just a sample of the issues considered during the first revisions of the Oral History Association's evaluation guidelines, and adopted by OHA members at the business meeting in Galveston in October, 1989. Originally prepared at the Wingspread Conference, in 1979, the evaluation guidelines offer a series of questions for evaluating the conduct, processing and preservation of oral history collections. Over the next ten years the Wingspread guidelines proved especially useful to funding agencies as criteria for judging oral history proposals. But as oral historians employed new technology, and explored new issues, the need for revisions of the guidelines became increasingly apparent.

In 1987, Ron Grele appointed Ronald Marcello and Don Ritchie as a task force to determine what revisions were necessary. They identified the legal and ethical guidelines as the section most in need of revision, and suggested three new sections on independent researchers, videotaping, and teaching. Rather than repeat a separate Wingspread meeting, they recommended that all members of the association be invited to participate in the process.

The following year, when Ronald Marcello became president, he proposed making the annual meeting in Galveston a second Wingspread. In preparation, he appointed four committees, coordinated by Don Ritchie, to address each of the major issues. Sherna Gluck chaired the committee on ethical/legal guidelines, whose members included Al Broussard, John Neuenschwander, and Linda Shopes. Terry Birdwhitall chaired the independent/unaffiliated research committee, with Jo Blatti, Maury Maryanow, and Holly Shulman. Pam Henson chaired the committee on the use of videotape, with James Murray, David Mould, Terri Schorzman, and Margaret Robinson. The committee on teaching, chaired by George Mehaffy, and including Andor Skotnes, Richard Williams, Patricia Grummer, Denise Joseph, and Rebecca Sharpless, prepared guidelines for teachers and students.

During the past year these committees prepared the draft guidelines that they presented during sessions at the Galveston meeting. Audience participation at these sessions was active, and a number of changes that members proposed were incorporated into the drafts before they were adopted at the Sunday morning business session. But the process should not end there. The OHA invites comments and suggestions about the new guidelines from all its members, including those who did not have the opportunity to attend the Galveston meeting. The full text of the new guidelines follows.

PROGRAM/PROJECT GUIDELINES[3]

Purposes and Objectives
    a. Are the purposes clearly set forth? How realistic are they?
    b. What factors demonstrate a significant need for the project?
    c. What is the research design? How clear and realistic is it?
    d. Are the terms, conditions and objectives of funding clearly made known to allow the user of the interviews to judge the potential effect of such funding on the scholarly integrity of the project? Is the allocation of funds adequate to allow the project goals to be accomplished?
    e. How do institutional relationships affect the purposes and objectives?

Selection of Interviewers and Interviewees
  a. In what ways are the interviewers and interviewees appropriate (or inappropriate) to the purposes and objectives?
  b. What are the significant omissions and why were they omitted?

Records and Provenance
  a. What are the policies and provisions for maintaining a record of the provenance of interviews? Are they adequate? What can be done to improve them?
  b. How are records, policies and procedures made known to interviewers, interviewees, staff and users?
  c. How does the system of records enhance the usefulness of the interviews and safeguard the rights of those involved?

Availability of Materials
  a. How accurate and specific is the publicizing of the interviews?
  b. How is information about interviews directed to likely users?
  c. How have the interviews been used?

Finding Aids
  a. What is the overall design for finding aids?
  b. Are the finding aids adequate and appropriate?
  c. How available are the finding aids?

Management, Qualifications and Training
  a. How effective is the management of the program/project?
  b. What provisions are there for supervision and staff review?
  c. What are the qualifications for staff positions?
  d. What are the provisions for systematic and effective training?

What improvements could be made in the management of the program/project?

ETHICAL/LEGAL GUIDELINES

What procedures are followed to assure that interviewers/programs recognize and honor their responsibility to the interviewee? Specifically, what procedures are used to assure that:
  a. the interviewee is made fully aware of the goals and objectives of the oral history program/project?
  b. the interviewee is made fully aware of the various stages of the program/project and the nature of her/his participation at each stage?
  c. the interviewee is given the opportunity to respond to questions as freely as possible and is not subjected to stereotyped assumptions based on race, ethnicity, gender, class or any other social/cultural characteristic?
  d. the interviewee understands her/his right to refuse to discuss cer-

tain subjects, to seal portions of the interview or in extremely sensitive circumstances even to choose to remain anonymous?

e. the interviewee is fully informed about the potential uses to which the material may be put, including deposit of the interviews in a repository; publication in books, articles, newspapers, or magazines; and all forms of public programming?

f. the interviewee is provided a full and easily comprehensible explanation of her/his legal rights before being asked to sign a contract or deed of gift transferring rights, title and interest in the audio and/or visual tape(s) and transcript(s) to an administering authority or individual; and whenever possible, the interviewee is consulted about all subsequent use of the material?

g. all prior agreements made with the interviewee are honored?

h. the interviewee is fully informed about the potential for and disposition of royalties that might accrue from the use of her/his interviews, including all forms of public programming?

i. the interview and any other related materials will remain confidential until he/she has released their contents for use?

j. care is taken when making public all material relating to the interview?

What procedures are followed to assure that interviewers/programs recognize and honor their responsibilities to the profession? Specifically, what procedures assure that:

a. the interviewer has considered the potential for public programming and research use of the interviews, and has endeavored to prevent any exploitation of or harm to interviewees?

b. the interviewer is well trained and will conduct her/his interview in a professional manner?

c. the interviewer is well grounded in the background of the subject(s) to be discussed.

d. the interview will be conducted in a spirit of critical inquiry and that efforts will be made to provide as complete a historical record as possible?

e. the interviewees are selected on the basis of the relevance of their experience to the subject at hand and that an appropriate cross-section of interviewees is selected for any particular project?

f. the interview materials, including tapes, transcripts, agreements, and documentation of the interview process, will be placed in a repository after a reasonable period of time, subject to the agreements made with the interviewee; and that the depository will administer their use in accordance with those agreements?

g. the methodologies of the program/project, as well as its goals and objectives, are available for the general public to evaluate?

h. the interview materials have been properly cataloged, including appropriate acknowledgment and credit to the interviewer, and that their availability for research use is made known?

What procedures are followed to assure that interviewers and programs are aware of their mutual responsibilities and obligations? Specifically, what procedures are followed to assure that:

    a. interviewers are made aware of the program goals and are fully informed of ethical and legal considerations?

    b. interviewers are fully informed of all the tasks they are expected to complete in an oral history project?

    c. interviewers are made fully aware of their obligations to the oral history program/sponsoring institution, regardless of their own personal interest in a program/project?

    d. programs/sponsoring institutions treat their interviewers equitably, including the establishment of provisions for appropriate compensation and acknowledgment for all products resulting from their work; and support for fieldwork practices consistent with professional standards whenever there is a conflict between the parties to the interview?

    e. interviewers are fully informed of their legal rights and of their responsibilities to both the interviewee and to the sponsoring institution?

What procedures are followed to assure that interviewers and programs recognize and honor their responsibilities to the community/public? Specifically, what procedures assure that:

    a. the oral history materials, and all works created from them, will be available and accessible to the community that participated in the project?

    b. sources of extramural funding and sponsorship are clearly noted for each interview or project?

    c. the interviewer and project endeavor to not impose their own values on the community being studied.

    d. the tapes and transcripts will not be used in an unethical manner?

TAPE/TRANSCRIPT PROCESSING GUIDELINES

Information About the Participants

    a. Are the names of both interviewer and interviewee clearly indicated on the tape/abstract/transcript and in catalog materials?

    b. Is there adequate biographical information about both interviewer and interviewee? Where can it be found?

Interview Information

    a. Are the tapes, transcripts, time indices, abstracts and other material presented for use identified as to the project/program of which they are a part?

    b. Are the date and place of interview indicated on the tape, transcript, time index, abstract, and in appropriate catalog material?

    c. Are there interviewer's statements about the preparation for or circumstances of the interviews? Where? Are they generally available to researchers? How are the rights of the interviewees protected against the improper use of such commentaries?

d. Are there records of contracts between the program and the interviewee? How detailed are they? Are they available to researchers? If so, with what safeguards for individual rights and privacy?

Interview Tape Information
a. Is the complete master tape preserved? Are there one or more duplicate copies?
b. If the original or any duplicate has been edited, rearranged, cut or spliced in any way, is there a record of that action, including by whom and when and for what purposes the action was taken?
c. Do the tape label and appropriate catalog materials show the recording speed, level and length of the interview?
d. Has the program/project used recording equipment and tapes which are appropriate to the purposes of the work and use of the material? Are the recordings of good quality? How could they be improved?
e. In the absence of transcripts, are there suitable finding aids to give users access to information on tapes? What form do they take? Is there a record of who prepares these finding aids?
f. Are researchers permitted to listen to or view the tapes? Are there any restrictions on the use of tapes?

Interview Transcript Information
a. Is the transcript an accurate record of the tape? Is a careful record kept of each step of processing the transcript, including who transcribed, audited, edited, retyped, and proofread the transcript in final copy?
b. Are the nature and extent of changes in the transcript from the original tape made known to the user?
c. What finding aids have been prepared for the transcript? Are they suitable and adequate? How could they be improved?
d. Are there any restrictions on access to or use of the transcripts? Are they clearly noted?
e. Are there any photo materials or other supporting documents for the interview? Do they enhance and supplement the text?

If videotaped, do the tape label and appropriate catalog information show the format (e.g. U-Matic, VHS, 8mm, etc.), scanning system, and clearly indicate the tracks on which the audio and time code have been recorded?

INTERVIEW CONTENT GUIDELINES

Does the content of each interview and the cumulative content of the whole collection contribute to accomplishing the objectives of the project/program?
- — In what particulars does each interview or the whole collection succeed or fall short?

In what ways does the program/project contribute to historical understanding?[7]
- — In what particulars does each interview or the whole collection succeed or fall short of such contribution?
- — To what extent does the material add fresh information, fill gaps in the existing record, and/or provide fresh insights and perspectives?
- — To what extent is the information reliable and valid? Is it eyewitness or hearsay evidence? How well and in what manner does it meet internal and external tests of corroboration, consistency, and explication of contradictions?
- — What is the relationship of the interview information to existing documentation and historiography?
- — How does the texture of the interview impart detail, richness and flavor to the historical record?
- — What is the basic nature of the information contributed? Is it facts, perceptions, interpretations, judgments, or attitudes, and how does each contribute to understanding?
- — Are the scope and volume, and where appropriate the representativeness of the population interviewed, appropriate and sufficient to the purpose? Is there enough testimony to validate the evidence without passing the point of diminishing returns? How appropriate is the quantity to the purposes of the study? Is there a good representative sample of the population reflected in the interviews?
- — How do the form and structure of the interviews contribute to make the content information understandable?
- — Does the visual element complement and/or supplement the verbal information? Has the interview captured interaction with the visual environment, processes, objects, or group interaction?

INTERVIEW CONDUCT GUIDELINES

Use of Other Sources
- a. Is the oral history technique the best means of acquiring the information? If not, what other sources exist? Has the interviewer used them, and has he/she sought to preserve them if necessary?
- b. Has the interviewer made an effort to consult other relevant oral histories?

    c. Is the interview technique of value in supplementing existing sources?

    d. Do videotaped interviews complement, not duplicate, existing stills or moving visual images?

Historical Contribution
    a. Does the interviewer pursue the inquiry with historical integrity?

    b. Do other purposes being served by the interview enrich or diminish quality?

    c. What does the interview contribute to the larger context of historical knowledge and understanding?

Interviewer Preparation
    a. Is the interviewer well-informed about the subjects under discussion?

    b. Are the primary and secondary sources used in preparation for the interview adequate?

Interviewee Selection and Orientation
    a. Does the interviewee seem appropriate to the subjects discussed?

    b. Does the interviewee understand and respond to the interview purposes?

    c. Has the interviewee prepared for the interview and assisted in the process?

    d. If a group interview, have composition and group dynamics been considered in selecting participants?

Interviewer-Interviewee Relations
    a. Do interviewer and interviewee motivate each other toward interview objectives?

    b. Is there a balance between empathy and analytical judgment in the interview?

    c. If videotaped, was the interviewer/interviewee relationship maintained despite the presence of a technical crew? Did the technical personnel understand the nature of a videotaped oral history interview, as opposed to a scripted production?

Adaptive Skills
    a. In what ways does the interview show that the interviewer has used skills appropriate to ...

       — the interviewee's condition (health, memory, mental alertness, ability to communicate, time schedule, etc.)?

       — the interview conditions (disruptions and interruptions, equipment problems, extraneous participants, etc.)?

Technique
    a. What evidence is there that the interviewer has ...

       — thoroughly explored pertinent lines of thought?

  — followed up on significant clues?
  — made an effort to identify sources of information?
  — employed critical challenge where needed?
  — thoroughly explored the potential of the visual environment, if videotaped?

b. Has the program/project used recording equipment and tapes which are appropriate to the purposes of the work and use of the material? Are the recordings of good quality? How could they be improved?

c. If videotaped, are lighting, composition, camera work and sound of good quality?

d. In the balance between content and technical quality, is the technical quality good without subordinating the interview process?

Perspective
  a. Do the biases of the interviewer interfere with or influence the responses of the interviewee?
  b. What information is available that may inform the users of any prior or separate relationship of the interviewer to the interviewee?

INDEPENDENT/UNAFFILIATED RESEARCHER GUIDELINES

Creation and Use of Interviews
  a. Has the independent/unaffiliated researcher followed the guidelines for obtaining interviews as suggested in the Program/Project Guidelines section?
  b. Have proper citation and documentation been provided in works created (books, articles, audio-visual productions or other public presentations) to inform users of the work as to interviews used and permanent location of the interviews?
  c. Do works created include an explanation of the interview project, including editorial procedures?
  d. Has the independent/unaffiliated researcher provided for the deposit of the works created in an appropriate repository?

Transfer of Interviews to Archival Repository
  a. Has the independent/unaffiliated researcher properly obtained the agreement of the repository prior to making such representation?
  b. Is the transfer consistent with agreements or understandings with interviewers? Were legal agreements obtained from interviewees?
  c. Has the researcher provided the repository with adequate description of the creation of the interviews and the project?
  d. What is the technical quality of the recorded interviews? Are the interviews transcribed, abstracted or indexed, and, if so, what is the quality?

EDUCATOR AND STUDENT GUIDELINES

Has the educator:
a. become familiar with the "Oral History Evaluation Guidelines" and conveyed their substance to the student?
b. ensured that each student is properly prepared before going into the community to conduct oral history interviews?
c. become knowledgeable of the literature, techniques and processes of oral history, so that the best possible instruction can be presented to the student?
d. worked with other professionals and organizations to provide the best oral history experience for the student?
e. considered that the project may merit preservation and worked with other professionals and repositories to preserve and disseminate these collected materials?
f. shown willingness to share her/his expertise with other educators, associations and organizations?

Has the student:
a. become thoroughly familiar with the techniques and processes of oral history interviewing and the development of research using oral history interviews?
b. explained to the interviewee the purpose of the interview and how it will be used?
c. treated the interviewee with respect?
d. signed a receipt for and returned any materials borrowed from the interviewee?
e. obtained a signed legal release for the interview?
f. kept her/his word about oral or written promises made to the interviewees?
g. given proper credit (verbal or written) when using oral testimony, and used material in context?

REFERENCES

1. Original version adopted November 25, 1968, with minor revisions since then.
2. Adopted October 27, 1979. Published in *Oral History Review,* 1980, revised October, 1989.
3. *Project* is here defined as a series of interviews or a single interview focused on a particular subject, theme or era. *Program* is defined as a set of projects under one management.

3

A CODE OF ETHICS FOR ARCHIVISTS

Society of American Archivists

Archivists select, preserve, and make available records and papers that have lasting value to the organization or public that the archivist serves. Archivists perform their responsibilities in accordance with statutory authorization or institutional policy. They subscribe to a code of ethics based on sound archival principles and promote institutional and professional observance of these ethical and archival standards.

Archivists arrange transfers of records and acquire papers in accordance with their institutions' purposes and resources. They do not compete for acquisitions when competition would endanger the integrity or safety of records and papers; they cooperate to ensure the preservation of these materials in repositories where they will be adequately processed and effectively utilized.

Archivists negotiating with transferring officials or owners of papers seek fair decisions based on full consideration of authority to transfer, donate, or sell; financial arrangements and benefits; copyright; plans for processing; and, conditions of access. Archivists discourage unreasonable restrictions on access or use, but may accept as a condition of acquisition clearly stated restrictions of limited duration and may occasionally suggest such restrictions to protect privacy. Archivists observe faithfully all agreements made at the time of transfer or acquisition.

Archivists appraise records and papers with impartial judgment based on thorough knowledge of their institutions' administrative requirements or acquisitions policies. They arrange records and papers selected for retention in conformity with sound archival principles and as rapidly as their resources permit. Archivists protect the integrity of records and papers in their custody, guarding them against defacement, alteration, theft, and physical damage, and ensure that their evidentiary value is not impaired in the archival work of restoration, arrangement, and use. They cooperate with other archivists and law enforcement agencies in the apprehension and prosecution of thieves.

Archivists respect the privacy of individuals who created or are the

Originally published in *The American Archivist* (Summer, 1980) p. 414–418.

subjects of records and papers, especially those who had no voice in the disposition of the materials. They neither reveal nor profit from information gained through work with restricted holdings.

Archivists answer courteously and with a spirit of helpfulness all reasonable inquiries about their holdings, and encourage use of them to the greatest extent compatible with institutional policies, preservation of holdings, legal considerations, individual rights, donor agreements, and judicious use of archival resources. They explain pertinent restrictions to potential users, and apply them equitably.

Archivists endeavor to inform users of parallel research by others using the same materials, and, if the individuals concerned agree, supply each name to the other party.

Archivists may use their institutions' holdings for personal research and publication if such practices are approved by their employers and are made known to others using the same holdings. Archivists may review and comment on the works of others in their fields, including works based on research in their own institutions. Archivists who collect manuscripts personally should not compete for acquisitions with their own repositories, should inform their employers of their collecting activities, and should preserve complete records of personal acquisitions.

Archivists avoid irresponsible criticism of other archivists or institutions and address complaints about professional or ethical conduct to the individual or institution concerned, or to a professional archival organization.

Archivists share knowledge and experience with other archivists through professional activities and assist the professional growth of others with less training or experience.

Archivists work for the best interests of their institutions and their profession and endeavor to reconcile any conflicts by encouraging adherence to archival standards and ethics.

COMMENTARY ON CODE OF ETHICS

The committee charged with the responsibility for writing a code of ethics for archivists decided that there should be a basic code that is short enough for easy reading—a summary of the guidelines in the principal areas of professional conduct. In addition there should be a longer COMMENTARY, to explain the reasons for some of the statements and to be a basis for discussion of all the points raised. The commentary contains general statements and some notes by members of the Ethics Committee.

I. The Purpose of a Code of Ethics

Codes of ethics in all professions have several purposes in common, including a statement of concern with the most serious problems of professional conduct, the resolution of problems arising from conflicts of interest, and the guarantee that the special expertise of the members of a profession will be used in the public interest.

The archival profession needs a code of ethics for several reasons: (1) to inform new members of the profession of the high standards of conduct in the most sensitive areas of archival work; (2) to remind experienced archivists of their responsibilities, challenging them to maintain high standards of conduct in their own work and to promulgate those standards to others; and (3) to educate people who have some contact with archives, such as donors of material, dealers, researchers, and administrators, about the work of archivists, and to encourage them to expect high standards.

A code of ethics is not a *moral* or a *legal* statement, but it implies moral and legal responsibilities. It presumes that archivists obey the laws and are especially familiar with the laws that affect their special areas of knowledge; it also presumes that they act in accord with sound moral principles. In addition to the moral and legal responsibilities of archivists, there are special professional concerns, and it is the purpose of a code of ethics to state those concerns and give some guidelines for archivists. The code will identify areas where there are or may be conflicts of interest, and indicate ways in which these conflicting interests may be balanced; the code will urge the highest standards of professional conduct and excellence of work in every area of archives administration.

II. Introduction to the Code

The introduction states the principal functions of archivists. Because the code speaks to people in a variety of fields—archivists, curators of manuscripts, records managers—the reader should be aware that not every statement in the code will be pertinent to every worker. Because the code intends to inform and protect non-archivists, an explanation of the basic role of archivists is necessary.

This code is compiled for archivists, individually and collectively. We hope that institutions' policies will not obstruct the archivists in their efforts to conduct themselves according to this code; indeed, we hope that institutions, with the assistance of their archivists, will deliberately adopt policies that comply with the principles of the code.

III. Collecting Policies

Among the members of the committee and among archivists generally there seems to be agreement that one of the most difficult areas is that of policies of collection and the resultant practices. This section of the code calls for cooperation rather than wasteful competition, as an important element in the solution of this kind of problem. We realize that institutions are independent and that there will always be room for legitimate competition. However, if a donor offers materials that are not within the scope of the collecting policies of an institution, the archivist should tell the donor of a more appropriate institution. When two or more institutions are competing for materials that are appropriate for any one of their collections, the archivists must not unjustly disparage the facilities or intentions of others. As stated later, legitimate complaints about an institution or an archivist may be made through proper channels, but

giving false information to potential donors or in any way casting asper-
sions on other institutions or other archivists is unprofessional conduct.

It is sometimes hard to determine whether competition is wasteful.
Because owners are free to offer collections to several institutions, there
will be duplication of effort and bidding that artificially increases the
price of some manuscripts. This kind of competition is an unavoidable
result of the present market system. Archivists cannot always avoid the
increased labor and expense of such transactions.
William Price:

"While members of the committee realize that governmental archives
operate under 'collecting policies' dictated by law, most of those archives also possess private, non-official collections as well. When such
collections exist, this portion of the code should be applied to them."
Meyer Fishbein:

"My chief official interest in this section concerns the acquisition of
institutional records (whether from public or non-public agencies) as
'manuscripts' by an inappropriate repository. Replevin by public agencies is a difficult legal process."

The phrase "appropriate repositories" is from a document entitled
"Selected Changes to Draft B of Code of Ethics for Archivists" written
by the SAA Committee on Collecting Personal Papers and Manuscripts
and discussed at an open forum during the SAA convention in
Nashville, 4 October 1978. The same document was used for some of
the wording of the next section. The document was presented and explained by Charles Schultz on behalf of the committee.

IV. Relations with Donors, and Restrictions

Many potential donors are not familiar with archival practices and do
not have even a general knowledge of copyright, provision of access, tax
laws, and other factors that affect the donation and use of archival materials. Archivists have the responsibility for being informed on these matters and passing all pertinent and helpful information to potential
donors. Archivists usually discourage donors from imposing conditions
on gifts or restricting access to collections, but they are aware of sensitive
material and do, when necessary, recommend that donors make provision for protecting the privacy and other rights of the donors themselves, their families, their correspondents, and associates.

In accordance with regulations of the Internal Revenue Service and
the guidelines accepted by the Association of College and Research Libraries, archivists should not appraise, for tax purposes, donations to
their own institutions. Some archivists are qualified appraisers and may
appraise records given to other institutions.

It is especially important that archivists be aware of the provisions of
the new copyright act (effective 1 January 1978) and that they inform
potential donors of the possible effects of such changes as the limiting of
protection of unpublished material (which was once perpetual but is
now life of the author plus fifty years).

Archivists should be aware of problems of ownership and should not accept gifts without being certain that the donors have the right to make the transfer of ownership as well as of literary rights.

Members of the committee writing this code realize that there are many projects, especially for editing and publication, that seem to require reservation for exclusive use. Archivists should discourage this practice. When it is not possible to avoid it entirely, archivists should try to limit such restrictions; there should be a definite expiration date, and other users should be given access to the materials as they are prepared for publication. This can be done without encouraging other publication projects that might not conform to the standards for historical editing.

V. Appraisal, Protection, and Arrangement

Archivists obtain material for use and must insure that their collections are carefully preserved and therefore available. They are concerned not only with the physical preservation of materials but even more with the retention of the information in the collections. Excessive delay in processing materials and making them available for use would cast doubt on the wisdom of the decision of a certain institution to acquire materials, though it sometimes happens that materials are acquired with the expectation that there soon will be resources for processing them.

Some archival institutions are required by law to accept materials even when they do not have the resources to process those materials or store them properly. In such cases archivists must exercise their judgment as to the best use of scarce resources, while seeking changes in acquisitions policies or increases in support that will enable them to perform their professional duties according to accepted standards.

VI. Privacy and Privileged Information

In the ordinary course of work, archivists encounter sensitive materials and have access to restricted information. In accordance with their institution's policies, they should not reveal this privileged information, they should not give any researchers special access to it, and they should not use specifically restricted information in their own research. They determine whether the release of records or information from records would constitute an unwarranted invasion of privacy (privacy concerns only living persons).

VII. Use and Restrictions

The committee has recommended that archival materials be made available for use (whether administrative or research) as soon as possible. To facilitate such use, archivists should discourage the imposition of restrictions by donors.

Once conditions of use have been established, archivists should see that all researchers are informed of the materials that are available, and are treated fairly. If some materials are reserved temporarily for use in a special project, other researchers should be informed of these special conditions.

VIII. Information about Researchers and Correction of Errors

The wording of the first sentence of this section is based on the "ALA-SAA Joint Statement on Access to Original Research Materials in Libraries, Archives, and Manuscript Repositories."

Archivists make materials available for research because they want the information in their collections to be known as much as possible. The same motive prompts them to inform researchers that other people are working in the same area; such information can avoid duplication and perhaps lead to cooperation among researchers. In many repositories, public registers show who have been working on certain topics, so the archivist is not revealing restricted information. By using collections in archival repositories, whether public or private, researchers assume obligations and waive the right to complete secrecy. Archivists do not reveal all the details of one researcher's work to others, and they do not prevent a researcher from using the same materials that others have used.

Meyer Fishbein:

"This section generated considerable discussion at our meetings. I have spoken to several researchers who prefer to deal with their subjects in a thorough, time consuming manner. They may not wish to have their topics discussed in any detail until their product is near completion. I offered the suggestion that researchers be asked whether they wish to know about others working in similar areas and whether they would reciprocate. A form of agreement could be devised.

"Misinformation in scholarly works is corrected by other researchers. There have been rare instances when researchers have deliberately misused documentary materials for propaganda purposes. We should then inform the public of the objective facts. Archivists, in their official duties, should remain reasonably objective about the use of information in their holdings. Some have let their prejudices appear in the acquisition and use of records."

Since the purpose of making archives available for research is the promulgation of information, an erroneous or misleading publication is contrary to the purpose of archival research. Concern for accuracy in scholarship should prompt archivists who are aware of such distortions to take the necessary steps to correct them. Such steps include any or all of the following: a note or call to the researchers; an open letter to an appropriate journal; or a review. Archivists may try to correct errors in publications researched in their archives; they decide whether to make a public correction by judging the seriousness or apparent deliberateness of the mistakes. Some archivists are members of a community of scholars and regularly engage in research, publication, and review of the writings of other scholars.

William Price:

Archivists should refrain from "publishing unsolicited reviews in publications issued by their institutions."

Carolyn Wallace:

"Before publicly correcting the work of scholars, archivists should try to persuade the scholars themselves to do so. Even though archivists may doubt that the errors are simply mistakes the scholars would be glad to have corrected, archivists should courteously inform them and permit them to make the corrections themselves if they will do so, rather than rushing into print."

David Kyvig:

"I would argue that archivists who wish to ought to be perfectly free to write reviews. Their knowledge of their own holdings puts them in an excellent position to evaluate the quality of work purporting to use such materials. Some may at first feel uncomfortable with the idea, but such reviewing ought to be regarded as no different from that done by any other scholar who has become familiar with a topic and relevant archival holdings. Researchers should be no more deterred by the thought of an archivist reviewing their work than by the prospect of any other serious, informed review."

IX. Research by Archivists

If archivists do research in their own institutions, there are possibilities of serious conflicts of interest—an archivist might be reluctant to show to other researchers material from which he or she hopes to write something for publication. On the other hand, the archivist might be the person best qualified to research in areas represented in institutional holdings. The best way to resolve these conflicts is to clarify and publicize the role of the archivist as researcher.

At the time of their employment, or before undertaking research, archivists should have a clear understanding with their supervisors about the right to research and to publish. The fact that some archivists are involved in this kind of research should be made known to the patron, and archivists should not reserve materials for their own use. Because it increases their familiarity with their own collections, this kind of research should make it possible for archivists to be more helpful to other researchers. Archivists are not obliged, any more than other researchers are, to reveal the details of their work or the fruits of their research. The agreement reached with the employers should include in each instance a statement as to whether the archivists may or may not receive payment for research done as part of the duties of their positions.

Carolyn Wallace:

"Many institutions want, even expect, archivists to do research in the archives, and sometimes even make ability and willingness to do so a qualification for employment. In such situations, archivists should try to balance performance of archival responsibilities and research, not neglect one for the other."

X. Complaints About Other Institutions

Disparagement of other institutions or of other archivists seems to be a problem particularly when two or more institutions are seeking the same materials, but it can also occur in other areas of archival work. If committees on ethics are set up by archival organizations, those committees should handle complaints about institutions or individual archivists. Perhaps the institutional evaluations now being considered by the SAA will help to correct some deficiencies. Distinctions must be made between defects due to lack of funds, and improper handling of materials resulting from unprofessional conduct.

Meyer Fishbein:

"Who handles complaints about institutions? I believe that institutions should note the facilities they have for processing and servicing their holdings. If rival institutions lack the facilities, the donors can infer criticisms."

XI. Professional Activities

Archivists may choose to join or not to join local, state, regional, and national professional organizations; but they must be well informed about changes in archival functions and they must have some contact with their colleagues. They should share their expertise by participation in professional meetings, or by publishing. By such activities, in the field of archives, in related fields, and in their own special interests, they continue to grow professionally.

Carolyn Wallace:

"Experienced archivists are often asked to assist beginners by giving advice, demonstrating techniques, and sharing information on procedures, and should do so as generously as time permits. There is still much on-the-job training and learning in the archival profession, and the aid given by experienced archivists to those of less experience is of great importance in professional development."

XII. Conclusion

The code has stated the "best interest" of the archival profession— such as proper use of archives, exchange of information, careful use of scarce resources. The final statement urges archivists to pursue these goals. When there are apparent conflicts between such goals and either the policies of some institutions or the practices of some archivists, all interested parties should refer to this code of ethics and the judgment of experienced archivists.

OTHER COMMENTS

1. William Price: "This new code represents the extent to which the archival profession has evolved since Wayne C. Grover wrote his code. The old distinctions between archivists and manuscript curators are not so clear as they once were. The problems and concerns of the archival profession as a whole share a commonality that was not so evident in Grover's day. Indeed, most younger members of the archival profession do not distinguish between those working with public records and those working with non-public collections. Thus, this proposed code repre-

sents an effort to speak to the archival profession in its entirety. If this effort at times seems to dwell more on the concerns of non-public as opposed to public archivists, that is because many non-public archivists lack the parameters defined by the statutes and regulations within which public archivists work.

"This proposed code addresses the common concerns of the contemporary archival profession in ways Grover's code simply does not. That is not a criticism of Grover; it is an observation on the evolution of the profession."

2. Carolyn Wallace: "Some archivists have said there is no need for a new code, that the one by Wayne C. Grover is admirable and should not be replaced. However, Grover's code, written for government archivists, is in some ways inapplicable, and in others inadequate, for many archivists. We have tried to write a code broad enough to apply to all. Some areas have caused great problems. For example, the acquisition of private papers involves matters of great ethical concern to manuscripts curators but not at all applicable to government or corporation archivists. In the same way, at the request of business archivists, we omitted the emphasis on serving research needs that many of us stress for our own institutions. We tried to keep in mind the wide variety of repositories that archivists serve, and we hope that members of the Society will do the same as they read and criticize the code."

4
CODE OF ETHICS AND STANDARDS OF RESEARCH PERFORMANCE

Society of Professional Archeologists

PURPOSE, ORIGINS, AND PHILOSOPHY

The discipline of archeology has primary responsibility in locating, investigating, interpreting, and curating those portions of human history and related environmental data which, for whatever reasons, are not a portion of the written record. Archeology's study of material remains and their contexts, and the information resulting from this research, enables archeologists, other scientists, and the public better to understand and relate to the complex interrelationships among human groups and between humans and their environment. Only with this understanding can we adequately relate to the present and plan for the future.

Archeology is a diverse discipline, with rather flexible boundaries, many internal specializations, diverse schools of thought, and is subject to influence by the broader encompassing disciplines to which it is related. Archeology, however, has one critical attribute not shared with other social sciences: its subject matter is finite, fragile, irreplaceable, and unique. It is incumbent upon everyone to exercise a stewardship over these fragile resources with vigor and a sense of urgency, for access to knowledge from the past is an essential part of everyone's basic heritage.

Accelerating construction and other land alteration activities have posed an ever increasing requirement for archeological investigations. This increased need necessitated a diversified employment base for archeologists who, traditionally, had been academically oriented. Thus there developed an urgent need to establish national (rather than institutional) standards for archeological practices and to identify those who possess both the ability and willingness to meet such national standards. A coordinated study by the archeological community led to the establishment of the Society of Professional Archeologists (SOPA) in 1976.

SOPA is designed to represent the professional practitioners of the discipline of archeology. A basic responsibility of SOPA has been to define professionalism in archeology; to provide a measure against which to evaluate archeological recommendations and research; and to furnish a forum for a challenge to such recommendations and research. Two things—review of an individual's qualifications prior to acceptance for Certification and/or Membership, and a mechanism for review of violations of the Code of Ethics or the Standards of Research Performance—set SOPA apart from other archeological organizations. The urgent need for these mechanisms, whereby professional competence can be recognized by employers and the public, and evaluated by peers, has become evident to the archeological community and those who officially or individually work with the profession.

SOPA also serves to represent the archeological profession. It works with other professional organizations; with federal, state and local agencies; with private enterprise; and with the general public to further the goals and the discipline of archeology.

Any suggestions as to how SOPA might better meet its responsibilities or provide better service should be directed to the Secretary-Treasurer of the Society.

CODE OF ETHICS AND STANDARDS OF RESEARCH PERFORMANCE

Code of Ethics

Archeology is a profession, and the privilege of professional practice requires professional morality and professional responsibility, as well as professional competence, on the part of each practitioner.

I. The Archeologist's Responsibility to the Public
    1.1   An archeologist shall:
        (a) Recognize a commitment to represent archeology and its research results to the public in a responsible manner;
        (b) Actively support conservation of the archeological research base;
        (c) Be sensitive to, and respect the legitimate concerns of, groups whose culture histories are the subjects of archeological investigation;
        (d) Avoid and discourage exaggerated, misleading, or unwarranted statements about archeological matters that might induce others to engage in unethical or illegal activity;
        (e) Support and comply with the terms of the UNESCO Convention on the means of prohibiting and preventing the illicit import, export, and transfer of ownership of cultural property, as adopted by the General Conference, 14 November 1970, Paris.
    1.2   An archeologist shall not:
        (a) Engage in any illegal or unethical conduct involving archeological matters or knowingly permit the use of his/her

name in support of any illegal or unethical activity involving archeological matters;

   (b) Give a professional opinion, make a public report, or give
legal testimony involving archeological matters without
being as thoroughly informed as might reasonably be
expected;

   (c) Engage in conduct involving dishonesty, fraud, deceit or
misrepresentation about archeological matters;

   (d) Undertake any research that affects the archeological resource base for which she/he is not qualified.

II. The Archeologist's Responsibility to Colleagues

   2.1 An archeologist shall:

   (a) Give appropriate credit for work done by others;

   (b) Stay informed and knowledgeable about developments in
his/her field or fields of specialization;

   (c) Accurately, and without undue delay, prepare and properly
disseminate a description of research done and its results;

   (d) Communicate and cooperate with colleagues having common professional interests;

   (e) Give due respect to colleagues' interests in, and rights to,
information about sites, areas, collections, or data where
there is a mutual active or potentially active research
concern.

III. The Archeologist's Responsibility to Employers and Clients

   3.1 An archeologist shall:

   (a) Respect the interests of her/his employer or client, so far as
is consistent with the public welfare and this Code and
Standards;

   (b) Refuse to comply with any request or demand of an employer or client which conflicts with the Code and Standards;

   (c) Recommend to employers or clients the employment of
other archeologists or other expert consultants upon encountering archeological problems beyond her/his competence;

   (d) Exercise reasonable care to prevent her/his employees, colleagues, associates and others whose services are utilized
by her/him from revealing or using confidential information. Confidential information means information of a
non-archeological nature gained in the course of employment which the employer or client has requested be held
inviolate, or the disclosure of which would be embarrassing or would be likely to be detrimental to the employer or
client. Information ceases to be confidential when the employer or client so indicates or when such information becomes publicly known.

   3.2 An archeologist shall not:

   (a) Reveal confidential information, unless required by law;

(b) Use confidential information to the disadvantage of the client or employer;

(c) Use confidential information for the advantage of herself/himself or a third person, unless the client consents after full disclosure;

(d) Accept compensation or anything of value for recommending the employment of another archeologist or other person, unless such compensation or thing of value is fully disclosed to the potential employer or client;

(e) Recommend or participate in any research which does not comply with the requirements of the Standards of Research Performance.

Standards of Research Performance

The research archeologist has a responsibility to attempt to design and conduct projects that will add to our understanding of past cultures and/or that will develop better theories, methods, or techniques for interpreting the archeological record, while causing minimal attrition of the archeological resource base. In the conduct of a research project, the following minimum standards should be followed:

I. The archeologist has a responsibility to prepare adequately for any research project, whether or not in the field. The archeologist must:

1.1 Assess the adequacy of her/his qualifications for the demands of the project, and minimize inadequacies by acquiring additional expertise, by bringing in associates with the needed qualifications, or by modifying the scope of the project;

1.2 Inform herself/himself of relevant previous research;

1.3 Develop a scientific plan of research which specifies the objectives of the project, takes into account previous relevant research, employs a suitable methodology, and provides for economical use of the resource base (whether such base consists of an excavation site or of specimens) consistent with the objectives of the project;

1.4 Ensure the availability of adequate staff and support facilities to carry the project to completion, and of adequate curatorial facilities for specimens and records;

1.5 Comply with all legal requirements including, without limitation, obtaining all necessary governmental permits and necessary permission from landowners or other persons;

1.6 Determine whether the project is likely to interfere with the program or projects of other scholars and, if there is such likelihood, initiate negotiations to minimize such interference.

II. In conducting research, the archeologist must follow her/his scientific plan of research, except to the extent that unforeseen circumstances warrant its modification.

III. Procedures for field survey or excavation must meet the following minimal standards.

    3.1   If specimens are collected, a system for identifying and recording their provenience must be maintained.

    3.2.   Uncollected entities such as environmental or cultural features, depositional strata, and the like must be fully and accurately recorded by appropriate means, and their location recorded.

    3.3   The methods employed in data collection must be fully and accurately described. Significant stratigraphic and/or locational relationships among artifacts, other specimens, and cultural and environmental features must also be fully and accurately recorded.

    3.4   All records should be intelligible to other archeologists. If terms lacking commonly held referents are used, they should be clearly defined.

    3.5   Insofar as possible, the interests of other researchers should be considered. For example, upper levels of a site should be scientifically excavated and recorded whenever feasible, even if the focus of the project is on underlying levels.

IV. During accessioning, analysis and storage of specimens and records in the laboratory, the archeologist must take precautions to ensure that correlations between the specimens and the field records are maintained, so that prevenience, contextual relationships, and the like are not confused or obscured.

V. Specimens and research records resulting from a project must be deposited at an institution with permanent curatorial facilities.

VI. The archeologist has responsibility for appropriate dissemination of the results of her/his research to the appropriate constituencies with reasonable dispatch.

    6.1   Results reviewed as significant contributions to substantive knowledge of the past or to advancements in theory, method or technique should be disseminated to colleagues and other interested persons by appropriate means, such as publications, reports at professional meetings, or letters to colleagues.

    6.2   Requests from qualified colleagues for information on research results directly should be honored, if consistent with the researcher's prior rights to publication and with her/his other professional responsibilities.

    6.3   Failure to complete a full scholarly report within 10 years after completion of a field project shall be construed as a waiver of an archeologist's right of primacy with respect to analysis and publication of the data. Upon expiration of such 10 year period, or at such earlier times as the archeologist shall determine not to publish the results, such data should be made fully accessible for analysis and publication to other archeologists.

6.4 While contractual obligations in reporting must be respected, archeologists should not enter into a contract which prohibits the archeologist from including her or his own interpretations or conclusions in the contractual reports, or from preserving a continuing right to use the data after completion of the project.

6.5 Archeologists have an obligation to accede to reasonable requests for information from the news media.

Institutional Standards

Archeological research involving collection of original field data and/or acquisition of specimens requires institutional facilities and support services for its successful conduct, and for proper permanent maintenance of the resulting collections and records.

A full-scale archeological field project will require the following facilities and services, normally furnished by or through an institution:

(1) Office space and furniture.
(2) Laboratory space, furniture, and equipment for analysis of specimens and data.
(3) Special facilities such as a darkroom, drafting facilities, conservation laboratory, etc.
(4) Permanent allocation of space, facilities, and equipment for proper maintenance of collections and records equivalent to that specified in the standards of the Association of Systemic Collections.
(5) Field equipment such as vehicles, surveying instruments, etc.
(6) A research library.
(7) Administrative and fiscal control services.
(8) A security system.
(9) Technical specialists such as photographers, curators, conservators, etc.
(10) Publication services.

All the foregoing facilities and services must be adequate to the scope of the project.

Not all archeological research will require all the foregoing facilities and services, but a full-scale field project will. Likewise, all institutions engaging in archeological research will not necessarily require or be able to furnish all such facilities and services from their own resources. Institutions lacking certain facilities or services should arrange for them through cooperative agreements with other institutions.

CERTIFICATION REQUIREMENTS

Field Research

The applicant must document a minimum of one year of field experience. "Field experience" in this context includes survey, reconnaissance, excavation, and laboratory processing/analysis. Documentation must indicate: 24 weeks of in-the-field experience under the supervision of a professional archeologist (defined as an individual who is a Certified Archeologist or meets the requirements for certification by SOPA), of which no more than 12 can be survey. An additional 20 weeks of in-the-field work must be in a supervisory capacity. Six of these weeks can qualify as part of the 24 weeks of supervised field work, provided the documentation clearly indicates who was supervisor, who was supervised, and whom the applicant supervised for what work and for what period of time. Eight weeks of laboratory experience must also be documented under supervision of a professional archeologist. Documentation must include a report written by the applicant on the field/lab work being cited for this emphasis.

Collections Research

The applicant must show 16 weeks of experience or training in collection research under supervision of a specialist as documented by a written report, a course transcript, or a letter of reference. The applicant must also document one year's independent experience in collections research, which results in a published or publishable report, equivalent in scope and quality to an M.A. thesis. Such study must focus principally on the comparative treatment of archeological materials themselves and on related data, and a specific archeological method of analysis must be used, such as stylistic analysis or ethnographic analogy. The simple description and typological identification of excavated materials that is found in a normal site report is NOT "collections research" since that is a necessary and basic part of field research. Examples of studies considered appropriate for this emphasis are a study of rim sherds for Late Woodland sites in the Mississippi Valley to determine function and technological changes, and microscopic analysis of edge wear on utilized flakes to determine function. The source and provenience of a collection used to fulfill the requirements for this emphasis must be sufficiently documented to ensure its authenticity and, if appropriate, to demonstrate that it has been acquired in accordance with the UNESCO Convention of 1970.

Theoretical or Archival Research

Persons will not be evaluated and certified in the Theoretical and Archival Emphasis subsequent to 1984. Persons certified prior to 1985 may retain Certification in that Emphasis as long as annual Certification is maintained.

Archeological Administration

The applicant must document a minimum of one full year in a position of administration of a program of archeological research. This emphasis is designed for those who direct archeological research programs, rather than those who administer academic departments (which may include archeology), or those who are responsible for programs which manage archeological resources. Administration of a specific field project, or acting as a principal investigator on a specific archeological project, is a basic and routine part of field research and is not appropriate documentation for this emphasis. Examples of positions which qualify an applicant for this emphasis would include: director of a unit within a university, a museum, or a corporate entity charged with undertaking archeological investigations; chief, head or primary administrative officer in a public agency charged with the conduct of archeological research (again, NOT management of archeological resources). Examples of appropriate responsibilities which could be documented are preparation of annual budgets, personnel and operating plans; and preparation of many proposals in response to many scopes of work or for grant requests which include research designs, personnel schedules, and budgets. Applicant should indicate administered projects which have been seen through to successful completion.

Archeological Resource Management

The applicant must document one year's experience in the management of archeological resources, through evidence of application of laws, regulations, policies, programs, and political processes directed toward the conservation of these resources. Documentation must include evidence of involvement on five major completed projects, at least two of which must involve archeological field investigations. This could include scopes of work written by the applicant; management plans which guide and/or direct decision-makers; comments on resulting reports of investigations; MOA's which include mitigation details written by applicant; and evidence of successful conclusion of each project relative to consideration of archeological research.

Archeological Resource Management begins with the earliest legal, fiscal, and political processes ensuring the appropriate consideration of archeological resources in a project area by an agency or other constituency. It includes identification of resources; evaluation of their scientific potential, public value, and legal status; the calculation of the impact of a project upon those resources; the development of management options which take into account all levels of concern; and the formulation of plans to preserve, conserve, mitigate the impact, and/or manage the resources. Management is the process which precedes, includes, and follows the various phases of archeological investigations to insure legally sufficient and ethically appropriate approaches to archeological resources in the best interests of science and of the public.

This emphasis is most appropriate to governmental positions (both state and federal) or to personnel attached to major corporations which manage or influence the management of archeological resources through legal, fiscal, or political mechanisms. Applicants will be considered appropriate also from directors of private organizations or entities, or principal investigators who can document drawing up and following through of recommendations relative to the conservation, the preservation, or the mitigation of impact which have been adopted by decision makers on at least five major projects.

Conducting archeological surveys or data recovery projects which are mandated by federal laws, regulations, policies, etc., is not considered appropriate for this emphasis, since they are a part of normal field and collections research. The development of a management plan in itself is not appropriate documentation, unless the applicant can show that the plan has been followed through to completion, whether by the applicant or by other decision makers.

Museology

The applicant must document one year's experience in the application of professional museological methods and techniques to archeological material and data. Internships do not qualify for any portion of this requirement. Service as a museum administrator or curator qualifies under this emphasis only if it involves the application of museological methods and techniques to archeological data. Examples of experience qualifying under this emphasis involve major responsibility for any of the following: educational programming and interpretation (e.g., design of exhibits) of archeological information for the public; conservation of archeological specimens; organization of modern classification and cataloguing systems for archeological collections. Since the title of "curator" is variously used in museums, applicants who serve in this capacity should describe their duties and responsibilities relative to archeological collections and information.

Teaching

The applicant must document one academic year of full-time teaching or the equivalent accumulated within any five-year period. Full-time teaching is considered 12 semester hours per year; at least six hours must be on archeological topics. Direction of a field school is not admissable experience for the emphasis. High school teaching experience is admissible, but it is the responsibility of the applicant to provide an accurate estimate of the high school teaching experience in terms of college semester hours. A person qualifying under this emphasis may satisfy the Archeological Report requirement (Section 2) by the production of a film on archeology, or publication of a report on archeology for use by students, colleagues, or the general public, provided the scope and quality of the film or publication are at least equivalent to those of an M.A. or M.S. thesis.

Marine Survey

The applicant must document one year's experience in the operation of remote sensing devices in a marine situation for the purpose of discovery and evaluation of archeological resources. (See Underwater Archeology emphasis for other types of marine archeology.) Six months of this time must be supervised by a specialist in the use of underwater remote sensing devices, and documentation must include evidence of at least two weeks offshore training (or the equivalent) in the operation of various remote sensing devices. The other six months of experience must be in a supervisory or independent role. The applicant must document his ability to set up, operate, and interpret the output of underwater remote sensing devices including magnetometer, side-scanning sonar, subbottom profiler, and bathymetric sounder. In addition, the applicant must document training in navigation and a background knowledge of coastal geomorphology and marine geology as these relate to discovery of archeological resources. The applicant should submit at least one report resulting from a marine survey made under her/his direction.

Historical Archeology

Historical archeology is defined as the application of archeological techniques to sites relating either directly or indirectly to a literate tradition. Historical archeology is most often devoted to the study of sites that date to the expansion of literate populations since the 15th century. An individual practicing historical archeology should be knowledgeable of the recovery and interpretation of both archeological and archival data, and familiar with the history of technology and its material remains including both artifactual components, as well as their conservation and preservation. The applicant must document a minimum of one year of field and laboratory experience, including 24 weeks of field work and eight weeks of laboratory work under supervision of a professional historical archeologist with sites and artifacts of an historical period, and 20 weeks in a supervisory or equally responsible capacity. A report on such field research, prepared wholly or in the majority by the applicant, must be cited. Also, the applicant must show experience or training in primary archival research under the supervision of a competent specialist as documented by a report, a course transcript, or letter of reference. Also, the applicant must show the design and execution of an historical archeological study as evidenced by an M.A. thesis, Ph.D. dissertation, or a report equivalent in scope and quality.

Archeometric, Physical Science, and Natural Science Laboratory Research

Professional archeologists now have at their disposal a vast range of analytical techniques and methods derived from physics, chemistry, geology, zoology, botany and other physical and natural science. Work considered under this emphasis involves the study, as part of the solution of archeological problems, of generally non-cultural phenomena that were parts of cultural systems or ecological systems. The emphasis is particularly intended for work in studies such as geochronology (radiocarbon, thermoluminescence, amino-acid racemization, neutron activation, archeo- and paleomagnetism, etc.); geoarcheology (including pedological studies, soil chemistry, etc.); archeobotanical and paleobotanical studies (including ethnobotany, palynology, dendrochronology, phytolith analyis, etc.); archeozoology (including trace-element analyses, mammalogy, vertebrate evolution, etc.); human biology; and other similar analytical studies. In addition to the postgraduate degree with an emphasis in archeology or archeological studies, applicants should demonstrate at least one year of relevant laboratory training followed by at least six months in a supervisory or independent research capacity, and the publication of a report interpreting analytical data.

Underwater Archeology

Underwater archeology can generally be divided into prehistoric or historic sites and nautical sites (ships and their related harbor structures). Underwater archeology is not so much a separate kind of archeology as it is archeology in a different environment. Since field techniques and artifact preservation differ from terrestrial sites, emphasis is placed on qualitative data retrieval and on preservation methods. For applicants specializing in prehistoric and historic underwater sites, experience and training similar to that specified in Field Research or Historical Archeology are expected with emphasis upon underwater sites, water-saturated artifacts, and preservation methods. Applicants specializing in nautical archeology should be knowledgeable about both archeological and archival data pertaining to ships.

Documents Research

Documents research involves the use of published and/or unpublished documentary data (field notes; collections; catalogues; historical, ethnohistorical and ethnographic data; environmental and paleoenvironmental data; etc.) as a basis for analysis. Persons wishing certification under this specialization must have at least one year's experience in any kind of archeological research under the supervision of a professional archeologist, and must have prepared at least one report, of at least the scope and quality of an M.A. thesis, that organizes a body of documentary data as defined above, and analyzes this body of data to reach predictions, conclusions, or interpretations concerning the archeological record. Noninterpretive summaries of information without analysis of such information do not qualify a person to be certified under this specialization. Summaries of information designed as preludes or accompaniments to fieldwork do not qualify a person under this specialization unless, by virtue of the quality of their analyses, they are capable of standing alone as contributions to the study and/or management of the archeological record.

GUIDELINES AND STANDARDS FOR ACADEMIC ARCHEOLOGICAL FIELD SCHOOLS

In 1974, the Society for American Archaeology passed the following resolution:

Whereas, each archeological site contains evidence of specific human activities and is therefore a unique source of data about past sociocultural behavior, no site can be written off in advance as unimportant or expendable. No site deserves less than professional excavation, analysis and publication, and;

Whereas, the training of students in archeological skills is an important part of an anthropological curriculum, and whereas such training is likely to be grossly inadequate and misleading to the student if it is not given in the context of a serious research commitment on the part of the instructor to the archeological resources in question;

Therefore, be it resolved that the practice of excavating or collecting from archeological sites solely or primarily for "teaching" purposes is contrary to the provision against indiscriminate excavation of archeological sites contained in Article I, Section 2 of the by-laws of the Society for American Archaeology. Such activities are to be deplored, whether conducted by anthropologists who are not adequately trained in archeological field techniques, or by trained archeologists who do not have continuing research interest in the resources in question, and;

Be it further resolved that such activities are unethical as defined in Article III, Section 4 of the by-laws of the Society for American Archaeology and by the guidelines of the ethics committee of the American Anthropological Association, and that members of these organizations who engage in such practices are subject to appropriate sanctions.

In accordance with these principles, and by virtue of its role in providing guidance and standards for the performance of archeological research, the Society of Professional Archeologists recommends that an academic archeological field school meet the following minimal criteria:

A. Purposes

1. The primary objective of an academic field school must be the training of students; explicitly, the field school give the initial field experience required as the first step in student career progress in her/his development as a professional (in accordance with SOPA standards) archeologist. Other goals (such as employment,

contract work or salvage of threatened resources) must be secondary.

2. The field program and recovered data must be part of an explicitly designed research or cultural resource management program, which includes evidence of conservation of resources, curation, and publication of results.

3. The field program and curriculum design should include an explicitly detailed schedule of instruction and supervision, evidence of adequate facilities (see E.1.), and provision for early analysis and reporting of data generated by the program. This should be provided to all participants.

B. Personnel

1. The Direction of the field program should meet SOPA qualifications in field research, and have dominant responsibility for direct supervision in the field and in the laboratory.

2. Assistant(s)/Supervisor(s) must be qualified by completion of at least one field school which meets these guidelines or by an equivalent combination of field and laboratory experience.

3. Other specialized instructors and lecturers should be used as may be appropriate.

C. Operational procedure should include:

1. Prefatory formal lectures on field excavation and survey observations, excavation procedures and hazards (stratigraphy, arbitrary versus "natural" levels, intrusions, reuse or rebuilding of structures), descriptive note writing, interpreting cross sections, survey, camp and dig logistics, administration, etc. Films, slides, models, and other techniques should be used as available and appropriate. At least 12 hours of lecture instruction should be devoted to this introduction prior to actual field excavation and survey.

2. Formal small group field instruction in topographic and plane table mapping, including nomenclature and terms by an experience instructor who should be a professional topographer or an archeologist skilled in topographic mapping.

3. Formal small group field instruction by a photographer skilled in archeological field photographic techniques and problems (lighting, angles, wide-angle lens, closeup, etc.)

4. Formal lectures in field or laboratory including but not limited to research plan, long-range goals, culture(s) being investigated, field problems, curation and reporting plans, etc.

5. Formal laboratory instructions and supervision in cleaning, labeling, sorting, identification of artifacts, and limited flotation exercises, mammal bone identification, etc., as appropriate. Field supervisors to alternate as lab supervisors, preferably scheduled so that field personnel process their own field data. Laboratory

experience should be organized to facilitate determination of length of supervised experience.

6. Some time devoted to reconnaissance level survey, not only to instruct in finding and recording data but also for instruction in the use of such data for defining archeological problems.

D. Field Procedures/structures

1. All students should be instructed in the use of all tools, equipment, and vehicles (as qualified), rotating as assistants with photography, grid mapping, provenience control, sketching, sampling of soils, and other specialized functions. All steps in procedures and evaluation of appropriate techniques should be repeatedly explained.

2. All students should be required to keep daily systematic notes as parts of the permanent record. All notes and records must be reviewed and critiqued by supervisors. Additional notebooks, photo records, etc., shall be maintained as necessary, under systematic supervision.

3. All field procedures should be guided by the concept of data and record responsibility as an integrated component of professional fieldwork, with responsibility and authority for field decisions and record keeping clearly defined.

4. All students should have access to type collections and relevant library materials (including maps, photographs, site reports, and literature on the archeology and environment relevant to the fieldwork). In most cases, this will require maintenance of such resources in both field and laboratory.

E. Sponsor

1. The institution sponsoring the field school must, by virtue of available resources, meet the minimal SOPA specifications for institutional support, including appropriate space for laboratory work, for storage, appropriate accessioning and cataloging procedures, adequate curation, and support for publication/distribution of the research results.

2. The institution sponsoring the field school must provide for the safety and health of participants.

F. A ratio of six to ten students per supervisor is optimal.

OUTLINE OF SOPA GRIEVANCE PROCEDURES

The guidelines for all SOPA grievance investigations and hearings are to be found in the document Disciplinary Procedures of the Society of Professional Archeologists. A copy of the Procedures may be obtained by writing to the Grievance Coordinator. The following is an abbreviated outline of the usual course of investigations.

1. Allegations of professional misconduct against SOPA accredited

archeologists may be filed with the grievance coordinator on a form designated by SOPA. Forms may be obtained from the grievance coordinator.

2. The grievance coordinator will consider allegations of professional misconduct against accredited archeologists which have occurred after the archeologist applied for SOPA accreditation and if the archeologist is listed in the current Directory of Professional Archeologists.

3. Upon receipt of an allegation the grievance coordinator makes a preliminary inquiry in order to determine if there is a reasonable cause to believe that the accused archeologist has violated a provision of the SOPA Code of Ethics or Standards of Research Performance which are published in the Directory. If it appears that a violation may have occurred, the grievance coordinator appoints two SOPA members who, along with the grievance coordinator, form a grievance investigating committee. The accused archeologist is then informed of the impending investigation. This committee investigates possible violations of the Code and Standards and prepares a report which is a finding of fact as well as a recommendation to the grievance coordinator.

4. Upon recommendation of the committee the grievance coordinator may ask the accused archeologist to accept admonishment.

5. Where the committee finds substantial violations of provisions of the Code or Standards the committee will direct the grievance coordinator to prepare and to file a complaint of misconduct with the Standards Board; this complaint constitutes the formal grievance. The Standards Board will hear the complaint and opposing arguments, making a ruling and where appropriate instituting penalties in conformity with those set forth in the Disciplinary Procedures.

5

EXCERPTS FROM *MUSEUM ETHICS*

American Association of Museums

PREFACE

Since the publication of the last Code of Ethics by the American Association of Museums in 1925, our museums have expanded their activities into disciplines and activities seldom a part of their institutional ancestors. Educational outreach, historical, environmental assessment and a host of other programs have become a normal and respected part of museum activity. Simultaneously, museum policy with respect to collecting has been influenced by expanded public awareness, a changing social conscience, and the decrease in intellectual isolationism and specialization among museum professionals. These expansive changes have caused the profession, one in which ethical requirements above and beyond the legal are everywhere apparent, to reexamine the ethical basis of its operational decisions. Some within the profession ask how their own views, or those of others, compare with the consensus or, for that matter, whether a consensus exists. Others question the ethical propriety of acts observed within their own institutions or others.

These thoughts were brought to the officers and council of the American Association of Museums during the mid-1970s. At the national meeting of the association in Fort Worth in 1974 President Joseph M. Chamberlain appointed a Committee on Ethics, which was continued in expanded form by his successor as AAM president, Joseph Veach Noble. This committee was to identify the ethical principles underlying museum operations in the broadest sense as viewed by the profession at this point in history.

For the complete text see, American Association of Museums, *Museum Ethics* (Washington, D.C.: American Association of Museums, 1978).

THE COLLECTION

Management, Maintenance and Conservation

Museums generally derive most of their prominence and importance from their collections, and these holdings constitute the primary difference between museums and other kinds of institutions. The collections, whether works of art, artifacts or specimens from the natural world, are an essential part of the collective cultural fabric, and each museum's obligation to its collection is paramount.

Each object is an integral part of a cultural or scientific composite. That context also includes a body of information about the object which establishes its proper place and importance and without which the value of the object is diminished. The maintenance of this information in orderly and retrievable form is critical to the collection and is a central obligation of those charged with collection management.

An ethical duty of museums is to transfer to our successors, when possible in enhanced form, the material record of human culture and the natural world. They must be in control of their collections and know the location and the condition of the objects that they hold. Procedures must be established for the periodic evaluation of the condition of the collections and for their general and special maintenance.

The physical care of the collection and its accessibility must be in keeping with professionally accepted standards. Failing this, museum governance and management are ethically obliged either to effect correction of the deficiency or to dispose of the collection, preferably to another institution.

Acquisition and Disposal

No collection exists in isolation. Its course generally will be influenced by changes in cultural, scholarly or educational trends, strengths and specializations developing in other institutions, policy and law regarding the traffic in various kinds of objects, the status of plant and animal populations, and the desire to improve the collection.

In the delicate area of acquisition and disposal of museum objects, the museum must weigh carefully the interests of the public for which it holds the collection in trust, the donor's intent in the broadest sense, the interests of the scholarly and the cultural community, and the institution's own financial well-being.

Every institution should develop and make public a statement of its policy regarding the acquisition and disposal of objects. Objects collected by the museum should be relevant to its purposes and activities, be accompanied by a valid legal title, preferably be unrestricted but with any limitations clearly described in an instrument of conveyance, and be properly cataloged, conserved, stored or exhibited. Museums must remain free to improve their collections through selective disposal and acquisition and intentionally to sacrifice specimens for well-considered analytical, educational or other purposes. In general objects should be kept as long as they retain their physical integrity, authenticity and usefulness for the museum's purposes.

Illicit trade in objects encourages the destruction of sites, the violation of national exportation laws, and contravention of the spirit of national patrimony. Museums must acknowledge the relationship between the marketplace and the initial and often destructive taking of an object for the commercial market. They must not support that illicit market. Each museum must develop a method for considering objects of this status for acquisition that will allow it to acquire or accept an object only when it can determine with reasonable certainty that it has not been immediately derived from this illicit trade and that its acquisition does not contribute to the continuation of that trade.

When disposing of an object, the museum must determine that it has the legal right to do so. When mandatory restrictions accompany the acquisition they must be observed unless it can be clearly shown that adherence to such restrictions is impossible or substantially detrimental to the institution. A museum can only be relieved from such restrictions by an appropriate legal procedure. When precatory statements accompany the acquisition, they must be carefully considered, and consultation with the donor or his heirs should be attempted.

The museum must not allow objects from its collections to be acquired privately by any museum employee, officer, volunteer, member of its governing board or his representative, unless they are sold publicly and with the complete disclosure of their history. Objects, materials or supplies of trifling value which the museum cannot sell and that must be discarded may be given to anyone associated with the institution or to the public.

In disposing of an object, due consideration must be given the museum community in general as well as the wishes and financial needs of the institution. Sales to, or exchanges between, institutions should be considered as well as disposal through the trade. In addition to the financial return from disposals, the museum should consider the full range of factors affecting the public interest.

While the governing entity bears final responsibility for the collection including both the acquisition and disposal process, the curatorial and administrative staff together with their technical associates are best qualified to assess the pertinence of an object to the collection or the museum's programs. Only for clear and compelling reasons should an object be disposed of against the advice of the museum's professional staff.

Appraisals

Performing appraisals or authentications can be useful to a museum and the public it serves; however, there should be institutional policy covering the circumstances where appraisals are desirable or permissible as an official museum-related function. Any appraisal or authentication must represent an honest and objective judgment, and must include an indication of how the determination was made.

Commercial Use

In arranging for the manufacture and sale of replicas, reproductions or other commercial items adapted from an object in a museum's collection, all aspects of the commercial venture must be carried out in a manner that will not discredit either the integrity of the museum or the intrinsic value of the original object. Great care must be taken to identify permanently such objects for what they are, and to ensure the accuracy and high quality of their manufacture.

Availability of Collections

Although the public must have reasonable access to the collections on a nondiscriminatory basis, museums assume as a primary responsibility the safeguarding of their materials and therefore may regulate access to them. Some parts of the collections may be set aside for the active scholarly pursuits of staff members, but normally only for the duration of an active research effort.

When a staff member involved in scholarly research moves to another institution, the museum should give special consideration to the need he may have of objects or materials that remain in the collections. Such needs should be accommodated, where possible, by loans to the staff member's present institution.

The judgment and recommendation of professional staff members regarding the use of the collections must be given utmost consideration. In formulating his recommendation the staff member must let his judgment be guided by two primary objectives: the continued physical integrity and safety of the object or collection, and high scholarly or educational purposes.

Truth in Presentation

Within the museum's primary charge, the preservation of significant materials unimpaired for the future, is the responsibility of museum professionals to use museum collections for the creation and dissemination of new knowledge. Intellectual honesty and objectivity in the presentation of objects is the duty of every professional. The stated origin of the object or attribution of work must reflect the thorough and honest investigation of the curator and must yield promptly to change with the advent of new fact or analysis.

Museums may address a wide variety of social, political, artistic or scientific issues. Any can be appropriate, if approached objectively and without prejudice.

The museum professional must use his best effort to ensure that exhibits are honest and objective expressions and do not perpetuate myths or stereotypes. Exhibits must provide with candor and tact an honest and meaningful view of the subject. Sensitive areas such as ethnic and social history are of most critical concern.

The research and preparation of an exhibition will often lead the professional to develop a point of view or interpretive sense of the material. He must clearly understand the point where sound professional judgment ends and personal bias begins. He must be confident that the resultant presentation is the product of objective judgment.

Human Remains and Sacred Objects

Research, which provides the very basic foundation for knowledge, is a dynamic and therefore continuing process. It is essential that collections of human remains and sacred objects upon which research is based not be arbitrarily restricted, be securely housed and carefully maintained as archival collections in scholarly institutions, and always be available to qualified researchers and educators, but not to the morbidly curious.

We have learned much about human development and cultural history from human burials and sacred objects. There is merit in continuing such investigations. But if we are to maintain an honorable position as humanists concerned with the worth of the individual, the study of skeletal material and sacred objects must be achieved with dignity. Research on such objects and their housing and care must be accomplished in a manner acceptable not only to fellow professionals but to those of various beliefs.

Although it is occasionally necessary to use skeletal and other sensitive material in interpretive exhibits, this must be done with tact and with respect for the feelings for human dignity held by all peoples. Such an exhibit exists to convey to the visitor an understanding of the lives of those who lived or live under very different circumstances. These materials must not be used for other more base purposes.

THE STAFF

General Deportment

Employment by a museum, whether privately or governmentally supported, is a public trust involving great responsibility. In all activities museum employees must act with integrity and in accordance with the most stringent ethical principles as well as the highest standards of objectivity.

Every museum employee is entitled to a measure of personal independence equal to that granted comparable professionals in other disciplines, consistent with his professional and staff responsibilities. While loyalty to the museum must be paramount, the employee also has the right to a private life independent of the institution. But museums enjoy high public visibility and their employees a generous measure of public esteem. To the public the museum employee is never wholly separable from his institution. He can never consider himself or his activities totally independent of his museum despite disclaimers that he may offer. Any museum-related action by the individual may reflect on the institution or be attributed to it. He must be concerned not only with the true personal motivations and interests as he sees them but also the way in which such actions might be construed by the outside observer.

Conflict of Interest

Museum employees should never abuse their official positions or their contacts within the museum community, impair in any way the performance of their official duties, compete with their institutions, or bring discredit or embarrassment to any museum or to the profession in any activity, museum related or not. They should be prepared to accept as conditions of employment the restrictions that are necessary to maintain public confidence in museums and in the museum profession.

To protect the institution and provide guidance to its employees, each museum should issue a comprehensive and well-understood policy covering ethical questions related to personal activities and conflicts of interest. That statement must define the procedures essential to the implementation of and compliance with stated policy.

Personal Collecting

The acquiring, collecting and owning of objects is not in itself unethical, and can enhance professional knowledge and judgment. However, the acquisition, maintenance and management of a personal collection by a museum employee can create ethical questions. Extreme care is required whenever an employee collects objects similar to those collected by his museum, and some museums may choose to restrict or prohibit personal collecting. In any event, the policies covering personal collecting should be included in the policy statements of each museum and communicated to its staff.

No employee may compete with his institution in any personal collecting activity. The museum must have the right, for a specified and limited period, to acquire any object purchased or collected by any staff member at the price paid by the employee.

Museum employees must inform the appropriate officials about all personal acquisitions. They also must disclose all circumstances regarding personal collections and collecting activities, and furnish in a timely manner information on prospective sales or exchanges.

A museum's policy on personal collecting should specify what kind of objects staff members are permitted or not permitted to acquire, what manner of acquisition is permissible and whether different types of employees have different rights. Policy should specify the method of disclosure required for the staff member. It also should specify the manner and time period within which the museum can exercise the rights it has to purchase objects staff members have acquired for their personal collections. Such a policy can be most effective if explicitly a part of the conditions of employment clearly understood by all employees.

Except by special agreement with individual staff members, the right of a museum to acquire from employees objects collected personally should not extend to objects that were collected prior to the staff member's employment by that museum. Objects that are bequests or genuine personal gifts should be exempt from the museum's right to acquire.

No museum employee may use his museum affiliation to promote his or any associate's personal collecting activities. No employee may participate in any dealing (buying and selling for profit as distinguished from occasional sale or exchange from a personal collection) in objects similar or related to the objects collected by the museum. Dealing by employees in objects that are collected by any other museum can present serious problems. It should be permitted only after full disclosure, review and approval by the appropriate museum official.

Outside Employment and Consulting

Certain types of outside employment, including self-employment and paid consulting activities, can be of benefit to both the institution and the employee by stimulating personal professional development. Remuneration may be monetary or nonmonetary, direct or indirect.

All employment activity must be undertaken within the fundamental premise that the employee's primary responsibility is to his institution; that the activity will not interfere with his ability to discharge this responsibility; and that it will not compromise the professional integrity of the employee or the reputation of the museum.

Museum employees often will be considered representatives of their institutions while they are engaged in activities or duties similar to those they perform for their museum, even though their work may be wholly independent of the institution. In other instances an employee's duties within or outside the institution may require little specialized knowledge of the functioning of a museum. In either case employees must disclose to the director or other appropriate superior the facts concerning any planned outside employment or consulting arrangements that are in any way related to the functions that such employees perform for their museums. Disclosure should not be required for small businesses or similar activities that are entirely unrelated to the work the individual carries out for his institution.

Appraisals, as an official museum activity and subject to well-defined policy, can be useful to a museum and its constituency. As an outside activity of an individual staff member it can present serious problems. No staff member should appraise without the express approval of the director. The related areas of identification, authentication and description, when pursued as an outside activity, should be subject to clearly defined museum policy.

The name of and the employee's connection with the museum should be sparingly and respectfully used in connection with outside activities.

In deference to the constitutional rights of museum employees to freedom of speech and association, disclosure should not be required for their activities on behalf of voluntary community groups or other public service organizations, except for those organizations such as other museums where the staff member could appear to be acting in his official capacity. Museum professionals should conduct themselves so that their activities on behalf of community or public service organizations do not reflect adversely on the reputation or integrity of their museum.

Gifts, Favors, Discounts and Dispensations

Museum employees and others in a close relationship to them must not accept gifts, favors, loans or other dispensations or things of value that are available to them in connection with their duties for the institution. Gifts include discounts on personal purchases from suppliers who sell items or furnish services to the museum, except where such discounts regularly are offered to the general public. Gifts also can include offers of outside employment or other advantageous arrangements for the museum employee or another person or entity. Salaries together with related benefits should be considered complete remuneration for all museum-related activities.

Employees should be permitted to retain gifts of trifling value when acceptance would not appear to impair their judgment or otherwise influence decisions. Meals, accommodations and travel services while on official business may be accepted if clearly in the interest of the museum.

Museum employees have the right to accept and retain gifts that originate from purely personal or family relationships. It must be recognized that genuine personal gifts may originate from individuals who have a potentially beneficial relationship with the museum. In such cases the staff member is obliged to protect both himself and his institution by fully disclosing the circumstances to the appropriate museum official.

Teaching, Lecturing, Writing and Other Creative Activities

Museum staff personnel should be encouraged to teach, lecture and write, as desirable activities that aid professional development. Museums should facilitate such activities so long as there is not undue interference with performance of regular duties, and employees do not take advantage of their museum positions for personal monetary gain or appear to compromise the integrity of their institution.

The employee must recognize that when an outside activity is directly related to his regular duties for the institution he is obliged to reach an agreement with the institution concerning all aspects of that activity.

Employees should obtain the approval of the institution of plans for any significant amount of outside teaching, lecturing, writing or editing. Any contemplated uses of the museum's research facilities, staff assistance and property such as copying machines, slides or objects from the collections should be described, and approvals should be obtained for uses of museum property in connection with such outside efforts.

The proprietary interest of both museum and individual in copyrights, royalties and similar properties should be a part of stated general institutional policy supplemented, through mutual agreement, to conform to the needs of the specific project.

Field Study and Collecting

Field exploration, collecting and excavating by museum workers present ethical problems that are both complex and critical. Such efforts, especially in other countries, present situations that can result in difficult interpersonal and international problems. The statements that follow are offered with the knowledge that any action also must be guided by good judgment, tasteful deportment and current knowledge.

Any field program must be preceded by investigation, disclosure and communication sufficient to ascertain that the activity is legal; is pursued with the full knowledge, approval, and when applicable the collaboration of all individuals and entities to whom the activity is appropriately of concern; and is conducted for scholarly or educational purposes. A general if not specific statement of the nature of the objects to be collected, the purposes that they are intended to serve and their final disposition must be prepared and should be fully understood by all affected parties.

Any field program must be executed in such a way that all participants act legally and responsibly in acquiring specimens and data; that they discourage by all practical means unethical, illegal and destructive practices associated with acquiring, transporting and importing objects; and that they avoid, insofar as possible, even the appearance of engaging in clandestine activity, be it museum-related or not. Normally no material should be acquired that cannot be properly cared for and used.

In both act and appearance participants must honor the beliefs and customs of host individuals and societies. General deportment must be such that future field work at the site or in the area will not be jeopardized.

On completion of field work, full and prompt reporting of the activity should be made to all appropriate parties; all precatory and mandatory agreements must be fulfilled or the failure to do so fully explained; and all material and data collected must be made available to the scholarly community as soon as possible. Materials incorporated into permanent collections should be treated in a manner consistent with recommendations and restrictions developed for their care and use by zoologists, botanists, archeologists, paleontologists or other discipline-specific groups.

MUSEUM MANAGEMENT POLICY

Professionalism

Members of the museum's administration and governing entities must respect the professional expertise of the staff, each having been engaged because of his special knowledge or ability in some aspect of museum activity. Museum governance must be structured so that the resolution of issues involving professional matters incorporates opinions and professional judgments of relevant members of the museum staff. Responsibility for the final decisions will normally rest with the museum administration and all employees are expected to support these decisions; but no staff member can be required to reverse, alter or suppress his professional judgment in order to conform to a management decision.

Collectively, the staff professionals are most familiar with the museum, its assets and its constituency. As such they should be heard by museum management and governance on matters affecting the general long-term direction of the institution.

Personnel Practices and Equal Opportunity

In all matters related to staffing practices, the standard should be ability in the relevant discipline. In these matters, as well as trustee selection, management practices, volunteer opportunity, collection usage and relationship with the public at large, decisions cannot be made on the basis of discriminatory factors such as race, creed, sex, age, handicap or personal orientation.

It must be remembered that the components of contemporary culture vary by reason of ancestry, experience, education and ability in the extent to which they can share in the museum experience, either as visitors or as a paid or volunteer participant. The museum must recognize that it is a significant force within its own social fabric and that these differences do exist. It should seize and indeed create opportunities whenever possible to encourage employment opportunity and the accessibility of the institution as a resource to all people.

Volunteers

Volunteer participation is a strong American tradition, and many museums could not exist without the contributions and personal involvement of devoted volunteers. Where volunteer programs exist, the paid staff should be supportive of volunteers, receive them as fellow workers, and willingly provide appropriate training and opportunity for their intellectual enrichment. While volunteers participate in most museum activities, those with access to the museum's collections, programs and associated privileged information work in areas that are particularly sensitive.

Access to the museum's inner activities is a privilege, and the lack of material compensation for effort expended in behalf of the museum in no way frees the volunteer from adherence to the standards that apply to paid staff. The volunteer must work toward the betterment of the institution and not for personal gain other than the natural gratification and enrichment inherent in museum participation.

Interinstitutional Cooperation

If museums intend to contribute to the preservation of humanity's cultural and scientific heritage and the increase of knowledge, each should respond to any opportunity for cooperative action with a similar organization to further these goals. A museum should welcome such cooperative action even if the short-term advantages are few and it will not significantly increase the individual institution's own holdings or enhance its image.

Ownership of Scholarship Material

The object, its documentation and all additional documentation accrued or developed subsequent to its acquisition are the property of the institution.

The analysis of an object for scholarly purposes usually includes the production of interpretive notes, outlines and illustrative material. It can be held that such material is essentially an extension of the intellect and the memory of the scholar, and that as such it is the property of the individual. An equally persuasive case can be made for institutional ownership of all such interpretive material, especially if a staff member was paid to render scholarly analysis. Either is ethically acceptable if the institutional policy is made known beforehand to the staff member, and if the administrative determination of ownership and access is not the result of vindictive or punitive motivation. The guiding ethical principle must be the most effective and timely dissemination of analytical information derived from the collection.

MUSEUM GOVERNANCE

General Responsibility

The governing body of a museum, usually a board of trustees, serves the public interest as it relates to the museum, and must consider itself accountable to the public as well as to the institution. In most cases the board acts as the ultimate legal entity for the museum, and stands responsible for the formulation and maintenance of its general policies, standards, condition and operational continuity.

Trustees must be unequivocally loyal to the purposes of the museum.

Each must understand and respect the basic documents that provide for its establishment, character and governance such as the charter, constitution, bylaws and adopted policies.

Each trustee must devote time and attention to the affairs of the institution and ensure that the museum and its governing board act in accordance with the basic documents and with applicable state and federal laws. In establishing policies or authorizing or permitting activities, trustees especially must ensure that no policies or activities jeopardize the basic nonprofit status of the museum or reflect unfavorably upon it as an institution devoted to public service.

Trustees should not attempt to act in their individual capacities. All actions should be taken as a board, committee or subcommittee, or otherwise in conformance with the bylaws or applicable resolutions. A trustee must work for the institution as a whole, and not act solely as an advocate for particular activities or subunits of the museum.

Trustees should maintain in confidence information learned during the course of their museum activities when that information concerns the administration or activities of the museum and is not generally available to the public. This principle does not preclude public disclosure of information that is properly in the public domain, or information that should be released in fulfilling the institution's accountability to the public.

The governing board holds the ultimate fiduciary responsibility for the museum and for the protection and nurturing of its various assets: the collections and related documentation, the plant, financial assets and the staff. It is obliged to develop and define the purposes and related policies of the institution, and to ensure that all of the museum's assets are properly and effectively used for public purposes. The board should provide adequate financial protection for all museum officials including themselves, staff and volunteers so that no one will incur inequitable financial sacrifice or legal liabilities arising from the performance of duties for the museum.

The board has especially strong obligations to provide the proper environment for the physical security and preservation of the collections, and to monitor and develop the financial structure of the museum so that it continues to exist as an institution of vitality and quality.

A critical responsibility of the governing board derives from its relationship to the director, the institution's chief executive. The selection of that executive and the continuing surveillance of his activities are primary board responsibilities which cannot be delegated and must be diligently and thoughtfully fulfilled.

In carrying out the duty to the collections, a policy must be developed and adopted by the board governing use of the collections, including acquisitions, loans and the disposal of objects. In formulating policies covering the acceptance of objects or other materials as gifts or loans, the governing board must ensure that the museum understands and respects the restrictions, conditions and all other circumstances associated with gifts and loans.

Conflict of Interest

Individuals who are experienced and knowledgeable in various fields of endeavor related to museum activities can be of great assistance to museums, but conflicts of interest or the appearance of such conflicts may arise because of these interests or activities. Guidelines for the protection of both individual and institution should be established by the governing board of every museum.

The museum trustee must endeavor to conduct all of his activities, including those relating to persons closely associated with him and to business or other organizations, in such a way that no conflict will arise between the other interests and the policies, operations or interests of the museum. The appearance of such conflicts also should be avoided. The reputation of the museum can be damaged should a trustee continue an inappropriate activity concurrent with his service in a position of institutional and public trust.

A procedure minimizing the vulnerability to individual or institutional embarrassment should be formulated and stated by every museum board. Every museum trustee should file with the board a statement disclosing his personal, business or organizational interests and affiliations and those of persons close to him which could be construed as being museum related. Such a statement should include positions as an officer or director as well as relationships to other organizations, if the purposes or programs are in any manner related to or impinge upon the purposes, programs or activities of the museum. Such statements should be made available to the board prior to the trustee's election to that body. As an aid to preparing such statements trustees should be provided relevant data on the museum's operations. Disclosure statements should be updated periodically or whenever significant changes occur.

A visible area for charges of self-interest at the expense of the institution, and of personal use of privileged information, arises whenever a trustee, a member of his family or a close associate personally collects objects of a type collected by the museum. Every museum governing board must clearly state its policy regarding such personal collections. The policy should contain statements to ensure that no trustee competes with the museum for objects; that no trustee takes personal advantage of information available to him because of his board membership; and that should conflict develop between the needs of the individual and the museum, those of the museum will prevail.

No trustee, person close to him, or individual who might act for him may acquire objects from the collections of the museum, except when the object and its source have been advertised, its full history made available, and it is sold at public auction or otherwise clearly offered for sale in the public marketplace.

When museum trustees seek staff assistance for personal needs they should not expect that such help will be rendered to an extent greater than that available to a member of the general public in similar circumstances or with similar needs.

Whenever a matter arises for action by the board, or the museum engages in an activity where there is a possible conflict or the appearance of conflict between the interests of the museum and an outside or personal interest of a trustee or that of a person close to him, the outside interest of the trustee should be made a matter of record. In those cases where the trustee is present when a vote is taken in connection with such a question, he should abstain. In some circumstances he should avoid discussing any planned actions, formally or informally, from which he might appear to benefit. Sometimes neither disclosure nor abstention is sufficient, and the only appropriate solution is resignation.

A museum trustee should not take advantage of information he receives during his service to the institution if his personal use of such information could be financially detrimental to the museum. Any such actions that might impair the reputation of the museum also must be avoided. When a trustee obtains information that could benefit him personally, he should refrain from acting upon it until all issues have been reviewed by an appropriate representative of the museum.

Trustees serve the museum and its public. They should not attempt to derive any personal material advantages from their connection with the institution. Trustees should use museum property only for official purposes, and make no personal use of the museum's collection, property or services in a manner not available to a comparable member of the general public. While loans of objects by trustees can be of great benefit to the museum, it should be recognized that exhibition can enhance the value of the exhibited object. Each museum should adopt a policy concerning the display of objects owned or created by the trustees or staff or in which the trustees or any person close to them have any interests.

6
STATEMENT ON PROFESSIONAL ETHICS

American Association of University Professors

The statement that follows, a revision of a statement originally adopted in 1966 by the American Association of University Professors, was approved by Committee B on Professional Ethics, adopted by the Council as Association policy, and endorsed by the Seventy-third Annual Meeting in June 1987.

INTRODUCTION

From its inception, the American Association of University Professors has recognized that membership in the academic profession carries with it special responsibilities. The Association has consistently affirmed these responsibilities in major policy statements, providing guidance to professors in such matters as their utterances as citizens, the exercise of their responsibilities to students and colleagues, and their conduct when resigning from an institution or when undertaking sponsored research.[1] The *Statement on Professional Ethics* that follows sets forth those general standards that serve as a reminder of the variety of responsibilities assumed by all members of the profession.

In the enforcement of ethical standards, the academic profession differs from those of law and medicine, whose associations act to assure the integrity of members engaged in private practice. In the academic profession the individual institution of higher learning provides this assurance and so should normally handle questions concerning propriety of conduct within it own framework by reference to a faculty group. The Association supports such local action and stands ready, through the general secretary and Committee B, to counsel with members of the academic community concerning questions of professional ethics and to inquire into complaints when local consideration is impossible or inappropriate. If the alleged offense is deemed sufficiently serious to raise the possibility of adverse action, the procedures should be in accordance with the 1940 *Statement of Principles on Academic Freedom and Tenure,* the 1958 *Statement on Procedural Standards in Faculty Dismissal Proceedings,* or the applicable provisions of the Association's *Recommended Institutional Regulations on Academic Freedom and Tenure.*

THE STATEMENT

I. Professors, guided by a deep conviction of the worth and dignity of the advancement of knowledge, recognize the special responsibilities placed upon them. Their primary responsibility to their subject is to seek and to state the truth as they see it. To this end professors devote their energies to developing and improving their scholarly competence. They accept the obligation to exercise critical self-discipline and judgment in using, extending, and transmitting knowledge. They practice intellectual honesty. Although professors may follow subsidiary interests, these interests must never seriously hamper or compromise their freedom of inquiry.

II. As teachers, professors encourage the free pursuit of learning in their students. They hold before them the best scholarly and ethical standards of their discipline. Professors demonstrate respect for students as individuals and adhere to their proper roles as intellectual guides and counselors. Professors make every reasonable effort to foster honest academic conduct and to assure that their evaluations of students reflect each student's true merit. They respect the confidential nature of the relationship between professor and student. They avoid any exploitation, harassment, or discriminatory treatment of students. They acknowledge significant academic or scholarly assistance from them. They protect their academic freedom.

III. As colleagues, professors have obligations that derive from common membership in the community of scholars. Professors do not discriminate against or harass colleagues. They respect and defend the free inquiry of associates. In the exchange of criticism and ideas professors show due respect for the opinions of others. Professors acknowledge academic debt and strive to be objective in their professional judgment of colleagues. Professors accept their share of faculty responsibilities for the governance of their institution.

IV. As members of an academic institution, professors seek above all to be effective teachers and scholars. Although professors observe the stated regulations of the institution, provided the regulations do not contravene academic freedom, they maintain their right to criticize and seek revision. Professors give due regard to their paramount responsibilities within their institution in determining the amount and character of work done outside it. When considering the interruption or termination of their service, professors recognize the effect of their decision upon the program of the institution and give due notice of their intentions.

V. As members of their community, professors have the rights and obligations of other citizens. Professors measure the urgency of these obligations in the light of their responsibilities to their subject, to their students, to their profession, and to their institution. When they speak or act as private persons they avoid creating the impression of speaking or acting for their college or university. As citizens engaged in a profession that depends upon freedom for its health and integrity, professors have a particular obligation to promote conditions of free inquiry and to further public understanding of academic freedom.

REFERENCES

1. 1961 *Statement on Recruitment and Resignation of Faculty Members*
1964 *Committee A Statement on Extramural Utterances* (Clarification of sec. 1c of the 1940 *Statement of Principles on Academic Freedom and Tenure*)
1965 *On Preventing Conflicts of Interest in Government-Sponsored Research at Universities*
1966 *State on Government of Colleges and Universities*
1967 *Joint Statement on Rights and Freedoms of Students*
1970 *Council Statement on Freedom and Responsibility*
1976 *ON Discrimination*
1984 *Sexual Harassment: Suggested Policy and Procedures for Handling Complaints*

7

THE COMMITTEE ON PROFESSIONAL STANDARDS AND RESPONSIBILITIES
American Political Science Association

(1968)

In 1967 the APSA created a committee with a broad mandate to explore matters "relevant to the problems of maintaining a high sense of professional standards and responsibilities."

That committee, chaired by Marver H. Bernstein,[1] published its report, "Ethical Problems of Academic Political Scientists," in the summer 1968 issue of *PS*. The Bernstein Report, as it came to be called, recommended the appointment of a Standing Committee on Professional Ethics and such a committee was duly created in 1968.

This Committee has evolved in ways not foreseen by the Bernstein Report as its responsibilities have been enlarged. Its original jurisdiction, for example, did not include individual cases. The Committee was at first envisaged as an educational body to "protect the rights of political scientists" by the issuance of Advisory Opinions to guide the professional behavior of political scientists.

The Bernstein Report did note, however, that although no formal written code of ethics for the profession was in existence, "a rather considerable unwritten code relating to questions of ethical behavior" was widely accepted. The enduring contribution of this Committee was the development of just such a written code consisting of twenty-one rules of professional conduct. The section of the Report containing these rules is reprinted here and may be regarded as the basic charter of the present Committee on Professional Ethics, Rights and Freedoms.

RULES OF CONDUCT

A. Teacher-Student Relations

Rule 1. A faculty member must not expropriate the academic work of his students. As a dissertation adviser, he is not entitled to claim joint authorship with a student of a thesis or dissertation. The teacher cannot represent himself as the author of independent student research; and research assistance, paid or unpaid, requires full acknowledgement.

Rule 2. The academic political scientist must be very careful not to impose his partisan views—conventional or otherwise—upon his students or colleagues.

B. Conduct of Officers and Employees of the Association

Rule 3. When an officer, member, or employee of the Association speaks out on an issue of public policy, endorses a political candidate, or otherwise participates in political affairs, he should make it as clear as possible that he is not speaking on behalf of the Association unless he is so authorized by the Association, and he should not encourage any inference that he acts for the Association unless he is so authorized by the Association.

Rule 4. Officers and employees of the Association are free to engage in activities outside their obligations to the Association provided that such activities are consistent with their duties and responsibilities to the Association. When doubts arise about the activities of subordinate staff members, they should be resolved by the Executive Director in consultation with the Executive Committee of the Association. Similarly when doubts arise about the activities of the Executive Director, they should be resolved by the Executive Committee.

Rule 5. An officer or employee of the Association should not knowingly participate in a transaction involving the Association in the consequences of which he has a substantial economic interest. In such an event, he should disqualify himself from participating in a transaction involving the Association when a violation of this rule would result. Procedures for such disqualification shall be established by the Executive Committee.

C. Political Activity of Academic Political Scientists

Rule 6. The college or university teacher is a citizen, and like other citizens, he should be free to engage in political activities insofar as he can do so consistently with his obligations as a teacher and scholar. Effective service as a faculty member is often compatible with certain types of political activity, for example, holding a part-time office in a political party or serving as a citizen of a governmental advisory board. Where a professor engages in full-time political activity, such as service in a state legislature, he should, as a rule, seek a leave of absence from his institution. Since political activity by academic political scientists is both legitimate and socially important, universities and colleges should have institutional arrangements to permit such activity, including reduction in the faculty member's work-load or a leave of absence subject to equitable adjustment of compensation when necessary.

Rule 7. A faculty member who seeks a leave to engage in political activity should recognize that he has a primary obligation to his institution and to his growth as a teacher and scholar. He should consider the problems that a leave of absence may create for his administration, colleagues and students, and he should not abuse the privilege by asking for leaves too frequently, or too late, or for too extended a period of time. A leave of absence incident to political activity should not affect unfavorably the tenure status of the faculty member.

Rule 8. Special problems arise if departments or schools endorse or sponsor political activities or public policies in the name of the entire faculty of the department or school. One of the purposes of tenure—to shelter unpopular or unorthodox teaching—is in some degree vitiated if the majority of a departmental faculty endorses or sponsors a particular political position in the name of the faculty of the department. The simple way out of this dilemma is to adhere strictly to the rule that those faculty members who wish to endorse or sponsor a political position or activity do so in their own names without trying to bind their colleagues holding differing views. Departments as such should not endorse political positions.

D. Freedom and Integrity of Research by Academic Political Scientists

Principles for Funding Agencies

Rule 9. Financial sponsors of research have the responsibility for avoiding actions that would call into question the integrity of American academic institutions as centers of independent teaching and research. They should not sponsor research as a cover for intelligence activities.

Rule 10. Openness concerning material support of research is a basic principle of scholarship. In making grants for research, government and non-government sponsors should openly acknowledge research support and require that the grantee indicate in any published research financed by their grants the relevant sources of financial support. Where anonymity is requested by a non-governmental grantor and does not endanger the integrity of research, the character of the sponsorship rather than the identity of the grantor should be noted.

Rule 11. Political science research supported by government grants should be unclassified.

Rule 12. After a research grant has been made, the grantor shall not impose any restriction on or require any clearance of research methods, procedures, or content.

Rule 13. The grantor assumes no responsibility for the findings and conclusions of the researcher and imposes no restrictions on and carries no responsibility for publication.

Principles for Universities

Rule 14. A university or college should not administer research funds derived from contracts or grants whose purpose and the character of whose sponsorship cannot be publicly disclosed.

Rule 15. A university or college that administers research funds provided through contracts and grants from public and/or private sources must act to assure that research funds are used prudently and honorably.

Rule 16. In administering research funds entrusted directly to its care, a university or college should do its best to ensure that no restrictions are placed on the availability of evidence to scholars or on their freedom to draw their own conclusions from the evidence and to share their findings with others.

Principles for Individual Researchers

Rule 17. In applying for research funds, the individual researcher should:
- (a) clearly state the reasons he is applying for support and not resort to stratagems of ambiguity to make his research more acceptable to a funding agency;
- (b) indicate clearly the actual amount of time he personally plans to spend on the research;
- (c) indicate other sources of support of his research, if any; and
- (d) refuse to accept terms and conditions that he believes will undermine his freedom and integrity as a scholar.

Rule 18. In conducting research so supported, the individual:
- (a) bears sole responsibility for the procedures, methods, and content of research;
- (b) must avoid any deception or misrepresentation concerning his personal involvement of respondents or subjects, or use research as a cover for intelligence work;
- (c) refrains from using his professional status to obtain data and research materials for purposes other than scholarship and;
- (d) with respect to research abroad, should not concurrently accept any additional support from agencies of the government for purposes that cannot be disclosed.

Rule 19. In managing research funds, the individual researcher should:
- (a) carefully comply with the time, reporting, accounting, and other requirements set forth in the project instrument, and cooperate with university administrations in meeting these requirements; and
- (b) avoid commingling project funds with personal funds, or funds of one project with those of another.

Rule 20. With respect to publication of the results of his research, the individual researcher:
- (a) bears sole responsibility for publication;
- (b) should disclose relevant source of financial support, but in cases where anonymity is justified and does not endanger the integrity of research, by noting the character of the sponsorship;
- (c) should indicate any material condition imposed by his financial sponsors or others on his research and publication;
- (d) should conscientiously acknowledge any assistance he receives in conducting research; and

(e) should adhere strictly to the requirements, if any, of the funding agency.

Contract Research Funded by the Federal Grant

Rule 21. Foreign Area research Guidelines.
A. Guidelines for Research Contract Relations between Government
and University:
  A1. The government has the responsibility for avoiding actions that
       would call into question the integrity of American academic in-
       stitutions as centers of independent teaching and research.
  A2. The fact of government research support should always be ac-
       knowledged by sponsor, university, and researcher.
  A3. Government-supported contract research should in process
       and results ideally be unclassified, but the practical needs of
       the nation in the modern world may require that some portion
       be subject to classification; the balance between making work
       public or classified should incline whenever possible toward
       making it public.
  A4. As a general rule, agencies should encourage open publication
       of contract research results.
  A5. Government agencies that contract with university researchers
       should consider designing their projects so as to advance
       knowledge as well as to meet the immediate needs of policy or
       action.
  A6. The government agency has the obligation of informing the
       potential researcher of the needs that the research should help
       meet, of any special conditions associated with the research
       contract, and generally of the agency's expectations concern-
       ing the research and the researcher.
  A7. The government should continue to seek research of the high-
       est possible quality in its contract programs.
B. Guidelines for the Conduct of Foreign Area Research Under Gov-
ernment Contract:
  B1. The government should take special steps to ensure that the
       parties with which it contracts have highest qualifications for
       carrying out research overseas.
  B2. The government should work to avert or minimize adverse for-
       eign reactions to its contract research programs conducted
       overseas.
  B3. When a project involves research abroad it is particularly im-
       portant that both the supporting agency and the researcher
       openly acknowledge the auspices and financing of research
       projects.
  B4. The government should under certain circumstances ascertain
       that the research is acceptable to the host government.
  B5. The government should encourage cooperation with foreign
       scholars in its contract research programs.

B6. Government agencies should continue to coordinate their foreign area research programs to eliminate duplication and overloading of any one geographic area.

B7. Government agencies should collaborate with academic associations on problems of foreign area research.

COMMITTEE ON PROFESSIONAL ETHICS, RIGHTS AND FREEDOMS GRIEVANCE PROCEDURES

The APSA's Committee on Professional Ethics, Rights and Freedoms is concerned about any ethical problem or personal abuse encountered by political scientists acting in their professional capacity. The primary responsibilities of the Committee fall into three major areas: (1) handling individual grievances and complaints, (2) writing ethical guidelines for the Association, usually in the form of advisory opinions, and (3) helping protect human rights of scholars in other countries.

(1) *Individual Grievances.* The Committee always acknowledges and responds to individuals' serious allegations of mistreatments, discrimination, or lack of due process in an action or series of actions that have adversely affected them. The Committee observes certain limitations on its participation in such cases, such as not publicizing cases, and (normally) not participating in cases if the dispute has been submitted to litigation in the courts. When the occasion warrants, the Committee, after completing its preliminary investigation, will appoint a "special representative" to do a comprehensive inquiry into the case. A special representative is a political scientist who lives in geographic proximity to both the initiator and target of the complaint and is considered to have the judgment and sensitivity necessary to win the confidence of those involved.

Political scientists and departments of political science are under an obligation to respond to the needs of special representatives for information (Advisory Opinion No. 17). The information collected is "treated with complete discretion." Individual cases are not publicized, nor does the Committee censure individuals, departments or institutions.

A special representative's first duty is to try to resolve the situation. Often special representatives have successfully mediated the disputes assigned to them. When mediation is not possible, special representatives compile a thorough report of their investigation for the use of the Committee. A special representative always approaches a dispute as a mediator and fact-finder, not as an advocate to either side.

At the completion of the fact-finding done by the Committee or its special representative, the Committee will take any actions it can to support those individuals who it concludes have been treated unfairly by other persons or institutions. The Committee does not have the power of censure, but it does make every effort to use persuasion and vigorous protest to rectify situations it is critical of. Where appropriate, the Committee will turn to the AAUP for assistance. The Committee is also developing a liaison with the American Civil Liberties Union. Although there are real limits to what the Committee can do by itself, it promises to do all that it can within its resources to protect political scientists from unjustifiable abuses.

(2) *Ethical Guidelines.* Unlike the individual cases that it takes up, which must remain confidential, the results of the work of the Committee in constructing ethical standards are published in *PS*. The Committee has adopted 19 advisory opinions to date and it will continue to formulate more of these guidelines as new problems emerge. These advisory opinions usually grow out of individual complaints that are received by the Committee. If an individual case appears to be indicative of a larger problem, an advisory opinion is the Committee's means of trying to prevent such occurrences in the future.

Political scientists faced with problems of ethics or academic freedom need direct assistance with their cases. Any advisory opinion that may be written in reference to a case is not a substitute for direct aid. It should be emphasized that although the review of individual grievances is closely intertwined with the development of advisory opinions, the Committee does not select cases on the basis of their relevance for prospective advisory opinions. The Committee does not select cases at all—it responds to all grievances that fall within its jurisdiction. The existence of an advisory opinion is not used as an excuse to disregard a recurrent problem. No matter how well-trodden the soil, the Committee stands ready to be of assistance.

(3) *Human Rights of Scholars in Other Countries.* According to guidelines established in 1982, the Committee will become involved in cases involving the human rights of scholars in other countries brought up by a reputable third-party information source. All requests for action are first cross-checked through the Clearinghouse on Science and Human Rights of the American Association for the Advancement of Science.

The Committee will respond to cases of human rights violation involving scholars whose fields correspond to those subsumed under the phrase "political science" in the United States. It will also take up cases that do not directly involve political scientists but have broad implications for all social scientists.

Given the limited time and resources of the Committee, it will consider only what appear to be the most egregious cases of human rights violations (the Committee will take up no more than six cases at a time). The standard to be used in making this choice will be the International Declaration of Human Rights and the two accompanying covenants.

The procedure the Committee will follow in human rights cases will be to write a letter of inquiry to the appropriate authorities and to follow up this letter with subsequent letters, if necessary. Other activities such as visits to embassies and site visits can also be considered by the Committee.

In discussing the grievance procedures available from the Committee of Professional Ethics, Rights and Freedoms a simple and basic part of the process should not be overlooked. The Committee cannot be of any help until it receives a formal request. Political scientists who feel they have been mistreated must take the first step and inform the Committee of the nature of the problem. After the initial contact is made the aggrieved political scientist should be ready to provide the Committee with as much detail and documentation of the alleged abuse as is possible.

It is common for grievances that come before the Committee to be communicated to it after an adverse action (e.g., denial of tenure) has been taken toward an individual. Sometimes a major decision, such as denial of tenure or rejection of a dissertation, is the first time the person perceives discrimination or the lack of due process. At other times, however, a decision of this sort is the culmination of a pattern of mistreatment that began earlier. The Committee on Professional Ethics, Rights and Freedoms encourages political scientists to approach it as soon as they begin to feel that they are the victims of discriminatory or arbitrary actions. The Committee is prepared to be of help in what might be termed "anticipatory situations." If mediation and the resolution of a problem can be achieved at its inception, so much the better for all parties concerned.

Political scientists who wish to get in touch with the Committee on Professional Ethics, Rights and Freedoms should write or phone its chairperson or the APSA at its Washington, D.C. headquarters.

ADVISORY OPINIONS OF THE COMMITTEE ON PROFESSIONAL ETHICS, RIGHTS AND FREEDOMS, AND APSA GUIDELINES ON EMPLOYMENT OPPORTUNITIES[1]

Scholarship

Books and Articles Stemming from Dissertations

When a thesis or dissertation is published in whole or in part, the following rules apply:

1. Authors are not ordinarily under an ethical obligation to acknowledge its origins.

2. Authors are free to decide what acknowledgment, if any, to give to the professor under whose supervision they worked.

Advisory Opinion No. 7 (August 28, 1970).

The Scholar's Ethical Obligation to Protect Confidential Sources

Scholars have an ethical obligation to make a full and complete disclosure of all non-confidential sources involved in their research so that their work can be tested or replicated. As citizens, they have an obligation to cooperate with grand juries, other law enforcement agencies, and institutional officials. Scholars also have a professional duty not to divulge the identity of confidential sources of information or data developed in the course of research, whether to governmental or nongovernmental officials or bodies, even though in the present state of

American law they run the risk of suffering some sort of penalty. Since the protection of confidentiality of sources is often essential in social science research, and since the continued growth of such research is clearly in the public interest, scholars have an obligation to seek to change the law so that the confidentiality of sources of information may be safeguarded. Scholars must, however, exercise appropriate restraint in making claims as to the confidential nature of their sources, and resolve all reasonable doubts in favor of full disclosure.

Advisory Opinion No. 13 (August 16, 1973).

Plagiarism

Political scientists, like all scholars, are expected to practice intellectual honesty and to uphold the scholarly standards of their discipline. Plagiarism, the deliberate appropriation of the work of others passed off as one's own, not only may constitute a violation of the civil law but represents a serious breach of professional ethics. Departments of political science should make it clear to both faculty and students that such misconduct will lead to disciplinary action and, in the case of serious offenses, may result in dismissal. Institutional rules and expected standards of conduct should be published in advance and distributed through such means as faculty and student handbooks. Disciplinary proceedings should conform to norms of fairness and academic due process as formulated in relevant AAUP statements.

Advisory Opinion No. 16 (May 17, 1975).

Joint Authorship

When a piece of writing is jointly authored, it is presumed to be the intellectual product of the authors collectively, not individually, and this fact should govern its further use including its use by any of the original authors. Passages of text and major themes and ideas used in subsequent work by any of the authors should be attributed to the original source following accepted standards for quotation and citation. Exceptions to this practice should occur only if a portion of the jointly authorized work has been clearly attributed in the original work to one of the authors.

Advisory Opinion No. 19 (December 3, 1982).

Publication

Multiple Submission of Manuscripts

The governing principle, in the opinion of the Committee, is that editors should be provided with information permitting them to judge how they can use their time, and that of readers, most effectively. Editors should not be permitted to assume that they have first claim on a manuscript if there is an expectation that it may be withdrawn regardless of their decision. On this basis, the Committee believes authors who submit manuscripts to more than one professional journal at the same time are obligated to inform each editor of the fact.

Advisory Opinion No. 1 (March 29, 1969).

Permission to Reprint

The Committee considered ethical principles related to permission to reprint copyrighted material.

Specifically with regard to the reprinting of previously published work, the Committee endorsed the following principles:

1. The copyright holder should permit the inclusion of previously published work only if the author consents. The copyright holder should either obtain the consent of the author or require that this be done by the party seeking permission to reprint.

2. Political scientists seeking to reprint previously published work have an ethical obligation to make sure that the consent of the author or authors is obtained. In cases where the copyright holder or the publisher of previously published work have not taken the steps necessary to this end, the political scientists involved, as compiler and editor of the book, should secure the consent of the author of the material. Political scientists are encouraged to include in contracts with publishers a provision that the publisher must obtain the consent of the author or authors before allowing reprinting of the work.

3. The copyright holder and the author are each entitled to a flat fee or a share of royalties in connection with permissions to reprint, specific terms depending on agreement with the party seeking permission. Either the copyright holder or the author may waive their right. Each may act on his or her own behalf, or by mutual consent one may act on behalf of both.

4. Permission must be renewed, and financial arrangements are subject to renegotiation, whenever a book goes into a new edition.

5. Any work reprinted may be changed only with the specific consent of the author.

An author is entitled to a complimentary copy of any publication in which is or her work is reprinted.

Advisory Opinion No. 3 (October 11, 1969, Revised May 17, 1975).

Employment Practices

The Academic Marketplace

The Committee considered several questions relating to the recruitment of faculty members. The Committee endorsed the following principles:

1. Once an employment institution clearly indicates that it is giving serious consideration to an applicant for a faculty appointment, e.g., by interviewing him or her, it should inform the applicant of the status of his or her application within a reasonable time.

2. Once an employing institution offers a faculty appointment, the individual to whom the offer is made should respond within a reasonable time with the decision or with a statement concerning his or her situation.

3. In connection with points 1 and 2 above, two weeks is to be considered a reasonable time unless the parties specifically agree to the contrary.

4. An employing institution that offers a faculty appointment orally should immediately communicate the offer in writing as well.

The Committee declined to endorse the view that it is improper for those interviewing the applicant to ask whether he or she is being considered elsewhere or has received offers from other schools.

Advisory Opinion No. 4 (October 11, 1969).

As the result of a specific complaint, the Committee on Professional Ethics has adopted the following language as an addition to the first paragraph of Advisory Opinion No. 4 *The Academic Marketplace.*

1. Once an employing institution clearly indicates that it is giving serious consideration to an applicant for a faculty appointment, e.g., by interviewing him or her, it should inform the applicant of the status of his or her application, and of any change in status, within a reasonable time. The employing institution has an obligation to inform a candidate for employment fully concerning the terms and procedures which are utilized in the making of offers of appointment.

Addition to Advisory Opinion No. 4 (June 11, 1971).

Fraud in Claiming Advanced Degrees

1. If a person who seeks an academic position falsely claims to have an advanced degree, and if the falsity of the claim becomes known to the department or other appointing authorities of the institution in which the position is located, the chair or other appointing authorities ordinarily have an ethical obligation to report the fraud to the institution alleged to have granted the degree.

2. If those who know of fraud are asked by a potential academic employer for an oral or written statement concerning the qualification of the guilty person, the statement should ordinarily include an appropriate description of the fraud, above all if there is reason to think that the guilty person may be persisting in it.

3. The judgment that a person is guilty of making a false claim must be made responsibly.

Advisory Opinion No. 6 (August 28, 1970).

Recommending Candidates for Faculty Appointments

1. Recommending a candidate for faculty appointment calls for honest and responsible judgment.

2. The scholarly achievements and promise of the candidate should be assessed as fairly as possible.

3. Also to be assessed are the characteristics of the candidate that relate to his or her probable effectiveness in the classroom and to the development of a stimulating rapport with professional colleagues.

4. Should there be clear basis for question about the compatibility of the candidate's past behavior with legitimate expectations of the employing institution, the fact may be mentioned. It is permissible for the employing institution to expect that members of its faculty will abide by those rules which do not violate academic freedom principles or political rights of citizenship, and refrain from inciting others to violate those rules.

5. A candidate should be informed if matters relating to paragraph 4 are in his or her record and should have an opportunity to place in the record a statement relating to such matters.

6. Matters pertaining to the candidate that have no bearing on the legitimate expectations of the employing institution should not be mentioned.

Advisory Opinion No. 11 (June 11, 1971).

The Confidentiality of Letters of Professional Evaluation

Recent legislation has required a new formulation of guidelines for letters of professional evaluation, as follows:

1. When an academic department requests from a scholar outside the institution an evaluation regarding a political scientist, the normal expectation in the profession is that the letter of evaluation will be treated as confidential. If it is the department's policy to place such letters in an open file, or otherwise make these letters available to those who may desire to see them, then the department has an ethical obligation to inform the individual from whom a letter is requested that the letter will not be regarded as a confidential document. If one who is requested to write an evaluative letter is informed in advance that the letter will be placed in an open file, then it is proper to exercise the option of not writing such a letter. Furthermore, the refusal to write a letter should not be a matter of record.

2. When the political scientist from whom a letter of recommendation is sought, at their own, or at some other institution, is still a candidate for a degree, letters placed in their file after January 1, 1975 are by law open for inspection by them, unless they have waived this right of access. If they have not waived that right the department has an obligation to inform the individual from whom a letter is requested that the confidentiality of his or her letter cannot be assured.

3. Under federal statute, postsecondary students' confidential letters of recommendation placed in files before January 1, 1975, are not open for their inspection. Letters placed in files after January 1, 1975 are open for inspection by students but this right to access may be waived by students.

Advisory Opinion No. 15 (March 16, 1974, Revised May 17, 1975).

Guidelines on Employment Opportunities

The Council of the APSA has adopted the following "Guidelines on Employment Opportunities":

1. *Open Listing Policy.* It is a professional obligation of all political science departments to list in the APSA Personnel Service Newsletter all positions for which they are recruiting at the Instructor, Assistant, and Associate Professor levels. In addition, the listing of openings at the Full Professor level are strongly encouraged. It is also a professional obligation for departments to list temporary and visiting appointments.

2. *Nepotism Rules.* Institutions employing political scientists should abolish nepotism rules, whether they apply departmentally or to an institution as a whole. Employment and advancement should be based solely on professional qualifications without regard for family relationships.

3. *Part-time Positions.* Institutions employing political scientists should make more flexible use of part-time positions for fully qualified professional women and men, just as is now done for those professionals with joint appointments or part-time research positions.

Part-time positions should carry full academic status, equivalent rank, promotion opportunities, equal rates of pay, commensurate departmental participation and commensurate fringe benefits, including access to research resources. The policy of flexible part-time positions is not intended to condone any practice such as moonlighting or any use of employers to circumvent normal career-ladder appointments.

4. *Equal Employment Opportunities.* It is Association policy that educational institutions not discriminate among job candidates on the basis of sex, race, color, religion, or national origin except in those cases in which federal law allows religious preference in hiring.

In accordance with this policy, therefore, the Association will not indicate a preference, limitation, or specification based upon these classifications in job listings, except that religious preference may be indicated when allowed by federal law.

It is Association policy to urge that educational institutions not discriminate against employees or applicants because of sexual orientation, marital status, or physical handicap.

It is Association policy to support the principles of affirmative action and to urge political science departments to aggressively pursue affirmative action programs and policies with regard to blacks, chicanos, women and other minorities.

Professional Conduct

Open Access to Documentation and Data

The Committee considered a proposal "that a condition of publication of quantitative articles in the *American Political Science Review* be that authors agree to make available to all interested scholars all the data directly related to the published study."

Though not endorsing the proposal as stated, the Committee recommended the following principles with regard to the obligations of authors:

1. Authors are obliged to reveal the bases of any of their statements that are challenged specifically, except where confidentiality is involved.

2. When statements that are challenged are based on reproducible data, authors are obliged to facilitate replication. They may expect the challenger to pay the costs of reproducing the relevant data.

3. Challenges are to be sufficiently precise to indicate to the author what documentation or data are needed. Challengers are themselves in the status of authors in connection with the statements that they make.

In addition, the Committee recommended that funding agencies should hereafter include in grants a stipulation that data gathered under the grants be made available to scholars at cost after a specified time, e.g., after a year has passed following the completion of the data-gathering process, or after the first substantial research report by the chief researcher has been completed.

The Committee made no recommendation concerning sanctioning measures that might be applied to reinforce the principles contained in its advisory opinion.

Advisory Opinion No. 2 (October 11, 1969).

Appraising Manuscripts and Reviewing Books

The Committee considered the problem of fairness and objectivity in connection with the appraisal of manuscripts and the reviewing of books.

The Committee endorsed the following statement:

"Appraising manuscripts and reviewing books are serious scholarly responsibilities. Those invited to make appraisals or to write reviews should disqualify themselves if there is in their minds reasonable doubt whether they can exercise the responsibility with scholarly detachment. Such doubt might be raised, for example, by an invitation to appraise the manuscript or review the book of a close personal friend or of a departmental colleague.

"Insofar as possible, editors and book-review editors should themselves act in conformity with the above principles. Moreover, in connection with the appraisal of manuscripts, editors should take all reasonable precautions to avoid revealing the names of the author and the reader to each other."

Advisory Opinion No. 5 (October 11, 1969).

Association Electioneering

In making statements or in sending communications to members of the Association in connection with the election of officers, there is an ethical obligation to speak with accuracy and appropriate restraint. All candidates and spokesmen are obligated to clear all claims and endorsements with all parties involved.

Advisory Opinion No. 9 (June 11, 1971).

Use of APSA Title for Political Purposes

Whereas a statement taking a position on American foreign policy was released to the public and published in the *American Political Science Review,* Vol. 64, p. 589 (June, 1970), over the signature of eight members of the Association, all of them identified as past, present or future Presidents of the Association; and

Whereas such identification is inconsistent with a proposed rule of conduct suggested by the Committee on Professional Standards and Responsibilities (Bernstein Committee) in its final report, as published in *PS,* Vol. 1 No. 3 (Summer, 1968), p. 11;

Therefore, the Committee on Professional Ethics formally endorses the following:

When past, present or future officers, members, or employees of the Association speak out on an issue of public policy, endorse a political candidate, or otherwise participate in political affairs, they should make it as clear as possible that they are not speaking on behalf of the Association unless they are so authorized by the Association, and they should not encourage any inference that they act for the Association unless so authorized by the Association.

The use of the title of the office held in the APSA in political advertisements, even if labeled "for identification purposes only," may well be seen by others as an endorsement of a political position by the Association and should be avoided.

Advisory Opinion No. 10 (June 11, 1971, revised December 3, 1982).

Cooperation in the Case of Complaints Charging a Violation of Professional Ethics or Academic Freedom

The Committee on Professional Ethics, Rights, and Freedoms has the mandate to formulate general policy on matters of professional ethics and academic freedom and to respond to grievances and complaints of members of the Association on such matters. When receiving a request for assistance from an individual or institution the Committee does not conduct a full-scale quasi-judicial investigation but generally appoints a senior member of the profession to serve as a consultant who provides advice and guidance to the complainant, seeks a resolution of the conflict through mediation, and prepares a report for the Committee.

In order to carry out its charge, the Committee on Professional Ethics, Rights and Freedoms requires the cooperation of institutions and of the Political Science profession. Specifically, individual political scientists and departments of political science are under an obligation to respond to the needs of consultants for information. All such information will be treated with complete discretion. The Committee does not publicize the cases handled nor does it censure individuals, departments or institutions.

Advisory Opinion No. 17 (May 17, 1975).

The Presentation of Personal Causes at Panels of Annual Meetings

It is improper for persons to use a panel at the Annual Meeting as a forum for the primary purpose of presenting their side of personal litigation in which they are or have been involved, since panels are not equipped or designed to serve as agencies for the adjudication of controverted evidential questions involved in litigation. The Executive Director and the Chairman of the Program Committee should make every possible effort to protect the Annual Meeting of the Association from such activity.

Advisory Opinion No. 12 (February 10, 1973).

Status of Profession

Deceptive Use of Scholarly Status for Purposes of Political Espionage

It has come to the attention of the APSA Committee on Professional Ethics, Rights and Freedoms that persons posing as political science students or scholars have been planted on the staffs of opposing candidates for public office allegedly for the purpose of collecting material of a research character. The Committee believes that it is highly unethical for any candidate for public office to trade on the credibility normally attached to objective scholarly research in the academic world. The Committee seeks to protect the valued symbols of political science scholarship, and expresses its strong disapproval of this practice. The Committee will taken every possible step to bring this advisory opinion to the attention of all bodies concerned with ethical practices in politics whenever such abuses occur.

Advisory Opinion No. 14 (March 16, 1974).

Procedural Rights of Graduate Students

Procedural Rights of Graduate Students

1. Students should be advised at the time of their admittance as to the departmental and institutional requirements of the degree program they will be entering. If a department of political science changes the requirements of a program, students already enrolled and making normal progress toward their degrees should have the right to be governed by the requirements in force at the time of their entrance if they so desire.

2. Students should be advised at the time of their admittance under what conditions written or oral major examinations ("prelims," "com-

prehensives," etc.) are given and whether such examinations, if failed, may be retaken.

3. After submitting a proposal for a thesis or dissertation, students should be informed by the chairperson of their committee of its action with regard to the acceptability of the proposal.

Action on a proposal should be taken within a reasonable time and communicated to the student in writing.

4. If, in the opinion of the supervising faculty, a student's thesis or dissertation does not show satisfactory progress and there should arise question of the acceptability of the final product, the student should be put on notice as soon as possible and in writing that his or her candidacy for the degree may be terminated.

5. Students should be advised on any changes in the composition of their thesis or dissertation committee. Faculty members should not participate in a thesis or dissertation examination unless they have had sufficient time to read the thesis or dissertation.

6. If students fail a written or oral major examination ("prelims," "comprehensive," etc.) or have a thesis or dissertation required for the degree rejected, they should be informed by the examiners or readers as to the reasons for such failure or rejection. Upon request, this explanation should be rendered in writing.

7. Students should be informed upon entering a graduate program about any departmental or university grievance procedures for handling disputes that may arise between faculty and graduate students pertaining to the interpretation of degree requirements or the administration of the graduate program. Departments that do not have any established grievance procedure are urged to develop such rules and to distribute them in writing to all their graduate students enrolled in degree programs. Universities should provide an appeals process beyond the department level to insure adherence to proper procedural standards.

Advisory Opinion No. 18 (June 12, 1976).

ACADEMIC FREEDOM AND TENURE

In 1947 APSA formally endorsed as Association policy the 1940 Statement of Principles on Academic Freedom and Tenure jointly developed by the American Association of University Professors and the Association of American Colleges. The Statement is reprinted here with later interpretive comments.

The Committee on Professional Ethics, Rights and Freedoms cooperates frequently with AAUP in individual cases. Also, as noted previously, institutions which have been censured by AAUP are listed annually in the summer issue of *PS*.

The Canadian Association of University Professors (CAUT) maintains a censure list as well.

The purpose of this statement is to promote public understanding and support of academic freedom and tenure and agreement upon procedures to assure them in colleges and universities. Institutions of higher education are conducted for the common good and not to further the interest of either the individual teacher[2] or the institution as a whole. The common good depends upon the free search for truth and its free exposition.

Academic freedom is essential to these purposes and applies to both teaching and research. Freedom in research is fundamental to the advancement of truth. Academic freedom in its teaching aspect is fundamental for the protection of the rights of the teacher in teaching and of the student to freedom in learning. It carries with it duties correlative with rights.[1][3]

Tenure is a means to certain ends; specifically: (1) Freedom of teaching and research and of extramural activities and (2) a sufficient degree of economic security to make the profession attractive to men and women of ability. Freedom and economic security, hence, tenure, are indispensable to the success of an institution in fulfilling its obligations to its students and to society.

Academic Freedom

(a) The teacher is entitled to full freedom in research and in the publication of the results, subject to the adequate performance of his other academic duties; but research for pecuniary return should be based upon an understanding with the authorities of the institution.

(b) The teacher is entitled to freedom in the classroom in discussing his subject, but he should be careful not to introduce into his teaching controversial matter which has no relation to his subject.[2] Limitations of academic freedom because of religious or other aims of the institution should be clearly stated in writing at the time of the appointment.[3]

(c) The college or university teacher is a citizen, a member of a learned profession, and an officer of an educational institution. When he speaks or writes as a citizen, he should be free from institutional censorship or discipline, but his special position in the community imposes special obligations. As a man of learning and an educational officer, he should remember that the public may judge his profession and his institution by his utterances. Hence he should at all times be accurate, should exercise appropriate restraint, should show respect for the opinions of others, and should make every effort to indicate that he is not an institutional spokesman.[4]

Academic Tenure

(a) After the expiration of a probationary period, teachers or investigators should have permanent or continuous tenure, and their service should be terminated only for adequate cause, except in the case of retirement for age, or under extraordinary circumstances because of financial exigencies.

In the interpretation of this principle it is understood that the following represents acceptable academic practice:

(1) The precise terms and conditions of every appointment should be stated in writing and be in the possession of both institution and teacher before the appointment is consummated.

(2) Beginning with appointment to the rank of full-time instructor or a higher rank,[5] the probationary period should not exceed seven years, including within this period full-time service in all institutions of higher education, but subject to the proviso that when, after a term of probationary service of more than three years in one or more institutions, a teacher is called to another institution, it may be agreed in writing that his new appointment is for a probationary period of not more than four years, even though thereby the person's total probationary period in the academic profession is extended beyond the normal maximum of seven years.[6] Notice should be given at least one year prior to the expiration of the probationary period if the teacher is not to be continued in service after the expiration of that period.[7]

(3) During the probationary period a teacher should have the academic freedom that all other members of the faculty have.[8]

(4) Termination for a cause of a continuous appointment, or the dismissal for cause of a teacher previous to the expiration of a term appointment, should, if possible, be considered by both a faculty committee and the governing board of the institution. In all cases where the facts are in dispute, the accused teacher should be informed before the hearing in writing of the charges against him and should have the opportunity to be heard in his own defense by all bodies that pass judgment upon his case. He should be permitted to have with him an adviser of his own choosing who may act as counsel. There should be a full stenographic record of the hearing available to the parties concerned. In the hearing of charges of incompetence the testimony should include that of teachers and other scholars, either from his own or from other institutions. Teachers on continuous appointment who are dismissed for reasons not involving moral turpitude should receive their salaries for at least a year from the date of notification of dismissal whether or not they are continued in their duties at the institution.[9]

(5) Termination of a continuous appointment because of financial exigency should be demonstrably bona fide.

1940 Interpretations

At the conference of representatives of the American Association of University Professors and of the Association of American Colleges on November 7–8, 1940, the following interpretations of the 1940 *Statement of Principles on Academic Freedom and Tenure* were agreed upon:

1. That its operation should not be retroactive.

2. That all tenure claims of teachers appointed prior to the endorsement should be determined in accordance with the principles set forth in the 1925 Conference Statement on Academic Freedom and Tenure.

3. If the administration of a college or university feels that a teacher

has not observed the admonitions of Paragraph (c) of the section on *Academic Freedom* and believes that the extramural utterances of the teacher have been such as to raise grave doubts concerning his fitness for his position, it may proceed to file charges under Paragraph (a) (4) of the section on *Academic Tenure*. In pressing such charges the administration should remember that teachers are citizens and should be accorded the freedom of citizens. In such cases the administration must assume full responsibility and the American Association of University Professors and the Association of American Colleges are free to make an investigation.

1970 Interpretive Comments

Following extensive discussions on the 1940 Statement of Principles on Academic Freedom and Tenure with leading educational associations and with individual faculty members and administrators, a Joint Committee of the AAUP and the Association of American Colleges met during 1969 to reevaluate this key policy statement. On the basis of the comments received, the discussions that ensued, the Joint Committee felt the preferable approach was to formulate interpretations of the Statement in terms of the experience gained in implementing and applying the Statement for over thirty years and of adapting it to current needs.

The Committee submitted to the two Associations for their consideration the following "Interpretive Comments." These interpretations were approved by the Council of the American Association of University Professors in April, 1970, and endorsed by the Fifty-sixth Annual Meeting as Association Policy.

In the thirty years since their promulgation, the principles of the 1940 *Statement of Principles of Academic Freedom and Tenure* have undergone a substantial amount of refinement. This has evolved through a variety of processes, including customary acceptance, understandings mutually arrived at between institutions and professors or their representatives, investigations and reports by the American Association of University Professors, and formulations of statements by that Association either alone or in conjunction with the Association of American Colleges. These comments represent the attempt of the two associations, as the original sponsors of the 1940 Statement, to formulate the most important of these refinements. Their incorporation here as interpretive Comments is based upon the premise that the 1940 Statement is not a static code but a fundamental document designed to set a framework of norms to guide adaptations to changing times and circumstances.

Also, there have been relevant developments in the law itself reflecting a growing insistence by the courts on due process within the academic community which parallels the essential concepts of the 1940 Statement: particularly relevant is the identification by the Supreme Court of academic freedom as a right protected by the First Amendment. As the Supreme Court said in *Keyishian v. Board of Regents* 385

U.S. 589 (1967), "Our Nation is deeply committed to safeguarding academic freedom, which is of transcendent value to all of us and not merely to the teachers concerned. That freedom is therefore a special concern of the First Amendment, which does not tolerate laws that cast a pall of orthodoxy over the classroom."

The numbers refer to the designated portion of the 1940 Statement on which interpretive comment is made recognized that membership in the academic profession carries with it special responsibilities. Both Associations either separately or jointly have consistently affirmed these responsibilities in major policy statements, providing guidance to the professor in his utterances as a citizen, in the exercise of his responsibilities to the institution and students, and in his conduct when resigning from his institution or when undertaking government-sponsored research. Of particular relevance is the *Statement on Professional Ethics,* adopted by the Fifty-second Annual Meeting of the AAUP as Association policy and published in the *AAUP Bulletin* (Autumn, 1966, pp. 290–291).

2. The intent of this statement is not to discourage what is "controversial." Controversy is at the heart of the free academic inquiry which the entire statement is designed to foster. The passage serves to underscore the need for the teacher to avoid persistently intruding material which has no relation to his subject.

3. Most church-related institutions no longer need or desire the departure from the principle of academic freedom implied in the 1940 Statement, and we do not now endorse such a departure.

4. This paragraph is the subject of an interpretation adopted by the sponsors of the 1940 Statement immediately following its endorsement which reads as follows:

> If the administration of a college or university feels that a teacher has not observed the admonitions of Paragraph (c) of the section on Academic Freedom and believes that the extramural utterances of the teacher have been such as to raise grave doubts concerning his fitness for his position, it may proceed to file charges under Paragraph (a) (4) of the section on Academic Tenure. In pressing such charges the administration should remember that teachers are citizens and should be accorded the freedom of citizens. In such cases, the administration must assume full responsibility and the American Association of University Professors and the Association of American Colleges are free to make an investigation.

Paragraph (c) of the 1940 Statement should also be interpreted in keeping with the 1964 *"Committee A Statement on Extramural Utterances" (AAUP Bulletin,* Spring. 1965, p. 29) which states inter alia: "The controlling principle is that a faculty member's expression of opinion as a citizen cannot constitute grounds for dismissal unless it clearly demonstrates the faculty member's unfitness to his position. Extramural utterances rarely bear upon the faculty members fitness to his position.

Moreover, a final decision should take into account the faculty member's entire record as a teacher and scholar."

Paragraph V of the *Statement of Professional Ethics* also deals with the nature of the "special obligations" of the teacher. The paragraph reads as follows:

As a member of his community, the professor has the rights and obligations of any citizen. He measures the urgency of these obligations in the light of his responsibilities to his subject, to his students, to his profession, and to his institution. When he speaks or acts as a private person he avoids creating the impression that he speaks or acts for his college or university. As a citizen engaged in a profession that depends upon freedom for its health and integrity, the professor has a particular obligation to promote conditions of free inquiry and to further public understanding of academic freedom.

Both the protection of academic freedom and the requirements of academic responsibility apply not only to the full-time probationary as well as to the tenured teacher, but also to all others, such as part-time and teaching assistants, who exercise teaching responsibilities.

5. The concept of "rank of full-time instructor or a higher rank" is intended to include any person who teaches a full-time load regardless of his specific title.[4]

6. In calling for an agreement "in writing" on the amount of credit for a faculty member's prior service at other institutions, the Statement furthers the general policy of full understanding by the professor of the terms and conditions of his appointment. It does not necessarily follow that a professor's tenure rights have been violated because of the absence of a written agreement on this matter. Nonetheless, especially because of the variation in permissible institutional practices, a written understanding concerning these matters at the time of appointment is particularly appropriate and advantageous to both the individual and the institution.

7. The effect of this subparagraph is that a decision on tenure, favorable or unfavorable, must be made at least twelve months prior to the completion of the probationary period. If the decision is negative, the appointment for the following year becomes a terminal one. If the decision is affirmative, the provisions in the 1940 Statement with respect to the termination of services of teachers or investigators after the expiration of a probationary period should apply from the date when the favorable decision is made.

The general principle of notice contained in this paragraph is developed with greater specificity in the *Standards for Notice of Nonreappointment,* endorsed by the Fiftieth Annual Meeting of the American Association of University Professors (1964). These standards are:

Notice of nonreappointment, or of intention not to recommend reappointment to the governing board, should be given in writing in accordance with the following standards:

(1) *Not later than March 1 of the first academic year of service,* if the appointment expires at the end of that year; or, if one-year appointment terminates during an academic year, at least three months in advance of its termination.

(2) *Not later than December 15 of the second academic year of service,* if the appointment expires at the end of that year; or, if an initial two-year appointment terminates during an academic year, at least six months in advance of its termination.

(3) At least twelve months before the expiration of an appointment after two or more years in the institution.

Other obligations, both of institutions and individuals, are described in the *Statement on Recruitment and Resignation of Faculty Members,* as endorsed by the Association of American Colleges and the American Association of University Professors in 1961.

8. The freedom of probationary teachers is enhanced by the establishment of a regular procedure for the periodic evaluation and assessment of the teacher's academic performance during his probationary status. Provision should be made for regularized procedures for the consideration of complaints by probationary teachers that their academic freedom has been violated. One suggested procedure to serve these purposes is contained in the *Recommended Institutional Regulations on Academic Freedom and Tenure,* prepared by the American Association of University Professors.

9. A further specification of the academic due process to which the teacher is entitled under this paragraph is contained in the *Statement of Procedural Standards in Faculty Dismissal Proceedings,* jointly approved by the American Association of University Professors and the Association of American Colleges in 1958. This interpretive document deals with the issue of suspension, about which the 1940 Statement is silent.

The 1958 Statement provides: "Suspension of the faculty member during the proceedings involving him is justified only if immediate harm to himself or others is threatened by his continuance. Unless legal considerations forbid, any such suspension should be with pay." A suspension which is not followed by either reinstatement or the opportunity for a hearing is in effect a summary dismissal in violation of academic due process.

The concept of "moral turpitude" identifies the exceptional case in which the professor may be denied a year's teaching or pay in whole or in part. The statement applies to that kind of behavior which goes beyond simply warranting discharge and is so utterly blameworthy as to make it inappropriate to require the offering of a year's teaching or pay. The standard is not that the moral sensibilities of persons in the particular community have been affronted. The standard is behavior that would evoke condemnation by the academic community generally.

REFERENCES

1. Its formal title was the Committee on Professional Standards and Responsibilities. The other members of the Committee were Stephen K. Bailey, Samuel H. Beer, William D. Carey, Manning J. Dauer, David Fellman, Jack W. Peltason, Douglas W. Rae, Randall B. Ripley, Wallace S. Sayre, Vernon Van Dyke, and Aaron B. Wildavsky.
2. The text of the advisory opinions has been edited to eliminate gender-specific pronouns when referring to members of the profession or the society at large except when such references are relevant to the context.
3. The word "teacher" as used in this document is understood to include the investigator who is attached to an academic institution without teaching duties.
4. Bold-face numbers in brackets refer to Interpretive Comments which follow.
5. For a discussion of this question, see the "Report of the Special Committee on Academic Personnel Ineligible for Tenure." *AAUP Bulletin,* Autumn, 1966, pp. 280–282.

APPENDIX A:
AUTHOR BIOGRAPHIES

THEODORE J. KARAMANSKI is an associate professor of history at Loyola University of Chicago. He is a specialist in North American frontier history and is director of Loyola's Program in Public History. From 1978 to 1979 he worked as a historic preservation consultant with American Resources Group, Inc. In 1980 he received his Ph.D. from Loyola University. Since that time he has been a member of the history department at Loyola and director of the Mid-American Research Center, a public history consulting organization. He is author of *Fur Trade and Exploration* (1983), *Deep Woods Frontier* (1989), numerous technical reports; and articles that have appeared in *The Alaska Journal, The Public Historian, The Beaver: Magazine of the North,* and the *Journal of Polar History.* From 1989–1990 he was chairman of the National Council on Public History.

RONALD C. TOBEY is professor of history and director of the Program in Historic Resources Management at the University of California, Riverside. He is also president of the Mission Inn Foundation. His publications include *The American Ideology of National Science, 1919–1931* (1971), and *Saving the Prairies: The Life Cycle of the Founding School of American Plant Ecology, 1898–1954* (1971).

ROY H. LOPATA received a Ph.D. from the University of Delaware in 1975. Prior to his appointment as planning director for the City of Newark in 1977 he served as administrative assistant to Newark's City Manager. The Newark Planning Department is responsible for zoning and land use regulation, economic and community development, historic preservation, transportation planning and public transit operations, environmental protection, planning for capital expenditures, and demographic data gathering and analysis. Mr. Lopata has published in *The Public Historian, Public Works, The International Transportation Engineers Journal, The Dictionary of American Biography, The Journal of the American Planning Association,* and was a contributor to the *Public History: An Introduction,* edited by Barbara J. Howe and Emory L. Kemp (Krieger Publishing, 1986). He also authored the recently published *City of Newark, Delaware: Comprehensive Development Plan II* (1987).

J. MORGAN KOUSSER was educated at Princeton and Yale, and has taught at the California Institute of Technology since 1969. He has also been a visiting professor at Michigan and Harvard. He is the author of *The Shaping of Southern Politics: Suffrage Restriction and the Establishment of the One-Party South, 1880–1910* (1974) and co-editor of *Region, Race, and Reconstruction: Essays in Honor of C. Vann Woodward* (1982). Recent articles include "Long-Linear Analysis of Contingency Tables: An Introduction for Historians" (*Historical Methods,* 1982), and "The Revivalism of Narrative" in *Social Science History, 1985*).

JOAN C. WILLIAMS is professor of law at American University. In 1974 she received a B.A. with distinction in history from Yale University. In 1980 she received a J.D. from Harvard Law School and an M.A. in city planning from Massachusetts Institute of Technology. Her publications have appeared in *Wisconsin Law Review, Texas Law Review, New York University Law Review, Urban Law Annual,* and *Tax Notes.* Her principal research interests are the history of municipal status in American law and legal historiography. She has participated in the Organization of American Historians and the Johns Hopkins/University of Maryland Seminar on Law and History.

CARL RYANT received his B.A. from Case Western Reserve University and his M.A. and Ph.D. from the University of Wisconsin-Madison. He is professor of history and codirector of the Oral History Center (Archives) at the University of Louisville. He has published articles on oral history, business history, and popular culture and a book, *Profit's Prophet: Garet Garrett (1878–1954)* (Susquehanna University Press, 1989). He is working on a comparative history of mass merchandising. He serves as chair of the International Committee of the Oral History Association.

DONALD PAGE is vice president for academic affairs at Trinity Western University in Langley, British Columbia. For sixteen years he was a historian with the Department of External Affairs. From 1986–1989 he was the senior historian in the department's Political and Strategic Analysis Division. He was responsible for all historical references and lessons drawn in the department's Policy Analysis Division and speeches dealing with international affairs. He is a graduate of the University of Toronto and was on the faculty of the University of Saskatchewan before joining the federal government. He is the author of more than five dozen published studies in Canadian foreign relations.

STANLEY M. HORDES is a consulting historian based in Santa Fe, New Mexico. He holds a Ph.D. in colonial Mexican history from Tulane University, and has served as curator of colonial manuscripts at the Louisiana State Museum in New Orleans, as historian for the Southwest Regional Office of the National Park Service, and as state historian for the State of New Mexico. He has published several articles on the history of Mexico and the Borderlands, and has directed a number of public programs to raise the level of historical consciousness in the New Mexico public schools and among the general community. He is the executive director of the New Mexico Committee for the Promotion of History, sits on the Board of Directors of the National Council for Public History, and represents the State Coordinating Committees on the Policy Board of the National Coordinating Committee for the Promotion of History. In addition, he teaches courses in applied and public history at the Santa Fe Graduate Center of the University of New Mexico.

A Ph.D. graduate of Duke University, **MARTIN REUSS** is the senior civil works historian for the U.S. Army Corps of Engineers. He specializes in the history of inland navigation, flood control, and hydraulic engineering. He served as the principal editor for two series published by the Corps of Engineers, one dealing with environmental history and the other covering the development of navigation in the United States. Dr. Reuss has published articles in various historical journals, including *Technology and Culture, The Public Historian, Environment,* and *Louisiana History.* He has written or contributed to a number of books in his field. He served on the nominating committee of the National Council on Public History, the editorial board of *The Public Historian,* and as president of the Society for History in the Federal Government (1988–89).

JAMES C. WILLIAMS is the director of the California History Center at De Anza College, Cupertino, California. He has been active in public history since 1976, serving as chair and executive secretary of the California Committee for the Promotion of History and on the board of the National Council for Public History (NCPH). He received his Ph.D. in public history from the University of California at Santa Barbara.